GUIDE TO ORGANISATION DESIGN

OTHER ECONOMIST BOOKS

Guide to Analysing Companies
Guide to Business Modelling
Guide to Business Planning
Guide to Economic Indicators
Guide to the European Union
Guide to Financial Markets
Guide to Investment Strategy
Guide to Management Ideas
Numbers Guide
Style Guide

Brands and Branding
Business Consulting
Business Miscellany
Business Strategy
China's Stockmarket
Dealing with Financial Risk
Economics
Emerging Markets
The Future of Technology
Globalisation
Headhunters and How to Use Them
Mapping the Markets
The City
Wall Street

Essential Director
Essential Economics
Essential Investment
Essential Negotiation

Pocket World in Figures

GUIDE TO ORGANISATION DESIGN
Creating high-performing and adaptable enterprises

Naomi Stanford

THE ECONOMIST IN ASSOCIATION WITH
PROFILE BOOKS LTD

Published by Profile Books Ltd
3A Exmouth House, Pine Street, London EC1R 0JH
www.profilebooks.com

Typeset in EcoType by MacGuru Ltd
info@macguru.org.uk

Printed in Great Britain by
Clays, Bungay, Suffolk

A CIP catalogue record for this book is available
from the British Library

ISBN 978 1 86197 802 8

The paper this book is printed on is certified by the © 1996 Forest Stewardship
Council A.C. (FSC). It is ancient-forest friendly. The printer holds FSC chain of custody
SGS-COC-2061

FSC
Mixed Sources
Product group from well-managed
forests and other controlled sources
Cert no. SGS-COC-2061
www.fsc.org
© 1996 Forest Stewardship Council

Contents

Acknowledgements

M Y THANKS TO the many people who have contributed directly and indirectly to this book. They include employees of many of the organisations I have worked with, colleagues who have reviewed chapters, friends who have tracked my progress and the family members who have lived with the process.

I am especially grateful to Hannah Barugh, Rosa Barugh, Roger Woolford, Rosie Stanford and Michael Stanford.

I would also like to acknowledge the good work of the Medical Foundation for the Care of Victims of Torture (www.torturecare.org.uk), to whom the royalties from this book are going.

Preface

ICAME TO write this book to answer the many repeated questions that people have about the constant "reorganisations" and "restructurings" that they willingly or unwillingly participate in during the course of their working life.

I currently work with both the initiators of these reorganisations and the people whose working lives are changed as a result of them. Both parties have similar concerns:

- How do I know that the reorganisation is really necessary?
- Is there any evidence suggesting that it is good to change things *per se*, or does it always depend on the specific change?
- How do you know if organisation redesign has worked?
- Is there any hard evidence about the absolute pros and cons of different structures?
- Is there a step-by-step guide I could follow?

In my previous work, as an employee of several large multinational companies, over time I too had to reapply for my job, was laid off, had five new managers in the course of six-months, was relocated, had to lay off staff myself, and so on – all as a result of various reorganisations. But during these experiences I also worked with the changes and helped people approach restructuring not with dread but with a certain sense of excitement and energy.

From these experiences I learned to think of organisations both in the more traditional way as whole systems that are inevitably shifting and responding as their context changes, and in the newer way as complex adaptive organisms evolving in order to survive. With these perspectives I discovered that there is a lot more to reorganisation than tinkering with the chart that represents the structure.

To answer the types of questions listed above (that I too had asked), I looked at all the components that contribute to organisational performance and found that organisational performance is more likely to improve if leaders and managers take a wider perspective than simply focusing on the structure: there is less rework, people are happier with the outcomes and it makes it easier to align all the organisational elements.

I also recognised that organisational alignment is always temporary, because things change. The design has to be adaptable; it must evolve and it must take into account the interests and views of all those with a stake in the business.

Lou Gerstner (former CEO at IBM) spoke well when congratulating his staff:

> In my eyes you stand tall. You did all this – the milestones passed, the victories just ahead, and those far down the road. Thank you. Take a bow. You've earned it. And, of course, I can't resist: let's all get right back to work because we've just begun!

As it is with milestones passed so it is with organisation design. One design gives way to the next. This book guides you along the path – not the straight and narrow path of restructuring, but the interesting and much more productive path of organisation design. It is written for leaders and managers looking for practical advice on tackling the business perform-ance issues that face them. Each chapter has information about the topic in hand, illustrative examples from organisations, a case study, and some practical and immediately usable tools. Note that all the examples given in this book report the situation as it was at that moment in time, and they are only partial: they serve as illustrations of points, not as enduring truths about any specific organisation. The case studies are all disguised and somewhat fictionalised examples of organisations I have worked with. The tools are all ones I find helpful and use regularly. I hope as you look through and read the book you will find hints, tips and approaches that you can apply to good result in your organisation.

Naomi Stanford
April 2007

1 Introducing organisation design

Design is a plan for arranging elements in such a way as best to accomplish a particular purpose.

Charles Eames, 1969

STORIES ABOUT COMPANY start-ups run like this: "We had a great idea. We got the funding. We hired people. We did well for a bit. Something happened. We fell apart." Unfortunately, 50% of start-ups do not survive beyond the first three years.

Business failure is not limited to start-ups. *Industry Watch*, published by BDO Stoy Hayward, an accounting firm, predicted that "17,043 businesses will fail [in the UK] in 2006, a further 4 per cent increase from 2005" and was not far wrong in its estimates.[1] It cited a range of factors that affect the success of businesses (see Figure 1.1).

Almost all businesses – established or start-up – fail. This failure is not necessarily total but is evident in some aspects: the businesses do not control costs, they let their customers defect, or they bring the wrong products or services to market. These failures result in low business performance and all-round stakeholder dissatisfaction.

Risk of failure in these and other aspects can be minimised or even completely avoided by consciously designing a new organisation or redesigning an existing one in such a way that it performs well and adapts readily to changing circumstances. This means assessing all the elements of an organisation and its operating environment and acting to bring them into alignment.

Organisation design, in this book defined as the outcome of shaping and aligning all the components of an enterprise towards the achievement of an agreed mission, is a straightforward business process that "is so critical it should be on the agenda of every meeting in every single department".[2] Curiously, however, executives rarely talk about it and even more rarely act to consciously design or redesign their business for success. What they often do instead is reorganise or restructure – it will become clear later in this chapter that a focus simply on organisation structure (the organisation chart) seldom has the desired effect. Peter Senge, in *The Fifth Discipline*, points out why intentional organisation design work is uncommon:[3]

Factors affecting business failures
2006–08

1.1

Indicator	Pushing business failures:	Main sectors affected
Gross domestic product	⬇	Our upward revisions to growth in gross domestic product in 2007 and 2008 have reduced the number of business failures forecast compared to those made three months ago.
Exchange rate	⬆	A less competitive sterling exchange rate against the dollar and euro will continue to put pressure on manufacturers, as well as businesses in the travel and transport and leisure sectors.
Energy prices	⬇	Energy costs have declined and this will support manufacturers and the travel and transport sector as their profit margins are relieved with lower costs; retail sales may pick up if lower fuel costs feed through to the consumer.
Business surveys	⬆	Business confidence is low in the wholesale sector and falling in the manufacturing sector as firms struggle with a less competitive exchange rate.
Consumer spending	⬇	Services should continue to benefit from UK consumer spending growth which should help limit business failures in the retail sector and help boost activity in the real estate and construction sector. However, with higher interest rates, consumer spending may become more restrained.
Housing market	⬇	Buoyancy in the housing market will help support the construction sector although we still expect activity in the sector to tail off towards the end of 2006.
Tourism	⬇	Tourism growth will help support firms in the leisure sector and the travel and transport sector. A less competitive exchange rate may damage tourism but has not yet had an impact. Any further shock such as another security alert could damage activity in the sector.
Business investment	⬇	Strong growth in business investment will support wholesalers and businesses in technology, media and telecoms – despite slipping confidence.

Source: www.bdo.co.uk/BDOSH/Website/bdouk/websiteContent.nsf/vAll/023F13FFCD2B07E380257243005538F2?OpenDocument

Part of the reason why design is a neglected dimension of leadership: little credit goes to the designer. The functions of design are rarely visible; they take place behind the scenes. The consequences that appear today are the result of work done long in the past, and work today will show its benefits far in the future. Those who aspire to lead out of a desire to control, or gain fame, or simply to be "at the center of the action" will find little to attract them in the quiet design work of leadership.

Leaders interested in the design of their organisation have an edge. They believe that an organisation behaves in the way it is designed to behave. If it is not designed correctly – an analogy is a poorly designed racing car – it will not be successful.

Believing that organisation design matters, these leaders act on five principles:

1 Design is driven by the business strategy and the operating context (not by a new IT system, a new leader wanting to make an impact, or some other non-business reason).
2 Design means holistic thinking about the organisation – its systems, structures, people, performance measures, processes and culture, and the way the whole operates in the environment.
3 Design for the future is a better bet than designing for now.
4 Design is not to be undertaken lightly – it is resource intensive even when it is going well.
5 Design is a fundamental process not a repair job. (Racing cars are designed and built. They are then kept in good repair.)

This chapter discusses what organisation design is and what it is not and then looks at these five principles. Note that throughout "organisation" means a discrete unit of operation or whole enterprise. Following the principles of hierarchy theory (see Glossary), departments and divisions can be designed independently as long as interfaces and boundaries with the wider organisation form part of the design. Herbert Simon's parable of the two watchmakers (see below) explains how complex systems, such as a whole organisation, will evolve much more rapidly from simple systems, such as departments, if there are stable and intermediate forms than if there are not. In organisation designs, getting the units aligned and organised coherently works to the benefit of the whole organisation.

The parable of the two watchmakers

There once were two watchmakers, named Hora and Tempus, who manufactured very fine watches. Both of them were highly regarded, and the phones in their workshops rang frequently. New customers were constantly calling them. However, Hora prospered while Tempus became poorer and poorer and finally lost his shop. What was the reason?

The watches the men made consisted of about 1,000 parts each. Tempus had so constructed his that if he had one partially assembled and had to put it down – to answer the phone, say – it immediately fell to pieces and had to be reassembled from the elements. The better the customers liked his watches the more they phoned him and the more difficult it became for him to find enough uninterrupted time to finish a watch.

The watches Hora handled were no less complex than those of Tempus, but he had designed them so that he could put together subassemblies of about ten elements each. Ten of these subassemblies could be put together into a larger subassembly, and a system of ten of the latter constituted the whole watch. Hence, when Hora had to put down a partly assembled watch in order to answer the phone, he lost only a small part of his work, and he assembled his watches in only a fraction of the time it took Tempus.

Source: Simon, H.A., *The Sciences of the Artificial*, 3rd edn, MIT Press, 1996

Organisation design: what it is and what it is not

As stated earlier, organisation design is the outcome of shaping and aligning all the components of an enterprise towards the achievement of an agreed mission. This definition implies that there are designed-in qualities that keep the organisation adaptable to the operating context (see Figure 1.2).

A reorganisation or restructuring that focuses – sometimes solely – on the structural aspects is not organisation design and is rarely successful. Ask anyone who has been involved in this type of reorganisation and there will be stories of confusion, exasperation and stress, and of plummeting morale, motivation and productivity. Most people who have worked in organisations have had this experience. So why is it that initiatives aimed at revitalisation, renewal and performance improvement so often miss the mark? The simple answer is that focus on the structure is both not enough and not the right start-point.

The following example illustrates the point that reorganising from a structural start-point is misguided. A new vice-president has been

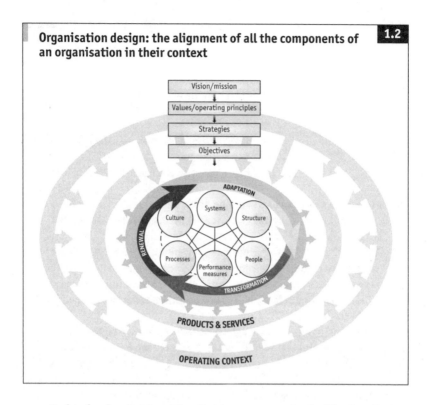

Organisation design: the alignment of all the components of an organisation in their context `1.2`

recruited to lead a division. The division structure looks like that shown in Figure 1.3.

The new vice-president decides (without consulting anyone) that the division would be more effective if the organisation chart looked like Figure 1.4.

So far, this looks like a simple change (or perhaps not a change at all). But the new positioning of employee 1 raises questions; for example:

- ◪ Why was this change initiated?
- ◪ Is employee 1 now in a different role?
- ◪ Is employee 1 now superior to employees 2 and 3, or has employee 1 been demoted to the role of the vice-president's assistant?
- ◪ Do employee 1's responsibilities change in the new role? If so, how – by adding to them and/or dropping some?
- ◪ If responsibilities are to be dropped, who, if anyone, is to take them on?

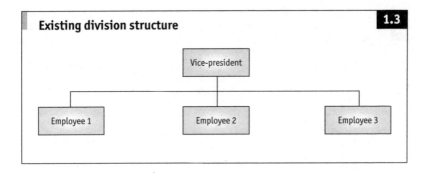

Existing division structure `1.3`

- How will this structural change affect information flow?
- How will this structural change affect relationships among the three employees?
- What effect will the change have on the business's systems if the work flow changes?
- How will customers be affected?
- What effect will this change have on other departments?

What seems a simple structuring tweak is actually complex, and the complexity is increased when more hierarchical levels are involved. Extending the example, Figure 1.5 shows that the new structuring could change the dynamics of the division substantially (depending on the answers to the various questions) and not only because the relationships between the players are changed.

This example shows why taking a structurally focused approach to organisational design is risky. Although it looks straightforward, it is likely

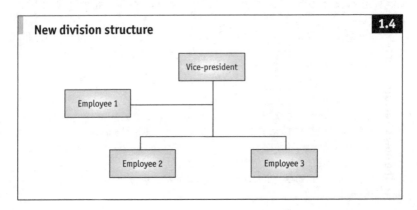

New division structure `1.4`

1.5 The new structure (right-hand side) has complex organisational impacts

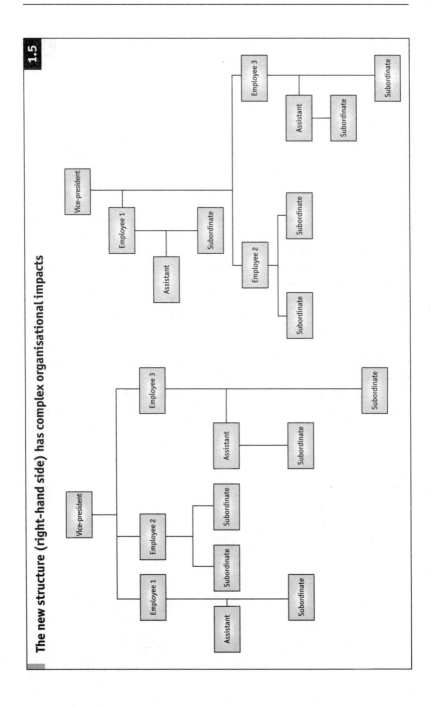

to have numerous impacts and consequences and bring with it potential derailers. Using the racing-car analogy again, it would be foolhardy to determine a new tyre configuration without thinking through the outcome and results of doing so. Simply changing the boxes on an organisation chart is tantamount to thoughtlessly reconfiguring tyres.

Organisation design is more than what is called reorganisation and different from a purely structural response to trying to solve a business problem. Organisation design starts with the business vision/mission (see Figure 1.2) and then involves consideration of all the elements of the organisation in its environment. Too little consistent, collaborative and strategic thought at the start of organisation design work almost guarantees failure. Although such work may (or may not) result in structure change, it involves much more than the structure.

To recap, organisation design is the whole sequence of work that results in an alignment of vision/mission, values/operating principles, strategies, objectives, tactics, systems, structure, people, processes, culture and performance measures in order to deliver the required results in the operating context. Just as in car racing, winning the Grand Prix is determined by much more than simply the structure of the car.

Designing is driven by the business strategy and the operating context

Look again at Figure 1.2 (page 5). The design process starts with leadership agreement on what the organisational vision/mission, values/operating principles, strategies, objectives and tactics are. This implies strategic thinking and strategic planning, which are different activities that should not be confused. Eton Lawrence summarises Henry Mintzberg's distinction between the two:[4]

> Mintzberg argues that strategic planning is the systematic programming of pre-identified strategies from which an action plan is developed. Strategic thinking, on the other hand, is a synthesizing process utilizing intuition and creativity whose outcome is an integrated perspective of the enterprise. Briefly put strategic thinking is the "what", and strategic planning is the "how", and you can't know how you're going to do something until you know what it is that you want to do.

Note that the operating context surrounds the graphic in Figure 1.2. It is constantly changing and is a critical variable in organisation design work.

Knowing the operating context helps determine the need for and scope of organisation design. Having determined the business strategy, the next step in organisation design is to assess the operating context. A simple tool such as the STEEPLE mnemonic illustrated in Table 1.1 will help (the cells have been completed for a hypothetical organisation).

Table 1.1 **Design the organisation with the operating context in mind**

	Context factors external to the organisation	Context factors internal to the organisation
Social	The characteristics of the available workforce change (eg, people want to work more from home or work part-time).	There is a new leader. Workforce demographics shift (eg, large numbers of employees are due to retire in a particular period.)
Technological	A new technology has an impact on the business (eg, VoIP).	System integration is proposed to iron out duplication of work.
Environmental	A new standard comes into play (eg, wood products sell better if they are made from sustainable forests).	There is a crisis with a product (eg, contamination or technical failure resulting in recalls).
Economic	Import/export barriers or tariffs change.	A new business strategy is initiated. A competitor suddenly starts to grab market share.
Political	There is a change in government requiring realignment of the organisation's lobbying.	The chairman and the CEO disagree. Board members take sides.
Legal	A new legal requirement requires compliance (eg, Operation and Financial Review in the UK).	An existing compliance standard has resulted in over-administration (eg, several departments may be collecting similar information).
Extras	Customers are drifting to competitors. The firm becomes the target of a hostile bid.	There is a disaster requiring recovery plans to be put into action.

The example operating context shown in Table 1.1 implies three things:

- ◪ Context factors do not come in neat single packets. Whether a business is new or established, it is usually necessary to respond to several simultaneously.

- The context is not static. As it changes elements become more or less important.
- Businesses must be designed to be adaptable to and accommodating of constant context changes.

Designing means holistic thinking about the organisation

Look once more at Figure 1.2. When the organisational vision/mission, values/operating principles, strategies, objectives and tactics have been determined and the operating context assessed, consider the six elements of the organisation labelled within the circle (systems, structure, people, performance measures, processes, culture). Organisation design work involves aligning these with each other, with the elements above them (vision/mission, and so on), and with the changing operating context. Imagine the organisation (as represented by Figure 1.2) is a gyroscope that needs to be kept both stable and moving. Organisation design work keeps the organisational alignment and also organisational flexibility and adaptability to the context.

Delivery of desired business results comes from aligning all the organisational elements towards the achievement of the vision/mission. The design is important because poor designs result in poor outcomes. Whether the business is new or established, good design decisions that involve the whole enterprise and its operating context will help give a competitive edge, minimise risk and raise performance levels.

This holistic approach to organisation design is evident in the case of Gore Associates, a privately owned company consistently rated as a high performer:[5]

> At Gore, we take our reputation for product leadership seriously, continually delivering new products and better solutions to the world. Gore's products are designed to be the highest quality in their class and revolutionary in their effect.
>
> Our founder, Bill Gore, created a flat lattice organisation. Since 1958, Gore has avoided traditional hierarchy, opting instead for a team-based environment that fosters personal initiative, encourages innovation, and promotes person-to-person communication among all of our associates. This kind of unique corporate structure has proven to be a significant contributor to associate satisfaction and retention, and continues to be a factor in our inclusion in the magazine's [Fortune] annual list of top companies. There are no chains of command or pre-determined channels of communication. Instead, we communicate

directly with each other and are accountable to fellow members of our multi-disciplined teams.

Note that to achieve its business strategy and maintain high performance, Gore has considered each of the elements. These are summarised from the extract above in Table 1.2.

Table 1.2 **Alignment of Gore's organisation elements**

Vision/mission	Our products are designed to be the highest quality in their class and revolutionary in their effect. We steadfastly live up to our product promises, and our associates address technical challenges with innovative, reliable solutions.
Structure	A flat lattice organisation.
People	A team-based environment.
Performance measures	Highest quality in their class.
Processes	New product delivery.
Culture	Fosters personal initiative, encourages innovation, promotes person-to-person communication.
Systems	Direct communication.

One of the strategies that Gore has determined is that no divisions in the company should comprise more than 150 people. By staying at this size Gore is able to retain the innovation, peer pressure and interconnectedness that enable it to consistently deliver outstanding results. However, this means that the company is constantly dividing and redividing to maintain its edge. (Note too that at Gore there are no standard job descriptions and there is a collaborative process for determining pay, both enabling internal job mobility.)

From this information it is clear that Gore's organisational elements are aligned. The strategy is clear, and the lattice structure, team-based working, lack of hierarchy, easy communication flows, reward systems and interpersonal accountability all promote consistent high performance that delivers the strategy.

Beware, however, of believing that there is a blueprint for design. Another company could not use the Gore design and achieve the same results. In the same way that there are many designs of vehicles (designed for specific customer segments and purposes), so the design of any company must reflect its particular styles and cultures of operation. Each enterprise has to determine its own design, and also its own timing and conditions for design work (but it must relate these to the business strategy and the operating context).

Having said that organisation design is both enterprise and context specific, there are nevertheless some generally applicable ways of approaching design work, starting with five rules of thumb.

Five rules of thumb for designing

1 Design when there is a compelling reason. Without a compelling reason to design it will be difficult to get people behind and engaged in any initiative. Business jargon talks about "the burning platform" needed to drive major change. Part of a decision to design rests on making a strong, strategic, widely accepted business case for it – based on the operating context. If there is no business case for design or redesign, it is not going to work.

2 Develop options before deciding on design. Scenarios or simulations can help to develop options. Mapping the workflow and identifying the impact that the context and circumstances have on it give clues on whether design is necessary or whether some other interventions (see Glossary) will be effective. Storytelling is another powerful technique to develop thinking on whether a new design is really necessary: ask people to tell stories about the work itself, about the nature of the work and how to do it better, and whether to do it at all. Larry Prusak, executive director of IBM's Institute of Knowledge Management and author of *Working Knowledge* and *In Good Company*, explains the value of storytelling:[6]

> What do you think people are going to do when a firm's in distress? They're going to talk to each other. They're going to try to tell stories. They're going to try to dig the firm out of whatever problems it's gotten into. They'll try to come up at least with local solutions. To help their offices as best they can. To help their branches. To help their division. The very worst thing you could tell people is: don't talk to your fellow workers when you have grave problems like that.
>
> And what we're really talking about here is a different model of how an organisation works. We're talking about a very non-mechanistic non-rationalist model, a model that is organic and self-adjusting, where people talk to each other, and things are not as crisp, not as clear, not as rational, not as scientific as they appear in the mechanistic models.

They're very little of those things. Organisations still have a lot of people in them. And that's what the people do: they talk to each other about work, mostly in the form of stories. There are many other studies of stories, but that's what they do, among other things.

Using a range of methods helps decide at a tactical level whether organisation design work makes sense or whether the issues can be addressed by other approaches (for example, technical skills training).

3 Choose the right time to design. Design work is undertaken in a dynamic environment in which the organisation, like a gyroscope, needs to be kept both stable and moving. Choosing the right time to intentionally design is a matter of judgment. However, for organisational change to be successful it is necessary to:

- establish a sense of urgency (the "burning platform" mentioned previously);
- form what John Kotter[7] calls a powerful "guiding coalition" – that is a group of people with enough power and influence to lead the organisation through the design;
- create a picture of the redesigned organisation in vivid terms that people will recognise and want to be part of (or can decide not to be part of – in this case plan to help them exit gracefully).

4 Look for clues that things are out of alignment. Assuming that there are frequent and regular measures of business results, look for clues that things are out of alignment. For example, Gore already knows that when unit size gets to more than 150, people issues arise, innovation is lost and associates stop seeing the whole picture. Organisations' blog sites are a good source of clues about organisational misalignment, as are the types of rumours or gossip that circulate as people talk to each other.

Lack of current alignment is a good signal for design work. However, if things are aligned, there is usually no reason to initiate design work (it is resource intensive even when going well).

5 Stay alert to the future. Identifying that things are currently aligned is no cause for complacency. The context is constantly shifting and this requires an alert, continuous and well-executed environmental scanning. Organisations must be aware that they may have to do design work at any point, so they should take steps to build a culture where change, innovation and forward thinking are welcomed. Gore's current situation illustrates this point:[8]

> A $1.6 billion company can't run on hope. Gore's next big challenge is to keep up its double-digit growth rate even as it gets bigger. As Gore grows from nearly 7,000 employees to 14,000 and then 21,000, it must continue to invent ways to protect its people from the harsh outside elements, even as it lets their big and creative ideas breathe – and prosper. That means venturing into the hazards of the greater world, where Gore might find it difficult to safeguard its unusual [innovative] culture. It means teaming up with giants like GM, the quintessential hierarchical organisation. It means expanding overseas to tap new markets and new sources of talent.

Gore has been a successful business since 1958. Even so, would it be safe to bet that the company is consciously considering how it should be designed for continuing and future success?

Designing for the future is a better bet than designing for now

Neither Gore nor any other company can accurately predict what the future will bring, but trend analysis, scenario planning, environmental scanning and a range of other techniques give clues on the context and the competitive environment. Organisations such as Shell that take the future seriously are less likely to be blindsided by events than organisations that are rooted in the present.

Shell has had considerable success over the past 30 years working with scenario planning. (See J. Van der Veer (ed.), *Shell Global Scenarios to 2025*, or look at the Shell website, www.shell.com, or www.well.com, a scenario planning website.) This has enabled the organisation to meet setbacks effectively with swift action and to perform well in difficult circumstances.

Conversely, the authorities in New Orleans did not heed the article by Joel K. Bourne published in *National Geographic* in October 2004, describing in great detail the devastating effects that a hurricane would have on the city. So when Hurricane Katrina hit in August 2005 the consequences were exactly as the journalist had predicted.

What many leaders fail to do is consider future possibilities. They are preoccupied by current and day-to-day issues. Frequently, they are caught off-guard even by predictable events and are equally unprepared for unpredictable events, having no plans in place to deal with either eventuality. (They would do well to heed the second habit Steven Covey discusses in his book *Seven Habits of Highly Effective People*: "begin with the end in mind".[9])

Systematic organisation design work involves creating a clear vision of the look and feel of the company in the future (the "to-be state"), assessing where it is now (the "as-is state") and then determining how to close the gap between the two. The gap-closing activity is the organisation design and implementation. Designers know that "the end" is a moving target, and they also know that the nature of the business issue any new design is seeking to address determines what is taken as the end – it may be anything from six months to ten years away.

Designing is not to be undertaken lightly – it is resource intensive even when going well

Because organisation design involves all the elements of an organisation (here organisation can mean the whole organisation, a division of an organisation, or a business unit – design work does not have to involve the entire enterprise), it is resource intensive. Keeping the day-to-day operation going while simultaneously trying, for example, to design for a new computer system, or merging divisions, or moving from a process to a market structure is not easy.

Be aware that organisation design, involving alignment of all organisational elements, may not be the right solution. This is why doing a careful assessment of the presenting issues, as well as the as-is and to-be states, is valuable and pays off in the long run. It may be that other types of interventions will solve the issues.

Take the example of Proctor & Gamble (P&G):[10]

> Outrageously high targets for revenues, earnings, and market share; a bold vision based on a striking new business model or groundbreaking technology; major strategic moves, such as acquisitions or partnerships, that change the game in an industry; a new CEO, freshly arrived from the outside and committed to shaking things up. Such shocks to the corporate system are widely assumed to be necessary for transforming a company's performance.
>
> Yet Alan G. Lafley's first five years as CEO of P&G show that none of these things is strictly necessary for achieving this sort of change. A large global company that has stumbled and lost some of its confidence can be led to new levels of performance through a more subtle form of leadership exercised by a long-term insider.

Alan Lafley, who became CEO after 25 years as a P&G operating manager, turned the company round by doing a number of things to align an existing design:[11]

> "I took P&G company goals down to 4 to 6 percent top-line growth, which still required us to innovate to the tune of one to two points of new sales growth a year," as well as some market share growth and, on average, a point of growth from acquisitions. "And then I committed to stretching but achievable double-digit earnings-per-share growth." The share price went down again "because the first thing I did was to set lower, more realistic goals".
>
> Lafley reined in the company's aspirations in a second, more subtle way: he defined what he calls "the core" – core markets, categories, brands, technologies, and capabilities – and focused his near-term efforts entirely on that.
>
> While management literature has emphasised the necessity of defining the core, Lafley underscores the importance of actually communicating the definition clearly. Indeed, he says that the need to communicate at a Sesame Street level of simplicity was one of his most important discoveries as CEO.
>
> Lafley realised that P&G, though struggling, was in better shape than press reports suggested. In particular, he recognised that the company's culture, far from being a hindrance, was an asset that could be leveraged in a transformation. So he reversed his predecessor's sharp critique of the culture and affirmed its competitive value in discussions with managers and employees across the company.
>
> Lafley clearly has strong faith in the transformative power of learning – a faith evident not only in his aspirations for the Gillette deal but also in the coaching role he regularly assumes with managers. It is clear, as well, in his initiatives to expand P&G's formal management and leadership training: for example, he founded the company's college for general managers and teaches leadership.

Lafley's approach was one of substantial change accomplished not by discarding what was in place but by making it work more effectively. His strategy successfully produced the desired results.

Unfortunately, there are no true signs of a need to "start over" the design rather than doing smaller-scale alignment work. Equally, it is not possible to determine whether a new design will have the intended outcome. Take the P&G example again:[12]

When Jager [Lafley's predecessor] left the company, news accounts cited his global reorganisation as a major contributor to his departure. Lafley, however, not only supported the reorganisation but had also served on the team that designed it. Rather than abandon Jager's new organisational structure, Lafley used it to support his own theme of returning to a stronger consumer orientation. The new market-development operations were charged with winning the first moment of truth, the new global business units with winning the second. The new structure, says Lafley, then "had a simple reason for being", and another apparent liability became an asset for the transformation.

By focusing on reorganisation (that is, structure changes), Jager appears to have omitted the crucial work of aligning all the other elements. By doing this Lafley brought success to the organisation.

Decisions on whether or not to design must be taken judiciously after doing a careful assessment of the circumstances and a risk assessment of the consequences. Bear in mind that the way the work is implemented is also a critical factor in its success or failure. In the P&G example, Jager apparently left the company partly because of the failure of his reorganisation work. Lafley picked it up, took a slightly different tack and made a success of it.

If organisation design is given the go-ahead, two things can help keep it on track without escalating disruption: strong governance; and tight project or programme management. Both of these involve finding people with the right skills, abilities and experience to manage and run the organisation design work and do so in a way that plays to the organisation's existing strength.

Designing is a fundamental process not a repair job

Racing cars are designed and built; they are then kept in good repair. Whether the design relates to a department, division, new enterprise or existing enterprise, it is important to remember that organisation design is a well-planned strategic change that fundamentally alters the way business is done. Take the example of IKEA:[13]

[IKEA] sought to redesign a specific product development and distribution system. The managers already knew that to restore their market advantage they had to flatten the hierarchy and broaden lines of communication.

The pipeline looked simple enough on paper. In fact, it described an interactive web of complex interdependencies. All 10,000 products were designed by IKEA employees in Sweden. Materials, from raw goods to finished products, were bought from roughly 1,500 suppliers in 55 countries and warehoused as close as possible to the stores. The 179 stores in 23 countries enjoyed more than 365m customer visits a year, and soon there would be 20 stores more.

The company a few years earlier had been reorganised into 11 business areas by product type, for example, upholstered seating, shelving, office, kitchen, and so on. The goal then was to shorten the path from supplier to customer by eliminating regional offices. Its unintended consequence was a proliferation of centralised staff in Sweden, seeking to co-ordinate the far-flung operations.

The organisation design work was undertaken using what is called the Future Search model (see Glossary). A year later the outcome was reported as follows:[14]

I previously had five managers reporting to me. Now I have two: one for supply, quality, and purchasing, and one for product range and commercial questions like advertising, rollouts, and marketing. Now the interfaces are clearer to all of us.

I realised that I needed another kind of leadership to help my organisation get all the way there. When it comes to product development at the suppliers, we have come far. Our latest example is a four-product programme called "Solsta" that was developed at a supplier in Romania, for the German market. The stakeholders developed a new distribution set-up to minimise the cost from supplier to customer as well as make it possible for the German stores to order different combinations of the four products. The first delivery was last week. The development time was less than half of what it was a year ago. (Catarina Bengtsson, business area manager, seating group)

In this example, the organisation design work related not to a department but to a product development and distribution system. The outcome was a fundamental change in the way this business was done. From the extract it is evident that the design affected all the elements of the organisation – systems, structure, people, performance measures, processes and culture – and to make the design work these had to be aligned.

Note that "the company a few years earlier had been reorganised into 11 business areas by product type" and the unintended consequence was "a proliferation of centralised staff in Sweden". This illustrates the point that without alignment of all the elements of the organisation the intended outcomes are difficult to realise.

The requirement to maintain a business designed for its context is a constant. This means knowing when and how to make design changes. What works in one time and environment does not work in another. If the business results and the environment are signalling that the current design fundamentally does not work, it is time to change it. The racing car that was designed in the 1990s is not going to win races against cars designed with the technologies available in the 2000s.

Summary

Organisation design is a series of activities aimed at aligning all the elements of an enterprise resulting in high performance and achievement of the business strategy. Because organisations behave the way they are designed to behave, conscious choices and decisions must be made on an individual enterprise basis on the right design for that organisation. Five principles govern effective organisation design:

1 Designing is driven by the business strategy and the operating context (not by a new IT system, a new leader wanting to make an impact, or some other non-business reason).
2 Designing means holistic thinking about the organisation.
3 Designing for the future is a better bet than designing for now.
4 Designing is not to be undertaken lightly – it is resource intensive even when it is going well.
5 Designing is a fundamental process not a repair job. (Racing cars are designed and built. They are then kept in good repair.)

Five rules of thumb guide the approach to organisation design:

1 Design when there is a compelling reason.
2 Develop options before deciding on design.
3 Choose the right time to design.
4 Look for clues that things are out of alignment.
5 Stay alert to the future.

Strong governance and effective project management minimise the risks of organisation design work.

2 Models, approaches and designs

All models are wrong but some are useful.

G.E.P. Box[1]

Models

Approaching the organisation as a system is a good start-point for organisation design. Figure 1.2 on page 5 shows one systems model, but several other organisation design models are available for use. These are all based in either systems theory or complexity theory, but because there are several models to choose from considerations of which is most appropriate for a particular situation come into play.

Knowing what a model is and the reasons for using one help determine which to use. A model can be defined as:

- an image or framework that presents a template for guidance; or
- a representation of a set of components of a process, system, or subject area, generally developed for understanding, analysis, improvement, and/or replacement of the process (US Government Accountability Office); or
- a representation of information, activities, relationships, and constraints (Treasury Enterprise Architecture Framework).[2]

The value of using a model lies in its ability to:

- help structure approaches to problems, improvements, or events;
- provide a framework for communication of changes and transitions;
- give the design process a common language and vocabulary;
- illuminate and help resolve design issues;
- illustrate interactions, interdependencies and alignments;
- help write a "new story"[3] of the organisation.

Without a model it is hard for a CEO or other senior executives to describe or think about their organisation in a holistic way. Their tendency is to think about only the structures (that is, the organisation chart), and with this narrow focus they cannot see the necessary alignment of all the elements that comprise a fully functioning organisation.

It is remarkable that models of organisation design are not usually part of an executive's toolkit. People are familiar with the use of models to clarify intention in all sorts of situations. For example, think of an architectural model of an apartment block. Prospective buyers know that the model is only an approximation of the unbuilt scheme, but even so it allows them to imagine themselves living in the apartment. They are able to use the model to project a whole lifestyle. Similarly, online clothing retailers such as Lands' End have developed the capability for buyers to "try on" clothes using a virtual model of themselves.

The modelling process allows a more complete (though not fully complete) assessment of the fit of the product to the requirements. Organisation design models do not result in a product like a physical building or a garment that meets customer requirements. But they do provide a good conceptual basis for developing an effective organisation design.

Systems models for organisation design in common use are those originated by consulting firms such as McKinsey, or individuals such as Jay Galbraith, Marvin Weisbord, David Nadler, Warner Burke and George Litwin (the Burke-Litwin model). The different models present various perspectives of the organisational system, in the same way that an astronomer standing on each of the planets would present a different perspective of the universe. No one perspective is "right" – the one that makes sense depends on circumstances, culture and context, among other things. So organisation designers at an airline might use the Galbraith model, and organisation designers at a large bank may favour the Burke-Litwin model.

The choice of model also depends on how complex users want it to be – how fancy, how usable, how costly in terms of implementation, how adaptable to changing circumstances, and so on.

Table 2.1 overleaf lists five systems models from the simplest to the most complex, noting some strengths and limitations of each. Comparing the models helps the selection process, which is discussed more fully later in this chapter.

The five models in Table 2.1 have been tried and tested over at least two decades. However, each was developed in an era of relative stability when organisations tended to have a single overarching business design that for the most part flowed down through the various divisions and business units.

Today's world is different: an organisation might comprise a portfolio of companies that operate differently one from another, might be simultaneously competing and collaborating with each other, and have to predict and respond in a chameleon-like way to a changing business

Table 2.1 **Systems models of organisation design in common use**

Originator	Model	Elements	Benefits	Limitations
McKinsey 7-S Model (developed by Pascale & Athos, 1981; refined by Peters & Waterman, 1982)		Systems Strategy Structure Style Shared values Staff Skills	Description of important organisational elements Recognition of the interaction between these	No external environment (input)/ throughput/output element No feedback loops No performance variables
Galbraith's Star Model		Strategy Structure People Rewards Process	Description of important organisational elements Recognition of the interaction between these	Does not "call out" some key elements including inputs/ outputs culture
Weisbord Six Box Model		Leadership (co-ordinates other five elements) Purpose Structure Rewards Helpful mechanisms Relationships	Includes some diagnostic questions in each box Requires the purpose to be stated	Focus on some elements may lead to overlooking of others
Nadler and Tushman Congruence Model		Informal organisation, formal organisation, work, people (with inputs and outputs)	Easy to follow Allows for discussion of what comprises "informal" and "formal" organisation Boxes must be congruent with each other	Few named elements may lead to wheel-spinning or overlooking of crucial aspects
Burke-Litwin Model		Mission/strategy Structure Task requirements Leadership Management practices Work unit climate Motivation Organisation culture Individual needs and values (Plus feedback loops)	Includes feedback loops "Calls out" more qualitative aspects (eg, motivation)	Very detailed Difficult to grasp at a quick glance

Note: The models are shown full size in Appendix 1.

environment. Because of the pace and extent of change, this relatively recent and crucial emphasis on having to be able to anticipate what the future operating environment will be like presents a substantial challenge to senior managers and organisational designers. Additionally, the models shown in Table 2.1 were developed with more of an inward-looking perspective (the organisation as a closed system) than an outward-looking one (the organisation as an open system).

Thus it is a moot point just how long the models discussed will be in circulation (and, of course, models are not set in stone – they can be adapted for best fit). New models are beginning to emerge as organisations respond to changes in society, technology, economics, environment, politics, legislation and everything else that bombards them. These models are emerging from arenas such as complexity theory, quantum theory (see Glossary) and non-western cultural traditions and patterns. Table 2.2 overleaf presents some of those which have potential for use in organisation design work.

The likelihood that traditional systems models (Table 2.1) are inappropriate for designing today's organisations is implied by Thomas Friedman in his book *The World is Flat*. He describes the way WPP – "the second largest advertising-marketing-communications consortium in the world" (comprising 130 companies) – changed its design to adapt to the current environment:[4]

> WPP adapted itself to get the most out of itself. It changed its office architecture and practices, just like those companies that adjusted their steam-run factories to the electric motor. But WPP not only got rid of all its walls, it got rid of all its floors. It looked at all its employees from all its companies as a vast pool of individual specialists who could be assembled horizontally into collaborative teams, depending on the unique demands of any given project. And that team would then become a de facto new company with its own name.

With this type of differently structured and temporary organisation, designers will find themselves using organisation design models in a different way than in the past. They will have to ensure that the model they select results in a design that is adaptive enough to keep pace with what Friedman calls the "ten flatteners" (see Glossary) – and their successors – which are having such a profound effect on the way work is done.

One way of developing an adaptive design is to look less at models and more at design principles or questions that are applicable to specific

Table 2.2 **New models with potential for use in organisation design work**

Originator	Model	Elements	Benefits	Limitations
Fractal Web Elizabeth McMillan[a] (after McMaster, 1996)		The fractal web principles of the organisation as an organism enable its characteristics to unfold or emerge as it learns and grows as a result of its own activities and its responses to the external environment	Based less in systems theory and more in complexity science. In this model the organisation is adaptive and self-organising, unlike the systems models which are more machine-oriented	Not easy to see how to apply it in practice
Ralph Kilmann's Five Track Model[b]		Five "tracks" for design: culture management skills team building strategy-structure rewards and systems	Kilmann developed this model because "the current view of organisations is rooted in a notion of reality that is false. This comes from the Newtonian paradigm that objects move through the universe and bounce off one another. There's nothing about life, consciousness, or people. The understanding of today's world was largely an outgrowth of the industrial revolution and the original economics"	Similar in scope and approach to a systems model
Ken Wilber's AQAL Model[c] (adapted here by Richard Barrett)		AQAL stands for all quadrants, all levels. Derived from an integrated philosophy of complementary ideas, theories, beliefs	Based in four quadrants (individual interior, individual exterior, collective interior, collective exterior) grounded in theories of developmental psychology	Not a fully formed organisational architecture model
Nadler's Updated Congruence Model[d]		One overarching vision with multiple competing strategies Multiple congruent relations between people, culture, formal organisation, strategy, and critical tasks	Allows for business unit differences	Requires strong leadership, mission and values to keep the units working autonomously but in the same direction

| Holonic Enterprise Model[e] | | Members are autonomous but coordinated In some cases the enterprise is time bound, ie it is formed to achieve the specific purpose and disbanded when this has been achieved. | Flexible organisational architecture combining the best features of top down (hierarchical) and bottom up/cooperative (heterarchical) enterprises e.g. Northern Italy where family affiliation and historic partnerships have created a lasting network of business arrangements to produce cheese and ham (Parmesan and Parma) | Requires capability to work in each other's interests and not just self-interest to achieve the common goal. |

Note: The models are shown full size in Appendix 1.

a McMillan, E., "Considering Organisation Structure and Design from a Complexity Paradigm Perspective", in Frizzelle, G. and Richards, H. (eds), *Tackling Industrial Complexity: The Ideas That Make a Difference*, Institute of Manufacturing, University of Cambridge, 2002.

b www.leadcoach.com/archives/interview/ralph_kilmann.pdf

c Wilber, K., *Summary of My Psychological Model – Or, Outline of An Integral Psychology*, 2000 (wilber.shambhala.com/html/archive/archive.cfm), in Barrett, R., *Building a Values-Driven Organization: A Whole-System Approach to Cultural Transformation*, Butterworth Heinemann, 2006.

d Nadler, D. and Tushman M., "The Organisation of the Future: Strategic Imperatives and Core Competencies for the 21st Century", *Organisational Dynamics*, Vol. 28, Issue 1, 1999, pp. 45–60.

e Ulieru, M. and Unland, R., "Enabling Technologies for the Creation and Restructuring Process of Emergent Enterprise Alliances", *International Journal of Information Technology and Decision Making*, Vol. 3, No. 1, 2004.

business strategies. This argues for a kind of "pattern book" of organisation design models for an enterprise rather than one model being used across the enterprise.

Raising its head, then, is the question: why even consider any of the traditional systems models? To which the answer is: because a large majority of organisations still have traditional architectures. The systems models described still fit most organisations and, used creatively or adapted, can help them move towards architectures that will accommodate the growing emphasis on decentralisation, cellular networks, internal markets, globalisation and employee empowerment.

Approaches

Choosing the right model for organisation design is one part of the process. The second part is to choose the right approach – the method for initiating the design work but also the way the design will be developed and implemented. The approach must match either the current organisational way of doing things or set the tone for doing things in future. So, for example, if things are currently done by leadership mandate in a command and control environment there may be lack of capability and behaviour to undertake design work using a participative and collaborative approach.

That said, organisations that are designed with the close involvement of stakeholders are more likely to be effective than those that are designed in a closed room by a few people. The more everyone in an organisation feels in some control of what's going on, and has input into things, the more likely it is that the end result will be one that they are motivated to work in: that is they will be committed rather than simply compliant. Advocates of employee empowerment are well aware of the value to the organisation of giving people at all levels in the organisation a voice and choices in their work, as the Zappos example demonstrates.

The Zappos culture book

Zappos runs a three-week training course for call-centre reps which starts with telling employees to forget everything they've learned. That's partly because Zappos, a six-year-old online shoe retailer with $184m in 2004 gross sales, isn't like many other companies. The training course's required reading? A 156-page handbook on Zappos culture, written entirely by employees themselves. In it, they quote Jimi Hendrix, praise the company-paid lunches, and tell stories about how they've felt empowered to help customers. Chairman and founder Nick Swinmurn, who calls Zappos "a service company that happens to sell shoes", (it offers free expedited shipping and free returns) believes empowerment means more than giving employees free rein to solve customers' problems. It's the power to help make the company better. "You need as many eyes, ears, and hands working toward the same goal for themselves, not for someone else," he says. An entry in the Zappos culture book by James G., a customer loyalty associate since 2003, shows that employees get it. "I'm helping write the book," he writes. "We all are."

Source: "Employee Innovator Runner-up", *Fast Company*, Issue 99, October 2005

This book strongly advocates stakeholder involvement – specifically employee involvement and empowerment – in organisation design, but if each of the traditional five design and implementation phases of assess, design, implement, embed and review (see Chapter 4) embraces widespread stakeholder participation using traditional approaches like surveys, focus groups, one-to-one interviews, problem surfacing, and so on, it can make the process feel laborious at best and never-ending at worst.

To manage the risk of feeling laborious, organisation designers are using a range of "engagement" approaches that are fun and energising. To manage the risk of feeling never-ending, large-scale "jumpstart" events that have representatives of all stakeholders in one place at one time are increasingly being used. Table 2.3 presents some examples in each of the two categories.

Table 2.3 **Examples of the engagement and jumpstart approaches**

ENGAGEMENT APPROACHES
(these can be used with or without the jumpstart approaches that follow)

	What it is	*How it works*
Storytelling	"A big part of a CEO's job is to motivate people to reach certain goals. To do that, he or she must engage their emotions, and the key to their hearts is story." (Robert McKee, *Harvard Business Review*, June 2003) "We are storytellers in this country. There is an oral tradition among what I call the skilled blue collar workers: miners, foundry workers, construction workers, deep sea fishermen, the military. You learn by working with someone who knows how to do your job. You are an apprentice. You are mentored." (Smith, S., "Preaching or Teaching: The Use of Narrative in Safety Training", April 13th 2005, www.occupationalhazards.com/Issue/Article/37525/Preaching_or_Teaching_The_Use_of_Narrative_in_Safety_Training.aspx)	Storytelling enables people to move away from a mechanistic linear approach to describing how something is done or works towards a more complex and "emergent" approach that richly describes the event, issue, or ways of approaching a solution. Storytelling approaches fit well with the newer organisation design models that are based in complexity theory.

Appreciative inquiry (AI)	Appreciative inquiry asks that people look for what works in an organisation and build designs from that. The result of this positive thinking inquiry process is a series of statements that describe where the organisation wants to be, based on the high points and good aspects of where they have been. For a variety of definitions of AI see: appreciativeinquiry.case.edu	Appreciative inquiry follows a four-phase approach: **Discover** Identify the actions and areas that have worked well in the past, asking such questions as: what did we do when we solved a similar problem before? **Dream** Envision possibilities and future states, asking such questions as: what is the best possible outcome we could get in solving this problem? **Design** Chart a course of action and develop an implementation plan, asking such questions as: where's the best place to start? What will it take to succeed? **Deliver** Move into implementation, asking such questions as: what's helping keep us on track? Where are things working well? What are we learning as we go along?
Positive deviance	"In every community there are certain individuals (the 'Positive Deviants') whose special practices/strategies/behaviours enable them to find better solutions to prevalent community problems than their neighbours who have access to the same resources. Positive deviance is a culturally appropriate development approach that is tailored to the specific community in which it is used." (www.positivedeviance.org) See also Pascale, R.T. and Sternin, J., "Your Company's Secret Change Agents", *Harvard Business Review*, May 2005. Here is a description, taken from the Harvard Business Online website, of the full article:	Positive deviance follows a four-phased approach: **Inquiry** Search for the positive deviants in the community or organisation who have got things done. Find out how they have made things work. **Design** Learn from their experiences. Structure questions and interventions that will help others change their behaviours. **Implement** Put the design into practice focusing on the skills adults have in learning new ways of doing things. **Sustain/establish** Make sure that new behaviours are embedded into the structure, systems and processes of the community or organisation.

"Organisational change has traditionally come about through top-down initiatives such as hiring experts or importing best-of-breed practices. Such methods usually result in companywide rollouts of templates that do little to get people excited. But within every organisation, there are a few individuals who find unique ways to look at problems that seem impossible to solve. Although these change agents start out with the same tools and access to resources as their peers, they are able to see solutions where others do not. These positive deviants are the key to a better way of creating organisational change." (harvardbusinessonline.hbsp.harvard. edu/b02/en/common/item_detail. jhtml?id=2874)

Positive psychology	The mission of the Positive Psychology Center (www.ppc.sas.upenn. edu/executivesummary.htm) – "To understand and build the strengths and virtues that enable individuals and communities to thrive" – serves to define positive psychology as an approach that draws on the positive rather than the negative aspects of life.	Positive psychology works from a perspective that individuals can stop their fears, anxieties, pessimism, negativity, and unhappiness from paralysing them and learn how to behave optimistically and positively, using their new ways of behaving to develop healthy and life-affirming outcomes.

JUMPSTART APPROACHES

The Axelrod Group's Conference Model	"People support what they have a hand in creating. When people understand the system they work in they feel empowered to make changes. Organisational capability builds when people learn principles rather than methods." (Axelrod, E.M. and Axelrod, R.H., *The Conference Model*, Berrett Koehler, 1999)	This model is series of two-day conferences with stakeholders. A typical route to the implementation of a design might be a visioning conference, a customer supplier conference, a technical conference, a design conference.

Future Search	"Future search helps people transform their capability for action very quickly. People tell stories about their past, present and desired future. Through dialogue they discover their common ground. Only then do they make concrete action plans." (www.futuresearch.net/method/whatis/index.cfm)	This is a conference-style approach involving large numbers of internal and external stakeholders jointly working on the design with facilitator support. Briefly, some initial questions are posed and the conference delegates use a combination of structured activities to agree answers/solutions. This approach has the benefit of generating feelings of ownership among the stakeholders with speed in getting to the implementation stage.
Open Space Technology	"Open Space gatherings are typically held to create a new vision, figure out how to implement a strategy, plan a significant change, solve a complex or intractable problem, invent a new product or prepare for community action." (www.openspaceworld.org)	"The rules are simple, although setting up the parameters for a meeting or conference in Open Space is based on the theories of complexity, self-organization and open systems. Do you know how sometimes when you go to a conference or a meeting, the best ideas, networking, brainstorming and deal making happen during the coffee breaks? Open Space Technology is designed to simulate that natural way people find each other and share ideas in all different cultures and countries. It is also based on the understanding that there is a great amount of wisdom and experience in any gathered group of people. "It all starts with a circle of chairs, without a pre-designed agenda. The group sets their own agenda by identifying issues and topics that have heart and meaning for them; topics for which they have passion and interest and for which they are willing to host a discussion group. Small group discussions happen throughout the day, with participants moving from group to group whenever they feel that they can no longer learn or contribute to a discussion, or when they feel drawn to another topic." (www.openingspace.net/openSpaceTechnology_method_DescriptionOpenSpaceTechnology.shtml)

| World Café | "World Café Conversations are an intentional way to create a living network of conversation around questions that matter. A Café Conversation is a creative process for leading collaborative dialogue, sharing knowledge and creating possibilities for action in groups of all sizes." (www.theworldcafe.com) | Use the guidelines in combination to foster collaborative dialogue and generate possibilities for action: Clarify the purpose Create a hospitable place Explore questions that matter Encourage everyone's contribution Connect diverse perspectives Listen for insights and share discoveries |

Note: Information taken from the websites listed.

Future Search was used in the IKEA example in Chapter 1 (see pages 17–18) to redesign the company's process and structure for product design, manufacture and distribution. Fifty-two stakeholders gathered to examine the current process, develop a new design, create a strategic plan and form task teams to implement it. It took 18 hours to develop a design and sign off on it. Note that this was not a sign-off meeting for something presented by top management – the design was developed with an implementable plan in a short space of time by people who had not met before.

Designs

When the function and purpose of the end-product is known the design process is started. In architecture, Louis Sullivan's phrase "form follows function" is commonly used and it is as useful and necessary a precept for organisation design as it is for architectural or product design. (Sullivan, 1856–1924, is considered the father of modern architecture.)

The selection of a model and an approach (or approaches) must be a conscious process because it forms the framework for the emerging design. In other words, the model and approach start to express the predetermined function of the design. Take a product analogy. Designers wanted a pocket knife that functioned well for a specific target group (young women). With this in mind they adopted the model of the Swiss Army knife. They followed this with a design approach that would appeal specifically to young women by virtue of its function. Thus with the function clear, a model in mind and some specific approaches, the designers were able to develop the knife.

Miss Army Kit

- A way to make your daily adventures easier.
- Everything a woman could possibly need in a compact little kit.
- Lightweight Miss Army Knife comes with 15 must-have female emergency items.
- Includes a flashlight, needle and thread, nail file, scissor, pill box, mirror, safety pin, tweezer.
- Secret compartment to put an emergency bottle of perfume.
- Very easy-to-carry in your purse or on a keychain.

Source: www.amazon.com

An architecture analogy further illustrates the use of models and approaches. If the design challenge is housing for older single people (the function), the model could be an apartment block. The approach is to design something that, within certain parameters, will appeal to that target group (and ideally unit purchasers will have been involved in the early design work). These parameters might include accessibility, utilities availability, market conditions, compliance requirements and cost to build matched to cost of purchase. The result is a form of housing for senior citizens that meets the brief.

In these two examples, the principle is that form follows function. So the Miss Army Knife has many of the constituents of the traditional Swiss Army knife: shape, size, price and elements that fold into the main body. The apartment block has all the constituents of many other buildings: metal, bricks or concrete, glass, ducting, cables, and so on. But in both cases something dictates that the final product is specifically a Miss Army Knife and not some other type of knife, or an apartment block for over 60s and not for upwardly mobile young people. This "something" is the function or purpose of the product in relation to its form. For the most part form is circumscribed by things like cost, quality, time to deliver, and so on.

Similarly, with organisation design the principle is that form-follows-function models and approaches follow when the boundaries – the things that circumscribe the form – are known. So as in a product:

- organisation design is an intentional construct;
- an organisation can be purposefully designed;
- an organisation will achieve successful results if a thoughtful process is used to develop its design.

Managers at Fujitsu described their picture of a well-designed organisation as follows:

> It has well-defined processes. There are clear links between the
> functions. We can see close fit between strategy, delivery, and output.
> People in the organisation understand their roles and can play their
> part without stress. Work flows smoothly through the organisation and
> the outcome meets customer expectations.

In the case of organisation design, the function or purpose is expressed by the business mission, vision and strategy. The boundaries of the organisation design are delineated by the values, operating principles and goals, among other things. In Figure 1.2 on page 5 the key purpose and boundary elements are shown at the top.

Now note that four of the five organisation models described in Table 2.1 (page 22) specify strategy or purpose as one of their elements. To emphasise the point, designing an effective organisation starts with agreeing its function (equated here with purpose, mission or vision). This is followed by getting clarity on the boundaries of the design. Once the aspects that comprise the function and boundaries of the design emerge, the form of it follows. This form-follows-function approach is implicitly endorsed by Michael Goold and Andrew Campbell who, in prescribing nine tests of organisation design, state:[5]

> The first and most fundamental test of a design, therefore, is whether
> it fits your company's market strategy. You should begin by defining
> your target market segments. The definitions will vary depending on
> which part of your organization is being evaluated. If GE, for example,
> were designing its overall corporate organization, it would use broad
> definitions such as "aircraft engines" or "broadcasting". But if it were
> looking only at the design of its financial services unit, it would use
> much narrower definitions, probably combining particular service
> lines with particular geographic markets: "aircraft leasing in Europe",
> for instance, or "receivables financing in Mexico". There should be no
> dispute about the relevant market segments; if there is, you need to do
> some fresh strategy thinking before you proceed with the design effort.

Sometimes a dilemma for organisation designers lies in the question: is the model chosen before the function is known, or is the function determined and then the design model chosen? This may seem a redundant question because there is an assumption that an organisation's leaders know what its function or purpose is. However, this is often not the case. An executive team can have as many different ideas about what the organisation exists to do or produce as there are team members. Often the first step in the design process is to get a common agreement (preferably deliverable in a single sentence) on the organisation's function. Members of the leadership team are then required to demonstrate through their behaviours and actions that they are committed to this purpose, will communicate it clearly and will work to make it "live". Google and Intel India Development Centre, for example, both have clear, one-sentence statements of what they are in business to do:

- Google's mission is to organise the world's information and make it universally accessible and useful.
- Intel India Development Centre's mission is to grow and sustain a design/development capability in India that delivers high-quality, cost-effective solutions for all major Intel divisions.

Any discussion on whether to determine function first or whether to choose the model first is immaterial. Most models force the clear declaration of the organisation's function. The choice of model and approach to develop the design is more a question of fit. Repeating the point made earlier, there is no single choice of model for an organisation design in the same way as there is no single choice of car for a family – making the choice usually involves trade-offs and compromises. But to help choose the model for the specific organisation, ask diagnostic questions such as the following:

- Does the model package the organisational elements in a way that stakeholders will recognise (are there enough, are they ones that are important in the organisation)?
- How will stakeholders react to the presented model (is it jargon-free, simple to understand and communicate)?
- Will the model find favour across the organisation or will it compete with other organisation design models?
- Does the model harbour implicit assumptions that might help or hinder design work? For example, does it include or exclude factors such as local culture (both national and organisational) and human factors (such as personalities), or does it suggest ways that elements may relate to each other?

◪ How adaptable is the model for the specific context and circumstances in which it will be used? Does it enable any new perspectives or innovative thinking? Is it scalable to small work-unit design and whole organisation design?

◪ Does the model work with other models in use in the organisation (for example, change management or project management models)?

◪ Are the costs to adopt the model acceptable (for example, training, communication and obtaining buy-in)?

◪ Does the model allow for new and unconventional organisation design that will help drive the business strategy?

◪ Does the model have a sponsor or champion who will help communicate it appropriately?

◪ Does the model allow for transformational design as well as transactional design? (Transformational means a design developed in response to environmental forces either internal or external to the organisation – for example, creation or closure of a business unit or a merger – that affects the mission, strategy and culture. Transactional means changes related to the business or work-unit structures, systems, processes, and so on that might be needed to carry out the mission and strategy but do not change them.)

Choice of approach takes place as the model is chosen. Approaches are not either/or – they can be used in combination. So, for instance, story-telling can be used in combination with appreciative inquiry, or Future Search can be used with positive psychology. An example is NASA'S ASK website, which was set up for storytelling.

Storytelling at NASA

One of the few things of value to survive the knowledge management movement of the late 1990s is an online site for managers at, interestingly enough, NASA. The site, with the awkward name of Academy Sharing Knowledge, or ASK, gives NASA managers the opportunity to tell each other stories about successes, failures and lessons learned. It is a publication every federal manager should read.

ASK uses a young technology, the Web, to disseminate the lessons, but it uses an ancient technique, storytelling, to help managers become better at their jobs. It's a refreshing change from consultant-speak books filled with jargon and catchphrases. It's far easier to peruse than Government Accountability Office and inspector general reviews, which force managers to read between the lines for leadership lessons. In ASK, managers tell stories in their own words.

Take a recent submission on risk management by Marty Davis, a Goddard Space Flight Center manager. He asked his employees to come up with a list of risks facing their weather satellite program. He told them not to use silly, unlikely risks such as someone dropping the satellite.

Shortly after, someone dropped the satellite.

"A 3,000-pound spacecraft dropping 3 feet onto a concrete floor gets damaged," Davis wrote. "How damaged was a bit more complicated, but estimates ran up to $200m."

The contractor on the program should have had 11 people moving the satellite, but had only six. The quality assurance officials who should have carefully observed the procedure didn't do so. An inspection of the cart to move the satellite didn't happen, and when someone noticed something on the cart looked different than usual, no one stopped to examine it. It turned out bolts were missing. After the team put the satellite on the cart, it fell.

Next came an investigation. Some of the contractor employees were fired. Davis discovered that similar accidents had happened in the past on other projects. What were the lessons learned? "None of these are simple cases where a team missed one step and so the accident happened," Davis wrote. "It's always a combination of skipped steps or miscommunications or dangerous assumptions."

"We need to properly identify the risk. ... The real risk wasn't necessarily 'dropping the spacecraft,' even though it was the end result. The risk in our case would more accurately be called 'complacency,'" Davis wrote. He said moving a heavy, expensive spacecraft is always risky, even though it is routine, and should always be treated as risky. "Safety requires strict adherence to procedures. Period!" he said.

A key strength of ASK is the goal to find lessons, not to assess blame. Managers feel free to talk about what happens without worrying that someone will take the fall for what they write. Davis, for example, was troubled by which employees lost their jobs. "The way I saw it, the people who got fired weren't necessarily the people who should have been blamed, because they weren't the root cause of the accident," he says. The source was the contractor's complacency about moving the satellite.

Storytelling is a way to bring out those kinds of lessons. Government often is ruled by the cover-your-butt method of management, in which people point fingers and eventually someone (usually a mid- or low-level supervisor or employee) takes the blame. Instead, ASK teaches managers that mistakes happen, lessons can be learned and people can improve.

Source: Friel, B., "For the ASKing", *Government Executive*, June 1st 2005

It is easy enough to see that storytelling could help in organisation design work at NASA, and indeed Michael Griffin, who became head of NASA in April 2005, instituted a sweeping new design for the agency.

NASA's new design

In July 2005, Griffin resurrected the 1970s executive position of associate administrator and promoted chief engineer Rex Geveden to fill it. With Geveden serving as chief operating officer, the administrator is free to tackle policy and strategy issues. Griffin also established an independent Program Analysis and Evaluation Office to "scrub" plans and budgets, and shifted reporting authority for the directors of NASA's 10 field installations from the mission directorates to Geveden. He's warned of a change in the structure of the Independent Technical Authority, which NASA formed in response to recommendations from the Columbia Accident Investigation Board.

In the 2005 operating plan update NASA submitted to the Senate Appropriations Committee in July, Griffin detailed several other organisational changes. When he was asked, "Which of these changes will have the greatest impact on NASA's ability to achieve its showcase mission of exploration?", Griffin replied, "I don't think any single change will have the greatest impact. The Columbia Accident Investigation Board report was not flattering about NASA organisation and institutions and programs. NASA needed a fresh look. The organisation hasn't adapted to the changes yet, but it will."

Source: Beth Dickey, "The New Regime", *Government Executive*, October 19th 2005

As with choosing a model, choosing an approach or approaches also involves posing a series of diagnostic questions such as the following:

- How will stakeholders react to the approach (is it pragmatic, not too fluffy)?
- Is it an approach that will work with other approaches in the organisation?
- Does the approach harbour implicit assumptions that might help or hinder design work? For example does it include or exclude factors such as local culture (both national and organisational) and human factors (such as personalities), or does it suggest ways that elements may relate to each other?

- How adaptable is the approach for the specific context and circumstances in which it will be used? Does it enable any new perspectives or innovative thinking? Is it scalable to small work-unit design and whole organisation design?
- Are the costs to adopt the approach acceptable (for example, training, communication and obtaining buy-in)?
- Does the approach facilitate new and unconventional organisation design that will help drive the business strategy?
- Does the approach have a sponsor or champion who will help communicate it appropriately?
- Does the approach allow for transformational design as well as transactional design?
- Do we need or want a jumpstart approach?

Again there is no single choice of approach. The general principle is to ensure that there is no conflict between the prevailing style of the organisation and the proposed approach.

CASE STUDY: choosing a model and an approach for a design

This case study illustrates how one organisation initiated a design and implementation project around a specific business issue. The choice of model and the approach chosen were part of the early thinking about how the design project should be set up. These choices formed the basis for resolving the issue in a participative and speedy way.

The organisation

A multinational pharmaceutical company with 91,000 employees in 140 countries. It is a world leader in offering medicines to protect health, cure disease and improve well-being. The organisation's stated goal is to discover, develop and successfully market innovative products to treat patients, ease suffering and enhance the quality of life. It has leadership positions in both patented and generic pharmaceuticals. It is strengthening its medicine-based portfolio, which is focused on strategic growth platforms in innovation-driven pharmaceuticals, high-quality and low-cost generics and leading self-medication over-the-counter brands. In 2005, the group's businesses achieved net sales of $32.2 billion and net income of $6.1 billion. Approximately $ 4.8 billion was invested in R&D.

The issue
Pricing of drugs is currently done within each geographic location. Thus there are many pricing teams each responding to local conditions and each with their own methods and criteria for pricing. There is a headquarters view that this model leads to overlap and duplication of work, inconsistent pricing for customers and lack of transparency on anticipated sales volume.

The requirement
An organisation design model and approach for designing and developing a pricing organisation and strategy that will result in cost savings, efficiency gains, appropriate standardisation of pricing policies and processes (allowing for local conditions if necessary), and local reinforcement of the desired business image of the global company.

Discussion
A group of managers met to look at new ways of thinking about pricing. They agreed that the design envisaged was transactional rather than transformational – that is, the overall business vision, mission and strategy would be unaffected. However, they felt it likely that thinking differently about pricing, how to price and pricing teams would result in a significant new design of many components of the organisation.

Before looking closely at the models the managers agreed that:

- the function of pricing was to determine the best price to cover costs and earn overall profit for the whole enterprise;
- pricing was determined by a relatively complex input, throughput, output process, shaped by the environment;
- they had to have a common, agreed and adhered to pricing strategy that dovetailed with the overall business strategy at the enterprise level but allowed for differentiation at the local level;
- the new "pricing organisation" should eliminate overlap, duplication and customer confusion.

This agreement ruled out a couple of the models immediately. The 7-S model does not specifically mention external environment and operating context and neither does Galbraith's Star Model, though both could be adapted.

The managers looked more closely at the remaining three models. The Burke-Litwin model with its many boxes, arrows and feedback loops looked too complex to be grasped easily and quickly by busy line staff operating in a range of geographies. The Weisbord 6-box model did not parcel the organisational elements in a way that seemed right to the group; for example, they were not clear what "helpful mechanisms" might look like across the current pricing process.

This left Nadler's Congruence Model as a possibility. This too had some constraints:

- It appeared to be a model for maintaining stability and consistency rather than encouraging adaptability to the environment.
- It appeared to militate against consideration of the different operating environments. In designing the characteristics of the pricing function, the managers were determined that this should include what Nadler calls the "twin principles of integration and differentiation" – integration meaning that each geography focused on the same business and pricing strategies; and differentiation meaning the ability for each geography to implement the strategies in a way that made sense locally.
- The managers were not convinced that it would result in a swift, innovative design and implementation. They were looking for a very different pricing function that would be operational within weeks rather than months, so they were not interested in going through the type of long-winded organisation design process they had experienced in the past. They were looking for speed in the design process and innovation in the resulting design.

However, they then realised that the Congruence Model had been updated to resolve these problems. The basic principles remain the same, but in the newer version[6] (see Table 2.2 on page 24) the model is applied at each business unit level but within a single enterprise vision.

The managers felt that in their case they could start to envisage an organisation design that built alignment, congruence and linkages (that is, integration) across all the geographic locations in the areas of formal organisation and work activities, and built differentiation for each geographic location in the areas of people and culture. The outcome would be people using the same systems and processes to carry out the same work activities but their ways of working could be different. The managers understood that the people and culture aspects of each geographic location would have to mesh with the formal aspects and the work activities, but they believed this was achievable.

Recognising that they were at an early stage in the process, the managers decided not to jump into an immediate solution to the business issue. Instead they worked through the diagnostic questions to see if their initial selection of the Updated Congruence Model made sense in their situation. By and large they felt that it would work, although they needed to check that it was in line with other models, and they wanted to see some of the costs associated with introducing it.

(The managers had been bitten in the past by external consultants using a range of models, each with its own vocabulary and style. The result was confusion, lack of consistency and money wasted as implementations collided on competing paths.)

The managers then started to consider the range of approaches they could use to develop and implement the design. As they went through the diagnostic questions, the discussion got more heated. Many group members felt that the prevailing style of the organisation was one of command and control, which was in direct conflict with the stated intention of being collaborative and "valuing the ideas of our people". With this disconnect between what was said and what was done, participants felt that trying to jumpstart the process through something like Future Search would be difficult to sell to some stakeholders because it could appear too soft in style and to others because they would not believe that anything they contributed would actually be used.

A challenger to this argument suggested that successfully using Future Search or other participative approaches could start to move the culture towards being a genuinely more involving one. In his view, this would improve organisation effectiveness because his experience was that participative business cultures were more highly performing than command and control ones.

The managers listened to him because they knew that although he was a relative newcomer to the business he had come from an organisation where collaboration was sought, valued and delivered excellent business results. He suggested that they examine their assumptions about involving people by looking for examples in the organisation where people had succeeded in collaborative ventures against the odds. (He decided not to label this as "positive deviance" but knew that this is what it was.)

However, he also made the point that if they were to choose a collaborative design process, they would probably have to change their own individual and collective management styles in order to "walk the talk" credibly. Bravely, he said that he thought this would be a bit of a stretch for some of them and a potential risk to the project, but he felt that if people could see their leaders visibly succeeding in becoming more collaborative this would be a great demonstration of ability to change and a good mitigation of that particular risk.

The discussion continued with people talking about the management challenges of being simultaneously global and local, particularly in terms of organisation design thinking. Some people started to suggest solutions to the whole pricing issue but were pulled back by someone stating that they had already agreed not to jump to a solution and to involve others in their thinking. The meeting ended with an agreement to:

- find out the costs of running a Future Search jumpstart, including preparation time;

◪ draw up a list of internal and external stakeholders to invite to the meeting, assuming they decided to go ahead;

◪ alert the communications group about the forthcoming piece of work;

◪ individually do some work on assessing their comfort levels with participative and collaborative approaches;

◪ make a decision on the boundaries of the project at their next meeting – they did not want to bite off more than they could chew, and they did want to agree clear parameters to the project.

Reflections on the case study

The selection of the model and discussion of the organisation design approach is not time wasted. It is not a sterile academic exercise rooted in ivory tower theory but something that provides a number of real-world benefits to the start-up of a successful design:

◪ It is a firm framework for everyone working through the design process, acting as a guide and a reference point right the way through.

◪ Communicated effectively, it shows stakeholders that there is a base from which a plan and a process will be developed. Too often restructuring or reorganisation is felt by those on the receiving end to be arbitrary, haphazard and not thought through.

◪ The discussion starts to reveal to senior managers their perspectives, attitudes and responses to the design issues. They learn where they need to develop their capability to work as a team to solve the problem.

◪ Using a model enables a number of possible solutions to be generated from the same platform. This makes comparing their relative advantages and disadvantages easier than simply presenting a range of possibilities.

◪ Discussion of different models or the aspects of a particular model encourages questions and debate about the intended design. For example, in the pricing case above, whether the critical pricing tasks were likely candidates for streamlining and consistency, and whether the way things were formally organised would need to be the same or similar across the locations.

◪ Using a model generates reflection on possible consequences of various types of design decisions. For example, what would be the consequences if they went for organisational consistency to enable mobility across locations in terms of roles, position in the hierarchy, and so on? Would there be any unintended consequences of going for such consistency?

Similarly, making conscious choices about the approach to the design helps move the organisation in a certain direction. In the pricing case, one of the design outcomes had to be to minimise customer confusion. This meant that people had to recognise customer confusion, care enough to do something about it, and have the capability and the means to do something about it. The managers realised that people knew when customers were confused but the prevailing attitude and behaviours were of the "so what, it's a management problem, we can't do anything about that" variety. Customer satisfaction surveys consistently pointed out these unhelpful attitudes.

Thus it was decided to use a design approach which gave people a say in the outcomes, developed attitudes and behaviours that improved customer service, and demonstrated a new commitment to making things transparent to all stakeholders.

Tools for this case

This debate could have gone wrong when it started to get heated. However, because of bad experiences in the past, the managers decided to get a facilitator to run their meetings and also to work on developing their individual skills in listening and questioning. What also helped them were two tools: the Learner/Judger Mindset Model; and electronic collaboration.

The Learner/Judger Mindset Model

This model was developed by Marilee G. Adams. Her engaging book, *Change Your Questions, Change Your Life: 7 Powerful Tools for Life & Work*,[7] teaches readers how to ask questions from a learning (curious) mindset rather than a judging mindset (see Table 2.4). Being an inquiring leader means asking questions like: What's the best thing to do? What are the choices? What's possible? What's the big picture? It also means listening carefully and not making assumptions, leaping to conclusions or closing down possibilities. Questions posed are constructive and open-minded rather than loaded with criticism or blame. This inquiring approach leads to innovation and creativity in thinking.

Table 2.4 **Ask questions from a learner mindset**

Judger mindset	Learner mindset
Human nature	Human spirit
Advocating	Inquiring
Automatic	Thoughtful
Judgmental, biased	Accepting, unbiased
Know-it-already	Inquisitive researcher
Inflexible, rigid	Flexible, adaptive
Point of view: only own	Point of view: includes others
Win-lose relating	Win-win relating
Debate	Dialogue
Feedback seen as hurtful	Feedback seen as helpful
Operates in "attack or defend" mode	Operates in resolution and innovation-seeking mode

Source: Adams, M.G., *Change Your Questions, Change Your Life: 7 Powerful Tools for Life & Work*, Berrett-Koehler Publishers, 2004

Electronic collaboration

Web-based collaboration tools such as GroupSystems (GroupSystems is a registered product of GroupSystems.com) come in a number of forms. These products are valuable in a number of ways:

- They can be deployed across multiple locations simultaneously, cutting down on travel costs, time taken to get to different sites, scheduling, and so on.
- They allow participants to "speak" in the electronic meeting environment. Participants answer questions or debate points by simultaneously typing in thoughts, ideas and responses. Each sees the input of others, stimulating more avenues of thought. This feature seems to produce more and higher-quality ideas than traditional meetings.
- The rapid collection of input enables substantive discussions with everyone seeing the same data.
- Everyone contributes anonymously and so participants are free to offer all kinds of ideas without fear of embarrassment or retribution.

- Each participant has an equal vote on an equal level. Each idea is evaluated on its own merits, rather than on the power, status, or persuasiveness of the contributor.
- Tools are fully integrated, which means that a group can brainstorm ideas, move their ideas into topics or categories, establish priorities for the ideas, look at alternatives, produce an outline of results and publish a report covering all stages of their work.
- Reports produced can be integrated into other software packages for easy editing and publication.
- A complete and accurate record of all ideas, evaluations and decisions is produced. This meeting "memory" is extremely valuable, especially if the participants change. Any new participant can read the decision record and rapidly come up to speed.

Summary

Organisation design works on similar principles to product or architectural design in that "form follows function". Traditional systems models of organisation design are giving way to models deriving from fields such as complexity theory and quantum theory. Nevertheless, traditional models can be adapted to take organisations into new forms. Organisation designs work best when a full range of stakeholders are engaged in the design thinking and process. Several approaches involving stakeholders are presented, all of which can be used with the various models. No one model or approach is recommended over another as the choice depends on the situation and the questions or issues that the organisation is aiming to address in the design. However, to help make the right choice of model and approach, some pertinent questions are listed. A short case study illustrates the points made and two tools to apply in this stage of the design process are briefly described.

3 Organisational structures

Structures are fine as long as they are controlled by the people who actually work within the structures, but they're dicey even there.

George Woodcock, Canadian poet and literary critic

HOW GREAT A role structural decisions play in organisation design projects depends on the outcomes sought. Structural decisions usually loom larger in leaders' minds than other decisions related to organisation design. But it is a mistake (often a costly one) to focus a design on changes in the structure. Structure is simply one of the elements to consider because, as previous chapters have pointed out, organisations should be viewed as complex and adaptive organisms rather than mechanistic and linear systems.

However, all design work requires at least an assessment of the current structure and its ability to support delivery of future results in a way that aligns with the other elements of the organisation. In making the assessment, it is useful to determine whether the current structure:

- directs sufficient management attention to the sources of competitive advantage in each market;
- helps the corporate centre add value to the organisation;
- reflects the strengths, motivations and weaknesses of the people;
- protects units that need distinct cultures;
- provides co-ordination for the unit-to-unit links that are likely to be problematic;
- has too many management levels and units;
- supports effective controls;
- facilitates the development of new strategies;
- provides the flexibility required to adapt to change;
- reflects complexity of markets and industry relationships while being sufficiently straightforward for stakeholders to work with.

Organisation structures seen in mature organisations (ones that have been around for two decades or so) have their roots mainly in classical organisation theory characterised by principles of scientific management. Based on these principles, organisations were structured to reflect economies of scale and standardisation of work. Financial capital was seen as a scarce resource and corporate headquarters exercised operational control over divisions, business units and departments. Many large organisations struggling today have had a hard time updating and renewing the legacy structure that has become entrenched. An example is General Motors. Jim Jubak, senior markets editor of *MSN Money* and formerly markets editor of *Worth*, comments:[1]

> Once upon a time, US industrial companies were designed to do everything themselves. Ford Motor marked a high point of this kind of corporate structure: the car maker made its own steel, for example, in the great River Rouge plant. General Motors builds its own cars from its own designs and then finances the cars. Independently owned – but company-affiliated – dealers sell the cars. Until recently, car makers built their own parts, too. General Motors and Ford Motor didn't begin spinning off part makers Delphi and Visteon respectively, until 1999.
>
> And once upon a time this structure worked well. By owning all parts of the process, these companies were able to make sure that all the raw materials and parts needed to mass produce cars were in the right place at the right time and of the right quality.
>
> But nobody would dream of building a company this way if they were starting a car maker today. Look at how Chery Automobile, an eight-year-old Chinese car maker, proposes to enter the North American market with six models in 2007. It has hired Visionary Vehicles (of the United States) for sales and marketing; Pininfarina and Bertone (of Italy, the designers of Peugeot sports cars, Ferraris and Lamborghinis) for body design; and Lotus Engineering (of the United Kingdom), Mitsubishi Automotive Engineering (of Japan) and AVL (of Austria) for engines and drive trains. Most other parts will be farmed out to Chinese suppliers.
>
> That gives the company a chance to focus on just two things – logistics and final assembly – and to put together a team of the world's best and world's cheapest overnight.

There are several reasons why traditional structures, largely stemming from the late 1800s and explained in Frederick W. Taylor's 1911 book *The Principles of Scientific Management*, are no longer valid. They are based in a world view that no longer holds, typified by a view that:

- management control and co-ordination are essential for maintaining productivity and performance;

◪ there is a "best" structure for any organisation;
◪ specialisation and division of labour increase the quality and quantity of production;
◪ changing the structure is the best way of dealing with perceived problems.

This so-called mechanistic perspective gave rise to the functional organisation structure characterised by a clear hierarchy in the workforce, a status-driven view linked to advancement (the perk of a corner office, for example) and an emphasis on vertical tasks with a focus on content.

Subsequent organisational theorists suggested that Taylor's view on the right structure for maximum productivity was too simple. They "proved" that it is numbers of complex, interacting variables that make the difference in motivating people and increasing productivity. The most widely known of these theorists is Elton Mayo, who between 1924 and 1932 conducted experiments in Western Electric's Hawthorne plant. His findings, popularly known as the Hawthorne Effect, propelled a wave of new thinking about organisational forms.[2]

Further thinking about organisations emerged, based on the view that organisations are systems. A change in one part of the system will produce different effects in the system as a whole, and because the operating environment changes frequently if not continuously, interactions within a system are inherently complex. This perspective resulted in structures that emphasised horizontal tasks, collaboration across units, a focus on process and a commitment model of worker productivity. Typical structures, discussed in subsequent sections of this chapter, reflecting early systems thinking are divisional (product, process, geographic/market, or customer) and matrix.

Later systems thinking and now complexity theories related to organisations have resulted in structures that aim to enable self-organising and interacting networks of agents, with leadership tied not to a hierarchy but to where it makes sense to have a leader. Structures reflecting open systems and complexity theories, also discussed later in this chapter, include project, network and cluster.

So the development of organisational theory gives rise to different organisational models (see Chapter 2), which in turn gives rise to different organisational structures. Table 3.1 simplifies the connections.

Table 3.1 **Organisational theory: models and structures**

Theory	Model	Structure
Scientific management	–	Functional
Systems theory (closed and open)	McKinsey's 7-S Model	Divisional
	Galbraith's Star Model	Matrix/project
	Nadler's Congruence Model	
	Weisbord's Six Box Model	
	Burke-Litwin's Model	
Complexity theory	Nadler's Updated Congruence Model	Network
	Kilmann's Model	Virtual (see Glossary)
	Wilber's AQAL Model	No structure yet emerging for this model
	McMillan's Fractal Web	Life-form (see Peter Senge *et al.* for further discussion of institutions as living beings[3])
	Holonic Enterprise Model	Cluster, virtual

Functional structure

A functional structure is a highly traditional structure deriving from the Taylorist view of organisations and is often found in strong command and control organisations such as the military. The key strategy of functionally focused organisations is to maximise margins through leveraging economies of scale and functional expertise. Functional structures are effective when:

- there are stable and undifferentiated markets with well-understood customer requirements;
- there is a successful, control-focused enterprise culture;
- there is a small, single product line;
- there is scale or expertise within each function;
- there are long product development and life cycles;
- the organisation works to common standards.

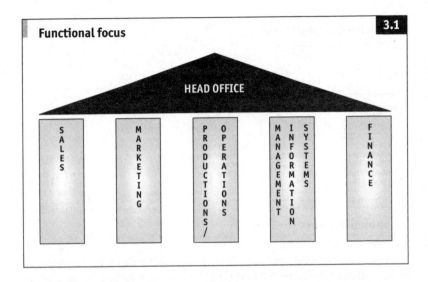

ExxonMobil's upstream operation

ExxonMobil's upstream operation is an "organisational design centred on a global functional approach", as Rex W. Tillerson, the company's senior vice-president, explained at the CERAWeek Conference in February 2004:

> Each ExxonMobil company will have different approaches as to how to meet the various challenges I've mentioned. I'll make a few comments regarding ExxonMobil's approach in the upstream portion of our business ... To maximize efficiency and adhere to a uniform high standard of business approach ... we have organized our upstream business by function, not geography, with each function operating as a global organization. We believe this global structure is the most efficient way to run our worldwide business. The global organization approach ensures that all exploration and development opportunities are pursued with a consistent eye toward quality and it ensures the right expertise and technologies can be deployed at the right time and with the right priorities.

Source: www2.exxonmobil.com/Corporate/Newsroom/SpchsIntvws/
Corp_NR_SpchIntrvw_RWT_090204.asp

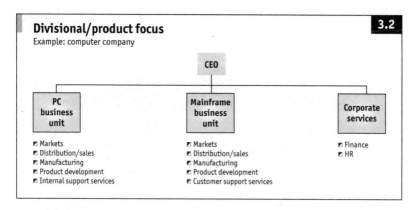

Divisional/product focus — 3.2
Example: computer company

CEO

PC business unit	Mainframe business unit	Corporate services
▪ Markets	▪ Markets	▪ Finance
▪ Distribution/sales	▪ Distribution/sales	▪ HR
▪ Manufacturing	▪ Manufacturing	
▪ Product development	▪ Product development	
▪ Internal support services	▪ Customer support services	

Divisional/product structure

A divisional/product structure is the most appropriate in a business where there are low synergies between the buyers and the distribution channels of the different divisions. Typically, in this structure each division runs as an independent business unit. Divisional/product structures are effective when:

- stakeholders perceive low synergies between products;
- there are different purchasing process/distribution channels;
- there are different operating requirements for success;
- there is a different competitive environment;
- there are short product development and life cycles;
- there is a minimum efficiency of scale for functions or outsourcing.

Danone is an example of an organisation structured on product lines as the following extract from its website illustrates.

Fresh dairy products, beverages, biscuits and cereal products – profitable growth on three fronts

The sale of Galbani's business at the beginning of 2002 marked a further step forward in a strategy pursued over the past five years, aiming for a focused business structure. Since 1998, Groupe DANONE has been organised in three business divisions worldwide which, in 2004, represented more than 97% of its consolidated sales: Fresh Dairy Products which groups together yoghurts, desserts and infant foods represent about 50% of the Group's consolidated sales, Beverages, essentially packaged water, which represent about 25% of consolidated sales and Biscuits and Cereal products, which represent about 22% of consolidated sales.

This focus on 3 dynamic categories allows the Group to have a determining strategic asset at its disposal to continue to display a growth rate that is higher than the average in the sector.

Source: www.danone.com

Divisional/geographic or market structure

As organisations expand domestically and internationally, the tendency is to organise by geographic markets enabling recognition of local cultures and operating conditions. These structures aim to operate under the slogan "Think Global, Act Local". Divisional/geographic or market structures are effective when:

- the business environment varies by geography – different customer needs, different competitive environment, different external constraints;
- the products produced have a low value-to-transport cost ratio (where the product value is considered in relation to the cost of transporting it). For example, potatoes are low value items and the

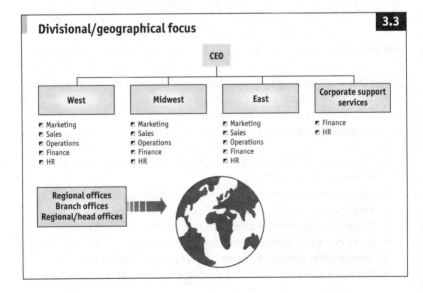

Divisional/geographical focus   **3.3**

CEO

West	Midwest	East	Corporate support services
Marketing	Marketing	Marketing	Finance
Sales	Sales	Sales	HR
Operations	Operations	Operations	
Finance	Finance	Finance	
HR	HR	HR	

Regional offices
Branch offices
Regional/head offices

cost of transporting them is high, so selling them close to where they are grown is a cost-effective strategy;
- the organisation is close to customers for delivery or support;
- the organisation wishes to be perceived as local.

Chevron/Texaco is an example of a geographic organisation structure.

Chevron/Texaco's organisation structure

In February 2001, Chevron and Texaco announced the organisation structure for the proposed post-merger company:

The worldwide downstream organisation reporting to Woertz [Pat Woertz, then executive vice-president downstream] will be segmented geographically into four operating companies for major refining and marketing operations, each headed by a president, plus a pipeline company. The refining and marketing organisations – North America, Asia/Middle East/Africa, Europe/West Africa, and Latin America – will have the scale and scope to create and share best practices within and across operating companies, will have a critical mass of competencies in each geographic area, and will share services at the lowest possible cost.

Divisional/process structure

In this structure the focus is on processes where core services are operated across the enterprise. Internal support services are frequently organised in this way but customer-facing services are equally well served by this structure, which is a good alternative to the functional structure. Process-focused structures work well when:

- there are well-defined processes serving different customers (internal/external);
- there is potential for new processes and/or radical change to processes;
- there is a requirement to reduce working capital;
- there is a need to reduce process cycle times;
- there is little interdependency between core processes;
- there are different cultures/workforces between core processes.

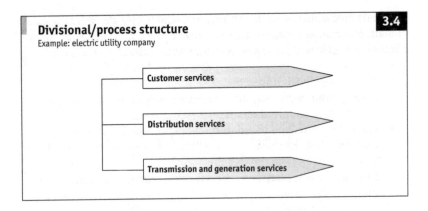

A US state government initiated a programme to streamline the situation outlined below.

Presentation to Finance Committee

Due diligence activities in 2005 uncovered an amazing situation. After surveying and interviewing 46 Executive Branch agencies regarding just 26 business processes, the following was discovered:

- 250 administrative, financial, human resource and supply chain management systems.
- All shapes, sizes and varieties – manual, spreadsheet, PC, server, mainframe and web.
- 4,750 FTEs (full-time equivalents, in other words the number of people) are needed to run/use these systems (this includes technical staff to support them).
- It costs $308m annually to keep this environment going.
- Extrapolated to the rest of the Executive Branch (minus higher education) the annual cost is estimated to be $441m.
- Redundant data entry and, therefore, duplicate data.
- Old and inflexible technology (such as COBOL) that is difficult to change and for which support is getting more and more difficult to find in the marketplace.

The desired outcome of the programme was clearly stated by the chief of staff. Summarised below, it is one where there are transparent, cost-effective and efficient processes across the enterprise:

- The primary goal of the Enterprise Applications Program is to redesign and implement new administrative, financial, human resource and supply chain processes and systems.
- The redesign will be based upon industry best practices and also accommodate the unmet needs of business staff in the Executive Branch as defined in the due diligence.
- Emphasis will be placed on process and system integration, data sharing, ability to adapt to business change and technology standards.
- Staff and technical inefficiencies will be identified and corrected.
- We will be able to see the whole enterprise. Management and staff will have the data and system functionality they need to operate the enterprise, closely track performance and make business changes to meet service demands of the state.

Divisional/customer structure

Structures around customer segments are successful where there are obvious customer segments defined by need, economics, distribution and other key attributes. Divisional/customer structures are effective:

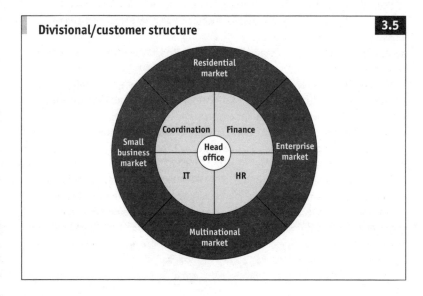

Divisional/customer structure 3.5

Residential market

Coordination | Finance

Small business market

Head office

Enterprise market

IT | HR

Multinational market

- where well-defined customer segments have been identified;
- when selling products/services unique to segment;
- when using buyer strength;
- when leveraging customer knowledge advantage;
- when requiring rapid customer service and product cycles;
- when perceiving minimum efficiencies of scale in functions or outsourcing;
- when promoting a strong marketing/customer-focused culture.

Royal Philips Electronics is an example of a customer-facing structure.

Royal Philips Electronics's drive to become customer centric

In the late 1990s, Royal Philips Electronics was a slow-footed behemoth whose products, from medical diagnostic imaging systems to electric shavers, were losing traction in the marketplace. By 2002, a new CEO, Gerard Kleisterlee, determined that the company urgently needed to address the dynamic global marketplace and become more responsive to consumers' changing needs.

Strategists recognised a huge opportunity: to be the company that delivered on the promise of sophisticated technology without the hassles. Philips, they said, should position itself as a simple company. Andrea Ragnetti, Philips's chief marketing officer, was dumbstruck. "I said, 'You must be joking. This is an organisation built on complexity, sophistication, brainpower.'" But he and Kleisterlee responded with an even more audacious plan. Rather than merely retooling products, Philips would also transform itself into a simpler, more market-driven organisation.

That initiative has been felt from the highest rungs of the organisation to the lowest. Instead of 500 different businesses, Philips is now in 70; instead of 30 divisions, there are 5. Even things as prosaic as business meetings have been nudged in the direction of simplicity: the company now forbids more than 10 slides in any PowerPoint presentation. Just enough, they decided, was more.

The campaign, christened "Sense and Simplicity," required that everything Philips did going forward be technologically advanced – but it also had to be designed with the end user in mind and be easy to experience.

Early results of the business reorganisation, particularly in North America, have been dramatic. Sales growth for the first half of 2005 was up 35%, and the company was named Supplier of the Year by Best Buy and Sam's Club [giant wholesale hypermarkets]. Philips's Ambilight Flat TV and GoGear Digital Camcorder won European iF awards for integrating advanced technologies into a consumer-friendly design, and the Consumer Electronics Association handed the company 12 Innovation Awards for products ranging from a remote control to a wearable sport audio player.

[John] Maeda, who, as a member of Philips's Simplicity Advisory Board has had a front-row seat for this transformation, is impressed. "The best indication of their sincerity is that they're embracing the concept at a management level," says Maeda. "It isn't just marketing to them. That's quite a radical thing."

Source: Linda Tischler, "The Beauty of Simplicity", *Fast Company*, November 2005

Matrix structure

Matrix structures typically operate in two dimensions (for example, function and product, as in Figure 3.6) and are usually one of three types: functional matrix, balanced matrix or project matrix.

The aim of the matrix structure is to provide customers with innovative solutions through effective teams of highly skilled individuals. Matrix structures are most effective in conditions where:

- core work is project-based or the work requires small groups of people;
- projects require highly specialised skills and knowledge;
- project skill requirements vary greatly;
- labour cost is a prime economic driver.

General Motors is an example of a matrix structure.

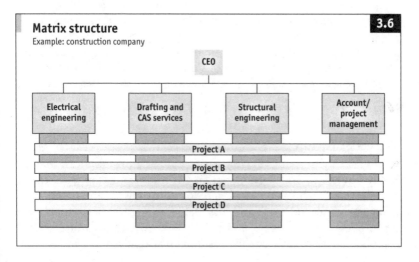

Matrix structure 3.6
Example: construction company

CEO

Electrical engineering | Drafting and CAS services | Structural engineering | Account/ project management

Project A
Project B
Project C
Project D

General Motors: a matrix in action

When Ralph Szygenda became GM's first corporate chief information officer (CIO) in 1996, EDS had just been spun off from GM, but it was still running all of the company's systems. Consequently, GM had no IT staff of its own. "There weren't any IT people to speak of; there was no IT leadership," Szygenda recalls. "How do you transform that?"

His answer, which got quite a bit of publicity at the time, was to build an organisational matrix of IT managers unlike that found in any other company. Szygenda hired five divisional CIOs to correspond roughly to GM's business divisions: North America; Europe; Asia-Pacific; Latin America, Africa and the Middle East; and finance. At the same time, he hired five process information officers (PIOs) to work horizontally in different specialities across all divisions around the world: product development, supply chain management, production, customer experience and business services (HR, legal and so on). These CIOs and PIOs came on board in 1997 to form the management organisation of GM's IT, formally known as Information Systems & Services (IS&S).

CIOs and PIOs work from divergent perspectives and have different reporting relationships. Each CIO reports not only to Szygenda but also to business heads; PIOs report to Szygenda alone. IT managers refer to "the matrix" or "the basket weave" to determine their relationship with one another and to explain their occasional clashes.

This matrix, proven over time, has been a critical part of how IS&S took control of IT spending from EDS. During the past seven years, Szygenda's team has lowered GM's IT budget by $1 billion (25%). Where previously GM used 7,000 different information systems, there are now fewer than 3,500.

By setting up overlapping, intersecting responsibilities among his direct reports, Szygenda designed the matrix to create internal competition, believing that was how to improve processes. "CIOs are driving efficiency in their world and PIOs are driving efficiency horizontally," says Cherri Musser, PIO for supply chain operations, who has twice been a CIO within IS&S and who was one of Szygenda's first hires.

Source: Prewitt, E., *CIO Magazine*, September 1st 2003 (www.cio.com/archive/090103/hs_reload.html)

Network structure

Network structures are valuable for fast-moving organisations that are highly innovative and operating in an environment that requires speed, flexibility and high levels of customer focus. In network enterprises work is organised around team and unit delivery, often because units have distinctively different ways of working. However, as the units work in combination, the delivery to the customer is seamless.

Network structure

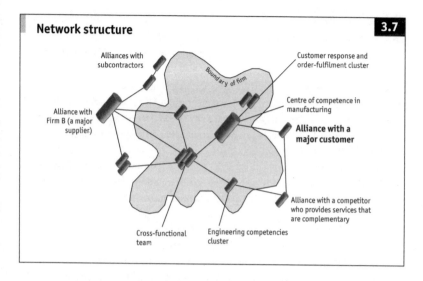

The movement of a parcel from point of despatch to point of delivery, via a company such as UPS, is an illustration of a network structure.

UPS: a networked organisation in action

UPS's financial strength is derived from its unique business model, combined with a company culture developed over 97 years. The business model is based on an integrated network where all systems work cohesively together.

One global network results in the most efficient use of assets and the highest reliability levels. And it makes it easier to bring products and services that are successful in the United States to the global market.

UPS invests hundreds of millions of dollars in its network annually for facilities, vehicles and aircraft. In Europe, construction continued on the expansion of the company's highly automated air hub in Cologne, Germany – the company's largest hub outside the United States. In addition, UPS's service portfolio was broadened to, from and within the ten countries that joined the European Union in 2004.

In the United States, network improvements reduced transit times by one day on UPS ground service between 20 metropolitan areas, including Atlanta, Baltimore/Washington DC, Chicago, Dallas, Houston, Kansas City, Los Angeles, Philadelphia and Pittsburgh. The company will continue enhancing transit times in the United States in 2005 and beyond.

Source: *UPS Annual Report 2004*

Cluster structure

The cluster model provides another example of an organisational style ideal for conditions requiring flexibility, innovation and change. It is a non-organisation in the sense that it does not exist as a physical entity. It is a subcontracting model where, as Gareth Morgan says in his book *Imaginization: New Mindsets for Seeing, Organizing, and Managing*, "the team at the centre steers the whole enterprise".[4] The subcontractors are the clusters around the central point. Specific and time-related contracts for work come from the central point.

The aim of the cluster model is to provide customers with innovative solutions through effective teams of highly skilled individuals. Cluster structures are most effective in conditions where:

- there is rapid pace of change;
- a market niche must be quickly exploited;
- subcontractors are required to do specific pieces of work;
- there is no requirement for direct reporting relationships;
- decision-making and accountability are delegated to those doing the work;
- clusters are linked by contacts among members.

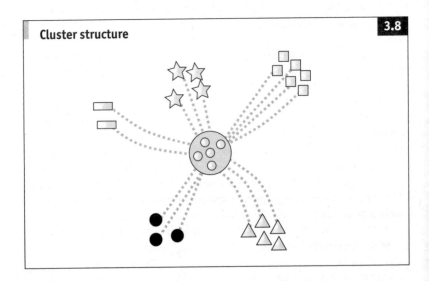

Cluster structure   3.8

Nike: a cluster approach

Firms such as Nike have stretched this idea to such an extent that some of them now make nothing: all Nike's shoes, for instance, are manufactured by subcontractors. Nike employs few people directly. Companies such as Nike have become the orchestrators of a brand. Their baton has only limited control over the musicians who play for them, but that does not prevent them from producing great music (or shoes).

Source: "Partners in wealth", *The Economist*, January 19th 2006

"Life-form" structure

The structures described so far all derive from thinking about organisations as an assemblage of discrete parts that can be taken apart, replaced, reassembled and re-formed as if they were a collection of Lego bricks. A different view of organisations comes from Aries de Geus, who talks of large institutions, particularly global corporations, as a new living species – at best, thoughtful evolutionary "beings" collectively participating in the evolution of our universe.[5] From this perspective it is impossible to disassemble the elements just as it is impossible to disassemble a human being and remodel one. As Peter Senge says:[6]

> Rather than attributing the changes sweeping the world to a handful of all-powerful individuals or faceless "systems", we can view them as the consequences of a life-form, that like any life form, has the potential to grow, learn, and evolve.

Theoretically, any of the structures described above could be part of a life form (in much the same way that a skeleton is part of a mammal). The difference in outcome is the way that the "mind" of the structure "thinks". Senge discusses a U-movement (Figure 3.9), not of a mechanistic structure but of an organisational life form with the capability to think and be in the world.

In organisations where the structure is integral to the organisational life form, characteristics that other living species have would be evident. For example, such organisations could:

◪ continuously recreate themselves (as the cells in a human body do);

Life-form structure

3.9

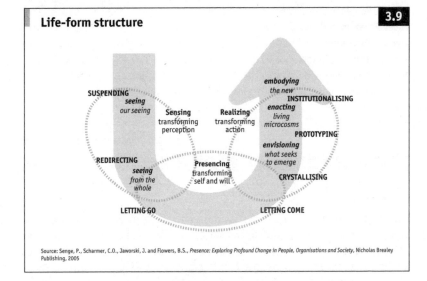

Source: Senge, P., Scharmer, C.O., Jaworski, J. and Flowers, B.S., *Presence: Exploring Profound Change in People, Organisations and Society*, Nicholas Brealey Publishing, 2005

- act from perceptions of where they are in relation to others;
- "conserve features essential to their existence and seek to evolve";[7]
- "learn to tap into a larger field to guide them toward what is healthy for the whole".[8]

Examples of this type of organisation are hard to find, but there are some "collectivities" that are perhaps moving in that direction. The Open Source Initiative is one, although it could be argued that this is closer to a virtual structure (see Table 3.3 on page 67).

Open Source Initiative: a life-form structure

Open Source Initiative (OSI) is a non-profit corporation dedicated to managing and promoting the Open Source Definition for the good of the community, specifically through the OSI Certified Open Source Software certification mark and program. You can read about successful software products that have these properties, and about our certification mark and program, which allow you to be confident that software really is "Open Source". We also make copies of approved open source licenses here.

The basic idea behind open source is very simple: When programmers can read, redistribute, and modify the source code for a piece of software, the software evolves. People improve it, people adapt it, people fix bugs. And this can happen at a speed that, if one is used to the slow pace of conventional software development, seems astonishing.

We in the open source community have learned that this rapid evolutionary process produces better software than the traditional closed model, in which only a very few programmers can see the source and everybody else must blindly use an opaque block of bits.

Open Source Initiative exists to make this case to the commercial world.

Source: www.opensource.org

Structure decisions

People in organisations are familiar with restructuring. Who has not enjoyed the Dilbert cartoons that exemplify the cynicism and weariness of the workforce as they get wind of the next round of downsizing, outsourcing, or similar? Restructuring an organisation can appear as a knee-jerk reaction to changing operating conditions, as Raymond Galvin (44 years in the petroleum industry, retired president, Chevron USA Production Company, and former director, Chevron Corporation) noted in a speech at the Petro-Safe '98 Conference and Exhibition:[9]

> For the last five years of my career, I presided over the restructuring of one of the largest oil and gas producing organisations in the United States. With oil and gas prices low and financial performance standards rising, we had to change. That reality, however, didn't alter the fact that cutting costs in health, environment and safety (HES) looked like a blend of hypocrisy and bad business judgment. To a good many employees, it looked like nothing more than putting profits ahead of safety.
>
> The years of downsizing and displacement had a big impact on morale – a lot of people left the industry feeling bitter. But a lot of others, whether they stayed on or left, appreciated the voluntary severance programmes, the redeployment efforts and the job placement services that many companies provided for surplus employees. These efforts were far from perfect, but I believe they made a big difference in HES performance during the roughest years of restructuring. In fact, it's a credit to the people of this industry that we were able to make behavioral and cultural progress in the HES area during such a traumatic period.

However, as leaders search for ways of increasing the speed, flexibility, integration and innovation of their organisation – without losing control of it – they turn first to its structure, perhaps because this appears to be an easy thing to do (compared with, say, looking at the culture, or the way people learn and apply things in the organisation). Basically, leaders want to know what structure will work best for the organisation and what the options are. The questions they want answers to are typically as follows:

- Speed
  - How often and how much restructuring is necessary to keep ahead of competitors?
  - What structures make for fast decisions and delivery of product or service?
  - What structures will enable keeping up to speed or ahead of the curve with changes in customer and market requirements?
  - What structures minimise bottlenecks without incurring risk?
- Integration (size and shape)
  - What structure will maximise the flow of knowledge and information through the organisation?
  - What effect do particular structures have on the relationships among business units, divisions, headquarters, customers, suppliers?
  - Does the way a department, business unit or organisation is structured get in the way of efficient and effective workflow?
  - What is the best balance between centralisation and decentralisation?
  - Does the structure allow everyone's voice to be heard (high participation) yet facilitate decision-making by more senior managers (centralisation)?
- Flexibility (role clarity)
  - How will jobs and pay levels be described and classified to maximise workforce flexibility?
  - What levels of autonomy, accountability and participation go with each of the potential structures?
  - What are the job designs that go with each type of structure?
  - How well do the relationships between individual departments and between departments and headquarters work?
- Innovation (specialisation/organisation identity)
  - What structure will best support the desired culture?
  - What structure will best support organisational values?

- Does the organisational structure attract the best and the brightest staff (and help retain them)?
- Will structuring differently help develop the organisation's market position and competitiveness?
- What structure would maximise the flow of knowledge and information through the organisation?
◪ Control
  - How will the balance between local and central control be attained?
  - How many layers of management make for effective and efficient control?
  - What is the optimum span (ie, number of people any one person can supervise) of control in a given set of circumstances?
  - How can structures be used to drive the desired/required behaviours?
  - What should be the chain of command/decision-making?
  - Who will report to whom and why?

Because the structure of an organisation is only one design element there are no straightforward answers to these questions as each has to be answered in relation to the other organisational elements. However, comparing the structures starts to give some useful information on the relative capabilities of each, as Table 3.2 overleaf shows.

Combining this information with the advantages and limitations of each structure (see Table 3.3 on page 67) gives a reasonable start-point on which to base discussions about current structures and structural alternatives. One point to bear in mind is that even within one organisation there may be no need for a single structural form across the whole organisation. For example, an internal audit department may require a different structure from a research and development department which may in turn need a different structure from a programme management department.

Table 3.2 **Comparing structures**

	Functional	Divisional	Matrix	Network	Cluster
Division of labour	By inputs	By outputs	By inputs and outputs	By knowledge	By skills and knowledge
Co-ordination mechanisms	Hierarchical supervision, plans and procedures	Division general manager and corporate staff	Dual reporting relationships	Cross-functional teams	Centralised hub co-ordinating across partner organisations
Decision rights	Highly centralised	Separation of strategy and execution	Shared	Highly decentralised	Within each contributing organisation
Boundaries	Core/periphery	Internal/external markets	Multiple interfaces	Porous and changing	Multiple changing interfaces
Importance of informal structure	Low	Modest	Considerable	High	High (hub to partner organisations)
Politics	Inter-functional	Corporate division and interdivisional	Along matrix dimensions	Shifting coalitions	Depends on contact between members
Basis of authority	Positional and functional expertise	General management responsibility and resources	Negotiating skills and resources	Knowledge and resources	Expertise, resources, position in marketplace
Resource efficiency	Excellent	Poor	Moderate	Good	Excellent
Time efficiency	Poor	Good	Moderate	Excellent	Excellent
Responsiveness	Poor	Moderate	Good	Excellent	Excellent
Adaptability	Poor	Good	Moderate	Good	Good
Accountability	Good	Excellent	Poor	Moderate	Good
Environment for which best suited	Stable	Heterogeneous	Complex with multiple demands	Volatile	Fast-paced
Strategy for which best suited	Focused/low cost	Diversified	Responsive	Innovative	Competitive

Source: Adapted from a presentation by BTR (now Invensys plc)

Table 3.3 **Advantages and limitations of structures**

Structure	Advantages	Limitations
Divisional/ product	Product focus Multiple products for separate customers Short product development and life cycle Minimum efficient scale for functions or outsourcing	High cost, loss of economies of scale Difficulty of co-ordinating geographic areas Lack responsiveness to local conditions New product development falls between the gaps
Divisional/ geographic	Low value-to-cost transport ratio Service delivery on site Closeness to customer for delivery or support Perception of the organisation as local	Conflict between regions and HQ Implementing new product lines or changes slow and difficult Difficult to apply global strategy Difficult to develop consistency and transfer learning
Divisional/ market	Important market segments Product or service unique to segment Buyer strength Customer knowledge advantage Rapid customer service and product cycles Minimum efficient scale in functions or outsourcing Geographic market segments needed	High costs, loss of economies of scale Difficulty co-ordinating geographical areas Less functional specialisation May lack responsiveness to local conditions
Divisional/ process	Best seen as an alternative to the functional structure Potential for new processes and a radical change to processes Reduced working capital Need for reducing process cycle times	Challenge to implement: need to redefine the operating culture of the business Clashes occur between HQ and divisions Increased likelihood of process overlap and duplication
Matrix	Flexible: teams may dissolve after task completion Specialist skills brought to bear where needed Attention paid to product/geography	Difficult to apply Supervisor power struggles/ overlapping responsibilities Need for a lot of co-ordination Greater transaction costs
Network	Quick response to markets High autonomy, ownership and accountability Less duplication of resources	Lack of deep functional expertise Difficulty with co-ordination between groups Accountability needs to be carefully thought through and made clear

Structure	Advantages	Limitations
Cluster	Partners focused on particular aspects of the value chain leading to: – greater economies of scale – superior skills developed – reduced redundancy of operations – lowering of barriers to entry – ability to create "a series of short term advantages"[10]	Clear central direction required Selection of capable partners an issue Keeping partners synchronised problematic
Virtual	Enables enterprises or individuals to organise and collaborate around an endeavour or project (often in real time over the internet) sharing ideas and information without being bound by any kind of formal organisation, royalty fees or legal risk, eg, the Oscar project (www.theoscarproject.org)	May clash with intellectual property rights Could enable competitors seize advantage
Life form	No real examples from which to draw conclusions on advantages	No real examples from which to draw conclusions on limitations

Layers and spans

Layers in an organisation refer to the number of levels of staff there are from the most junior to the most senior. Traditionally, government organisations have many layers: for example, US government agencies typically have 15 layers (with ten pay grades within each). The trend is to reduce the numbers of layers in an organisation by merging or removing them in order to place accountability at the lowest possible layer.

A span of management is the number of employees that a single manager is responsible for, usually in terms of allocating work and monitoring performance. There is no right number of people that one person can manage (though a commonly held view is that five is the optimum) as various factors affect a manageable span. The relationship between spans and layers is not straightforward either, although wide spans of management are typical of organisations that have few layers.

There are two frequently asked questions related to structure that managers and HR staff are anxious to get a right answer for:

◪ How many layers of management should there be?
◪ What is the right span of control?

Neither of these questions has one right answer. Layers and spans are structured to help managers get work done, so the first part of an organisational decision on the number of management layers and the span of a manager's control requires discussions and agreement on what managers are there to do.

In general, managers plan, allocate, co-ordinate and control in order to achieve what the late Peter Drucker described as their three tasks:[11]

1 To contribute to the specific purpose and mission of the enterprise.
2 To make work productive and the worker achieving.
3 To manage the social impacts and social responsibilities of the organisation.

Clearly, determining what configuration of layers and spans is likely to work in a given organisation depends on the situation, organisational purpose and a host of other factors related to the interpretation of what the three tasks entail and the weighting given to each of them. When John Browne became chief executive of BP in 1995, he reduced the management layers significantly and changed their spans of control and decision-making in order to introduce speed, flexibility and integration. According to an article in *The Economist*:[12]

> The oil giant had traditionally had a highly centralised hierarchical structure, but Lord Browne cut its head-office staff by some 80% and pushed decision-making down to 90 newly established separate business units. The hierarchy was flattened so much that the head of each of the 90 units reported directly to the company's nine-man executive committee – though as BP subsequently grew through takeover, some intermediate layers were introduced again. Individual managers also had much of their head-office support removed. The top of their silo had suddenly been lopped off.

Note that in this case some layers were later reintroduced, demonstrating that what may be the right configuration in one state of play may need to be changed if a different game starts.

To help get a good enough answer to the "how many layers" question, there are four rules of thumb (related to the four management activities of planning, co-ordinating, controlling and allocating). Each layer should:

- be flexible and adaptable enough to enable managers to forward plan in a context of constantly changing operating environments;

- facilitate co-ordination between business units (Michael Goold and Andrew Campbell suggest there are six forms of business unit to unit co-ordinating activity: leveraging know-how; sharing tangible resources; delivering economies of scale; aligning strategies; facilitating the flow of products or services; creating new business[13]);
- have appropriate control and accountability mechanisms (note that any task, activity, or process should have only one person accountable for it and accountability and decision-making should be at the lowest possible level in the organisation; overlap and duplication, fuzzy decision-making and conflict resolution processes are all symptoms of lack of adequate controls);
- enable its managers to allocate effectively the range of resources (human, time, equipment, money, and so on) they need to deliver their business objectives.

If these four attributes are working well, it is likely that the layer is adding value to the organisation, in that it is facilitating speed of operation, innovation, integration, flexibility and control. If it is not evident that the layer is doing this, it may be redundant and the reason for its existence should be questioned.

Determining a sensible span of control is possible (though infrequently done) both for an individual manager and for the type of work carried out in a business unit or organisation. The method involves considering the following:[14]

> The diversity and complexity of the work performed by the organisation, the experience and quality level of the workforce, the extent to which co-ordination or interdependence is important between employees and groups, the amount of change taking place in the work environment, the extent to which co-ordinating mechanisms exist and are effective, geographic dispersion, the extent to which job design and tools allow direct performance feedback to the employee, administrative burdens on each level of management, and expectations of employees regarding development and career counselling.

Robert Simons suggests that any job comprises four different spans: control (including people, working capital, facilities, infrastructure and intangibles), accountability, influence and support.[15] Each of the spans can be adjusted (see Figure 3.10) to reflect the business strategy and meet

The four spans `3.10`

Managers can adjust the spans of job design to create positions that are tuned for optimum performance

SPAN	TO NARROW THE SPAN	TO WIDEN THE SPAN
	Narrow	Wide
Span of control	Reduce resources allocated to specific positions or units	Allocate more people, assets, and infrastructure
Span of accountability	Standardise work by using measures (either financial, such as line-item budget expenses, or non-financial, such as head count) that allow few trade-offs	Use non-financial measures (such as customer satisfaction) or broad financial measures (such as profit) that allow many trade-offs
Span of influence	Require people to pay attention only to their own jobs; do not allocate costs across units; use single reporting lines; and reward individual performance	Inject creative tension through structures, systems, and goals – for example, cross-unit teams, dotted lines, matrix structures, stretch goals, cross-unit cost allocations, and transfer prices.
Span of support	Use leveraged, highly individualised rewards, and clearly single out winners and losers	Build shared responsibilities through purpose and mission, group identification, trust, and equity-based incentive plans

Source: Simon, R., "Designing High Performance Jobs", *Harvard Business Review*, July–August 2005

current organisational requirements, but to ensure high performance the spans related to the supply of resources (control and support) must be in equilibrium with the spans related to demand for resources (accountability and influence).

CASE STUDY: the effects of restructuring rather than designing

ATD Consulting was founded in 1992 as a two-person entrepreneurial venture to meet a need in the marketplace for consulting services focusing on collaboration techniques. It is now an 80-person company operating primarily as a consultant to government departments in a range of roles from staff augmentation to strategic partner.

For several years it remained a small company, but in 2000 it embarked on a new growth strategy combined with a branding campaign. By 2005 the company employed 85 people, had moved offices twice, had acquired a smaller organisation and had been named as one of the area's fastest growing companies.

ATD's mission was:

To drive peak performance, to enable clients to collaborate and structure solutions that achieve maximum efficiency and profitability, to build trusted partnerships and to help clients navigate through changing business environments with project and transformation management.

The company also cited seven organisational values:

- Collaboration: Bringing together disparate people, ideas, thoughts and experiences and blending them to create greater quality and highest value
- Mutual Respect: Treating everyone as you would like to be treated and valuing the contributions of others
- Integrity: Acting with high values; doing what is right rather than what is expedient
- Organisation-centric: All for one, one for all
- Client-centric: Dedicated to making our clients successful
- Trust and Safety: Having faith in fellow employees, the organisation and an atmosphere that enables individuals to try new things, voice opinions and be themselves without retribution
- Professional Excellence: Acting with the utmost professionalism, quality, proficiency, respect, integrity and class in all aspects of the work environment

On the company's website there was an assurance that "the two partners and the executive team work constantly to ensure cross-company collaboration and communication at all times, particularly during this period of rapid growth". In the reception area on a TV screen visitors could see information on the company mission, its staff and products, and the nine competency areas it focused on:

- Strategic and action planning
- Programme management and oversight
- Culture and communications
- Organisation change
- Business process evaluation
- Economic and financial analysis
- Information security management
- Technology studies and assessments
- Requirements management

Until October 2005 ATD was organised according to these nine competences, each with a competency director. The senior management team comprised the two owners, a chief operating officer, a chief finance officer and a head of business development. Two small support teams were headed by a chief information officer and an HR director. All these people had their own offices and the consultants were housed in cubicles. The organisation had three layers with an average span of eight people.

The offices were located on two floors of a new building. A special leasing deal, and an eye to future growth, meant that the company had a lot more space than people to fill it. There were a number of empty offices and several areas of open space with nothing in them.

In the early summer of 2005, discussions started with the competency directors about the future shape and size of the company. The feeling was that the structure was unwieldy, difficult to operate and confusing for clients. The company was also beginning to lose work to competitors. The two owners said that the organisation should be more speedy, flexible and innovative, and integrated with more appropriate control mechanisms.

Agreeing with this, the competency directors discussed the options among themselves and with their teams, and made recommendations that included clearly defining the business strategy and then designing an organisation to deliver it. They had assumed, from their current information, that the strategy included growth, attraction of commercial clients, and a move away from programme management (see Glossary) and towards strategic planning. With this and the organisation values in mind, they consulted their team members and drafted a design and implementation plan that ensured alignment of all the organisational elements and supported the collaborative principles on which ATD was founded.

The suggested structure (one aspect of the design and implementation plan) included combining some of the competence areas which would then operate as self-managing teams in a way that minimised organisational layers and optimised spans. Their plan included aligning all organisational elements.

At a staff meeting in October 2005, a new structure that had not been discussed with the competency directors or the consultants was revealed in a PowerPoint presentation. It showed the eight competency areas as five lines of business (LOBs), headed by a senior vice-president who had joined the company two weeks previously (see Figure 3.11).

Each LOB was headed by a vice-president: two were former competency directors, two were acting heads and one was someone who had joined the company the previous week. Thus seven competency directors lost their roles (if not their jobs) publicly and with immediate effect. During the presentation the consultants were told which line of business they were now in and to whom they would be reporting.

The new structure did not incorporate any of the recommendations or suggestions of the competency directors and added another layer of management (vice-presidents, senior vice-presidents, CEO and president). It named one of the new staff members senior vice-president operations (giving rise to speculation that he had been recruited with the promise of this although nothing had been

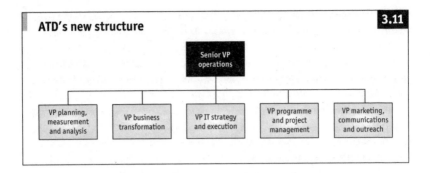

communicated at the time of his joining). The two owning partners became president and CEO.

Following the presentation and taking almost no questions about the new structure, the CEO moved to the meeting's next agenda item on organisational values. The stunned workforce was asked to form small discussion groups to discuss the values of "mutual respect" and "professional excellence".

A few days after the staff meeting the seven ex-competency directors were e-mailed a request to leave their offices and relocate to office cubicles within 30 days – even though this would add more empty offices to the existing ones. The new vice-presidents were each given a large office and the latest electronic communication devices.

Six weeks after the staff meeting all staff received an e-mail from the CEO mandating them to attend a workshop, the purpose of which was to "do some visioning – picturing ATD Consultants in the future". The owning partners noted in the invitation: "This is the first step in our strategic review process. We want to hear from you, so be there and be part of it!"

Four months later 16 people had resigned (six of these were the demoted competency directors), leaving clients unhappy as much of the work had to be covered by contractors. The informal organisation communications were about colleagues looking for jobs in other organisations, and the senior vice-president operations was being consistently described as someone with "no people skills" and "ice water in his veins" who expected staff to "salute and execute". The owning partners were struggling to keep their growth plans going in the midst of loss of organisational knowledge and skill, lower productivity, negative messages seeping out into the environment, and a developing culture of compliance rather than collaboration and commitment.

Reflections on the case study

Using the model shown in Figure 1.2 (page 5) and applying it to ATD Consulting's case exposes some basic design faults.

Although the impetus for the new design was, rightly, driven by the input elements in the model – customer requirements for clearer definition of the consultancy "offering" and by the operating context – the first principle of robust design is form follows function. In this case the new structure (only one part of form) was determined before the business strategy (function) had been developed. The values were in place but were compromised by the manner in which the restructuring was announced and took place. The other organisational elements were not aligned with the structure.

The net effect of introducing a new structure was that it started to dictate how the stated strategic desires – to enter the commercial market, focus on strategic planning capabilities rather than programme management and grow from 85 to 250 people within two years – could be formulated (or not) into an executable strategy. For example:

- The five lines of business reflected a government parlance and orientation that did not translate well into the commercial market.
- The loss of staff with specific and marketable skills made both changing strategic direction and responding to government requests for proposals (the predominant way ATD won work) hard as the organisation had less knowledge to draw on and fewer staff to act as key personnel on proposed projects.
- The inability to bid effectively for new work, because of staff attrition, led to increasing pressure on remaining staff to get themselves to 100% billable on current projects and to develop follow-on work from existing clients. This change of approach was not lost on the company's clients, some of whom became less favourably disposed towards it.
- Requiring consultants to be 100% billable meant that training, administration, research and collaboration had to be done in consultants' own time, leading an already demoralised workforce into further disaffection.

By overriding the company's stated values and operating principles (see Figure 1.2 on page 5), ignoring the work already done on a new design and simply presenting a new structure in a staff meeting, the owning partners lost the goodwill of their workforce. As well as compromising the values of collaboration and mutual respect, the structural change also compromised the value of trust and safety. People began to feel that speaking out about the changes was dangerous, and an intranet site put up for people to ask questions of the president, CEO and senior vice-president operations remained unused. Instead people gossiped and speculated informally among themselves.

As stated, structure was the only element addressed in the new design. The other five elements that comprise the model – systems, people, performance measures, processes and culture – were not aligned in tandem with the new structure. Inevitably, they were all negatively affected by the changes, leading to disruption and operational downtime. For example:

- Many staff felt that their capabilities were not congruent with the LOB in which they now sat. For several this signalled that the skills they had were no longer valued by the company.
- Some business processes stalled as the methods for operating them in the new system had not been considered. One was the process for responding to requests for proposals, another was the process for project reviews – both were essential in maintaining high-quality business.
- Conflicts surfaced around who owned which projects, which staff and which clients, as several of the projects in hand before the new structure did not necessarily fit neatly into one of the new LOBS.

Thus the five elements of speed, integration, flexibility and innovation, with adequate control, which the CEO and president said they were aiming to achieve, were compromised by a design process that began (and ended) with a restructuring. The resulting output was less than satisfactory. Six months later ATD had still not realised any growth, gained any commercial clients, or moved from programme management towards strategic planning.

Tools for this case

Had ATD's owning partners approached the design from a whole system perspective rather than a structural one they would probably have been more successful and carried more staff with them. The lesson is that structural changes affect all other aspects of the operation and it is essential to identify the right organisational structure as part of the organisation design process. Being mindful of the business issues the design is seeking to address and initiating a reflective discussion on potential structures are key steps in designing an efficient organisation. Two tools that help frame a discussion are structural evaluation and structural flexibility.

Structural evaluation
This tool (shown in Table 3.4), preferably used as part of a whole system design, helps identify a structure that will support business objectives.

Structural flexibility
Invite a mixed group of managers (who represent each level of management) and staff (who represent each level of staff) to a workshop. Select participants not just for the organisation level that they come from but also for their depth of knowledge about the business (its internal and external operating environment) and their ability to discuss future business possibilities. Ask them to suggest at least ten issues or opportunities that are in the pipeline or that might present within two years (or present them with some).

Now look at the current or planned structure and ask the group members to assess how they would flex and adapt to meet the new situation if it arose. They should focus particularly on aspects of planning, controlling, co-ordinating and allocating for each issue or opportunity, and should check that enough structural flexibility is in place to ensure that there is continued contribution to the mission, that the work is motivating, and that the social impacts and responsibilities of the organisation are not compromised.

For each issue or opportunity assess and, using the four rules of thumb, decide whether the current or proposed structure will help or hinder solving of the issue or realising the opportunity. If there appears to be a lack of flexibility or adaptability ask the group to develop a configuration that can cope with changes. This might be by modifying the existing structure, for example specifying roles and accountabilities, or clarifying decision points and co-ordination mechanisms. Or it might be by making more substantial structural changes, for example merging units. (If substantial changes are involved, the exercise is likely to become a full-scale design programme.)

Summary
The aspects of structure discussed in this chapter aim to give enough information to demonstrate that making changes to an organisation chart requires:

Table 3.4 **Structural evaluation tool**

	Yes	Somewhat	No
1 Do you consciously and periodically structure the organisation to reflect the changing priorities of your organisation?			
2 If so, have you consciously determined your current organisational structure?			
3 Do you have a set of measures that enable you to assess the effectiveness of your current structure?			
4 Do you evaluate your organisational structure on its ability to nourish entrepreneurialism, reduce bureaucracy and maintain control?			
5 Does your organisation currently have different structures in it?			
6 If so, have you identified factors that make these work well and less well?			
7 Do you know the advantages and limitations of the structures you could move to?			
8 Have you assessed the importance of the structural element in relation to the other elements in the overall organisation design process (eg, business processes, technology, systems, capabilities)?			
9 Have you considered the costs and benefits of changing the current structure?			
10 Do your staff members currently have the skills, knowledge and experience to work in a different structural form?			
11 Have you considered the effect that changing your structure will have on internal and external interfaces and boundaries?			
12 Have you considered the unintended consequences of changing your structure?			
13 Have you considered the risks inherent in changing your structure?			
14 Are you able to say what you have learned from past efforts to change your structure?			
15 If so, do you have the capability to apply the lessons learned?			

Scoring key: If more than 75% of your answers (12–15) are "Yes", your company is addressing the challenge of choosing the right organisation structure. If 50–75% of your answers (8–11) are "Yes" or "Somewhat", there is more work to be done to choose the right structure. If less than 50% of your answers are either "Yes" or "Somewhat", your company needs to re-evaluate its approach to selecting an organisational structure.

- assessment of the current structure;
- reflection on how any new structure can best support the business strategy;
- consideration of various internal and external operating factors that will affect the type of structure chosen and the layers and spans that comprise it.

The case study repeats the message of this book that changing the structure without due consideration of the other operational elements of an organisation is unwise. However, the point is also made that examining the structure is an essential part of designing an organisation, and changing it may be critical to delivery of the business strategy.

4 Planning and sequencing the organisation design

A plan is a list of actions arranged in whatever sequence is thought likely to achieve an objective.

John Argenti, author and founder of the Strategic Planning Society

DESIGNS THAT ARE simple, sustainable and deliver business results are the outcome of careful planning followed by well-managed implementation. They do not just happen. But if they do, the result is likely to be bad design rather than no design. Planning organisation design work involves:

- recognising that the time is right to design by assessing the problem or issue confronting the organisation;
- being clear about the design objectives, in order to develop a detailed plan;
- getting support for the implementation, so that the transition to the new design runs smoothly;
- monitoring the new design with appropriate performance measures that enable corrective action to be taken if there are signs of inability to embed it.

A question that is often asked is: how long does it take to get through the process from business case to embedding the new design? The answer is "it depends …". This is not a helpful response but it is the truth. Finishing to budget and schedule depends on a range of factors including the scope and scale of the design and the model and approaches used. Go into any project manager's office and on the wall are likely to be quotes like "Overruns are as certain as death and taxes" or "Any project can be estimated accurately (once it's completed)".

However, some designs can be complete and functioning effectively within a few weeks, as again an IKEA example shows:[1]

> IKEA, applying the principle of "whole system in the room", created a new structure and process for product design, manufacture, and

distribution, decentralizing an agglomeration of "silos" that no longer served. Some 52 stakeholders examined the existing system, developed a new design, created a strategic plan and formed task forces led by key executives to implement it. In 18 hours, the plan was developed and signed off on by the company president and key people from all affected functions, with active support from several customers. (Note: The process was operational within eight weeks.)

Other designs can take several years, as in the case of Barclays Bank (see page 103).

This chapter explains how taking a programme management approach provides a robust framework for planning and sequencing organisation design work.

High-level design plan and sequence

In an ideal world a new organisation design has a beginning, middle and end, each of which has been carefully initiated, structured and thought through in a logical sequence. Figure 4.1 provides the high-level view of a structured design process that is clear to visualise and straightforward to work with.

The organisation design programme starts with the business case (first row of Figure 4.1). Once the business case is accepted the organisation design programme is established: the governance and day-to-day operational management of the work (second row). The third row names the four phases that a design programme typically goes through – assess, design, implement and embed. Critical to organisation design success are five aspects – the change enablers – that must be built into the detailed plan (fourth row). The fifth row calls out these five enablers of success: leadership support, stakeholder engagement, change readiness, communication and training.

Although it is presented as a neat hierarchy with a linear sequence, in practice the process is much more iterative and messy – one thing merges with another, things happen and the edges become blurred. View the process as a map of how to get from A to B: experience proves that following the map will often involve getting lost, doing U-turns, backtracking and going along dead-end streets. The map may be accurate, but using it may not be as straightforward as it seems. Just like following a map, following a systematic process for planning and sequencing the design does give the basis for a high degree of transparency and control and does help things to get back on track as necessary, but it is not necessarily an easy and sequential journey from start to finish.

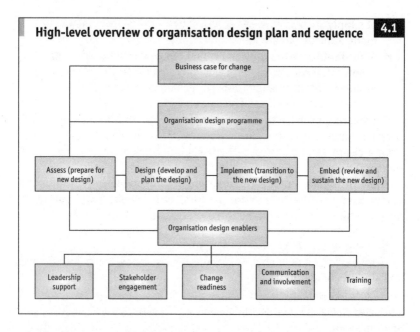

4.1 High-level overview of organisation design plan and sequence

The business case for change

A business case (first row of Figure 4.1) puts the argument for changing from the current design to a different design. If the case is well presented, it helps organisation decision-makers make the right investment decisions related to a range of social, technological, economic, environmental, political, legal, financial and other factors that have an impact upon the proposed design (see Table 1.1, page 9).

Organisations usually have some kind of template for the making of a business case. For most large organisations these include sections on five aspects:[2]

- **Strategic fit.** How well does the proposed way of meeting the requirement support the organisation's objectives and current priorities? Does the scope need to change?
- **Options.** Has a wide range been explored, including innovation and/or collaboration with others?
- **Achievability.** Can this project be achieved with the organisation's current capability and capacity (given other projects with a high priority that must be delivered at the same time)?
- **Value for money.** Can this be obtained from proposed sources

of supply such as current suppliers? Does the project need to be made attractive to a wider market?

◪ **Affordability.** Is the budget available to deliver what is required? If not, can the scope be reduced or delivery extended over a longer period, or funding sought from other sources?

Considering each of these areas helps ensure that a proposed new design is congruent with strategic objectives, that it is workable and that it has a clearly defined purpose. Without a tightly defined business case and sometimes even with one, things can go disastrously wrong, as the example of the FBI's major organisation design programme centred on a new case management system demonstrates. This had a less than adequate business case and the results showed.

The FBI's Virtual Case File

By late 2004, the writing was on the wall. The FBI's Virtual Case File, a much anticipated program to electronically organize and store mountains of investigative information, was coming unglued. The project was over budget. It was late. And a veritable revolving door of chief information officers and project managers meant that VCF was dangling in the wind with no one to save it.

Zalmai Azmi, who had been named the bureau's latest CIO in spring 2004, recalls FBI director Robert Mueller asking him, "How did this happen, Zal? How did this happen?" Looking back now, after VCF has been scrapped and the FBI has wasted $170m and three years of work, Azmi says the answers were obvious.

VCF was too ill-defined, it was too ambitious and it didn't receive appropriate managerial attention, Azmi says, ticking off the reasons as if he'd not only committed them to memory, but believed them with a certainty bordering on faith. To hear him tell it, you'd think the FBI's plans were doomed from the beginning.

Azmi has learned from past mistakes. "We should have developed [VCF] in phases ... not asked people to swallow it all at once," he says. With new controls over who buys what systems, his staff now ask offices to explain their business case for buying any new technology.

Source: Shane Harris, "The Turnaround", *Government Executive*, September 1st 2005

The organisation design programme

The second row in Figure 4.1, Organisation design programme, is the "office" of the new design. Regardless of the scope or scale of the design, a governance structure for it must be established to provide a framework for the upheaval that a new organisation design inevitably creates.

Governance comprises the way the organisation design programme is directed, controlled, organised, managed and administered through various policies and procedures (see the UK Office of Government Commerce example).

The UK Office of Government Commerce

The governance arrangements must deal with issues such as:

- the establishment and operation of best practice for the allocation and management of information and physical/human resources;
- the distribution of organisational responsibilities for managing change, and the relevant decision-making processes;
- the policies, procedures and practices implemented to ensure that the organisation derives maximum business benefit from its investments in business change;
- meeting requirements for the effectiveness, efficiency, confidentiality, integrity, availability, compliance and reliability of its information and information-based services;
- the implementation of effective standards and controls for the design, development, implementation, maintenance, use, acquisition and management of services and assets to support new ways of working.

A governance structure can be simple or complex depending on the organisation design programme. Figure 4.2 illustrates the governance structure of a British Airways (BA) programme to introduce a global human resources system to the organisation. A smaller project is likely to have a governance structure that in this graphic is labelled "project management" (that is, only that below the dotted line).

Given the scale and size of the BA programme, it was imperative to have a robust programme management office. One of the lead external consultants working with BA on this project noted that:

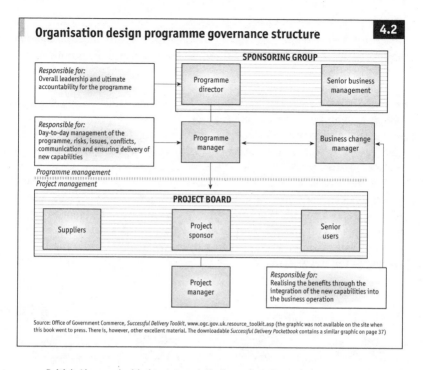

Organisation design programme governance structure 4.2

SPONSORING GROUP

Responsible for:
Overall leadership and ultimate accountability for the programme → Programme director | Senior business management

Responsible for:
Day-to-day management of the programme, risks, issues, conflicts, communication and ensuring delivery of new capabilities → Programme manager ⟷ Business change manager

Programme management
Project management

PROJECT BOARD

Suppliers | Project sponsor | Senior users

Project manager | Responsible for:
Realising the benefits through the integration of the new capabilities into the business operation

Source: Office of Government Commerce, *Successful Delivery Toolkit*, www.ogc.gov.uk.resource_toolkit.asp (the graphic was not available on the site when this book went to press. There is, however, other excellent material. The downloadable *Successful Delivery Pocketbook* contains a similar graphic on page 37)

British Airways decided to set up an independent Programme Management Office. It's made a world of difference to me, as one of the systems integrators. The requirements are clearly specified, at last I have access to the people and information I need. Everyone can see what this system is designed to achieve and where it fits into the greater whole. There's no more stone-walling between the stakeholders.

It's been really refreshing to learn from other projects and share our successes and failures with them. Not that there have been many failures with this new approach. People are involved in the project and participating – the culture and behaviours are measurably changing. I feel I'm doing a good job and the client is going to be really happy with the end product. Not only that, we're tackling all the other issues that go with systems implementation – organisation design, change management, transition management, communication, and the other stuff that gets dropped off the list when you're battling alone in your silo without a clear direction. I'm now firmly convinced that independent Programme Management Offices are a requirement for project success.

The four phases of the design process

The third row of Figure 4.1 shows the four phases of an organisation design programme: assess, design, implement, embed. Figure 4.3 illustrates the activities that typically take place in each of the phases. Note that the activities embrace the change enablers shown on the fifth row of Figure 4.1 (leadership support, stakeholder engagement, change readiness, communication, training) and the six organisational components (systems, structure, people, performance measures, processes, culture – shown in Figure 1.2 on page 5) that need to be aligned as the design work proceeds.

The blueprint discussed in the following sections forms the basis for planning during each of the phases of the organisation design work. Among the documents that come from working with the blueprint are a detailed plan with activities, tactics, milestones, critical success factors and other measures aimed at helping employees make the transition from the current to the future state.

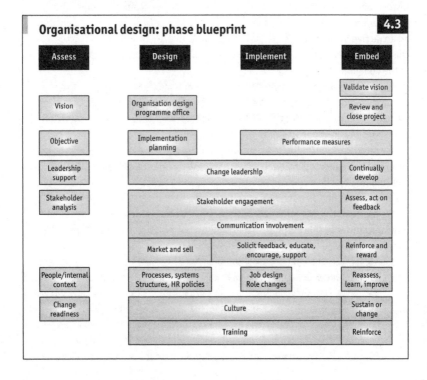

Organisational design: phase blueprint — 4.3

Assess	Design	Implement	Embed
			Validate vision
Vision	Organisation design programme office		Review and close project
Objective	Implementation planning	Performance measures	
Leadership support	Change leadership		Continually develop
Stakeholder analysis	Stakeholder engagement		Assess, act on feedback
	Communication involvement		
	Market and sell	Solicit feedback, educate, encourage, support	Reinforce and reward
People/internal context	Processes, systems Structures, HR policies	Job design Role changes	Reassess, learn, improve
Change readiness	Culture		Sustain or change
	Training		Reinforce

Phase 1: Assess
Vision (also mission or purpose)

All proposed organisation designs require a description of what they will look like when they are complete. In much the same way that an architectural model of a building describes what the completed building will look like, so an organisation design vision tells people what to expect in terms of new capabilities, service levels, competitive position, and so on.

An example is a description of a vision for the Commonwealth of Virginia developed when the Council on Virginia's Future started to consider ways of designing the Commonwealth's government agencies to make them fit to meet the future.

A vision for the Commonwealth of Virginia

Building on a centuries-old heritage of leadership, achievement and commitment to the success of all its citizens, and with an abiding commitment to the rich historic and natural resources of this Commonwealth, we aspire to responsibly grow our economy to provide an enviable quality of life. To do so, we must ensure an attractive business environment, challenging and rewarding jobs reflective of a changing marketplace, and strong growth in personal income throughout all regions in the Commonwealth.

We aspire to increase the levels of educational preparedness and attainment of our citizens throughout all regions in the Commonwealth because an educated, well-trained citizenry, committed to lifelong learning, provides the greatest opportunity to responsibly grow our economy.

We have a responsibility to be the best-managed state in the country. To do so, we must have a focused vision, and a fiscally responsible system that provides clear, measurable objectives, outcomes and accountability, and that attracts, motivates, rewards and retains an outstanding state workforce.

We aspire to have an informed and engaged citizenry so that our citizens can provide knowledgeable input to shape the vision of the Commonwealth, identify appropriate service levels and assess progress.

Source: Interim Report of The Council on Virginia's Future. Report Document No. 15 (Rd 15), 2005, Commonwealth of Virginia, Richmond, Virginia, January 12th 2005 (Reference HB 2097 – § 2.2-2687)

Note that this vision is for the whole enterprise. If the new organisation design programme is for only part of an enterprise – a department or business unit – be certain that the vision for the design is completely aligned with the vision for the whole enterprise. (Nadler's Updated Congruence Model shown in Table 2.2 on page 24 illustrates the need for a single overarching vision that business-unit visions must "play into".)

Every leader and manager directly and indirectly affected by the new design must be able to communicate its vision to their people in a compelling way. People have to understand why the new design is required right now and in the way proposed. They also need to know what part they will play in realising the vision and why they should make the effort to participate. The vision must then be communicated consistently within and across the enterprise, allowing for different slants to reflect the different circumstances of business units or departments. As mentioned above, part of communicating the vision includes leaders showing their belief in it through personal passion and emotional energy. They need to convey that everyone, including themselves, is affected by the new design. They must also acknowledge the human elements that will be involved: stress, fear, resistance and concern about long-term security.

Objectives
Frame the objectives of the organisation design programme in a way that aligns with the vision/mission, values and strategies. (Figure 1.2 on page 5 illustrates the flow-down of objectives from vision.) In the case of WPP, a worldwide advertising and marketing company, the objectives reflect the organisation's mission.

Our mission
To develop and manage talent;
to apply that talent,
throughout the world,
for the benefit of clients;
to do so in partnership;
to do so with profit.

Future objectives
We will continue to focus on our key objectives – improving operating profits and margins, increasing cost flexibility, using free cash flow to enhance share owner

value and improve return on capital employed, continuing to develop the role of the parent company in adding value to our clients and people, developing our portfolio in high-revenue growth areas, both geographically and functionally, and improving our creative quality and capabilities.

Source: WPP Annual Report, 2004

In the assess phase of an organisation design programme the links between the vision/mission and the objectives are confirmed. In later phases specific performance measures for each objective are determined, implemented and embedded. Measures are discussed further in Chapter 5.

Leadership support
This is one of the change enablers shown in the fifth row of Figure 4.1 (see page 82) as well as in the blueprint currently being discussed. Building leadership support is integral to getting the business case for the design work accepted and continues during the assess phase. A high level of leadership support is essential for any size of organisation design work, and it must be obvious and demonstrated. If leaders are signed up and understand their role, they will:

- make the change vision clear, inspiring and shared;
- communicate the compelling rationale for change that will motivate people to make it work;
- make resources available and clear blockages;
- demonstrate commitment and energy to the new design;
- ensure that the design work is given a clear priority in relation to the business plan;
- maintain the design as a high priority on the organisation's agenda;
- enrol and develop their own management team, keeping them on side;
- model new behaviour and ways of working;
- increase visibility and availability in order to answer questions, tell a compelling story and keep stakeholders on board;
- celebrate and publicise the reaching of milestones and success points as the new design is implemented;

Not every leader is able to do this effectively or skilfully. Many leaders fail to appreciate that taking people through a change process has a different emphasis from the role of operational or strategic leadership. In these instances the type of approach Allan Loren took in turning round D&B (formerly Dun & Bradstreet), a business information provider, is a good example:[3]

> The culture we've created here is all about leadership. Leadership development is virtually the most important control lever you have for achieving success. You can't control customers; there are too many of them, and they are, of course, independent. You can't control the environment; look at all we've been through in the past four or five years. But if you have leaders who are adaptable and capable of leading just about anything you can be successful. To make better leaders we have to modify their behaviour not their personality. We spend a lot of energy helping team members become better leaders.

Stakeholder analysis and engagement

Stakeholder engagement is one of the change enablers shown in the fifth row of Figure 4.1 and an area of activity in the blueprint. It is important to identify early on the individuals and groups who can have a good or

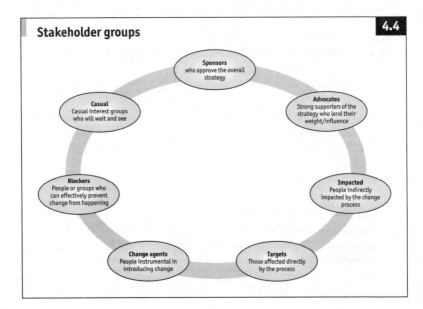

4.4

Stakeholder groups

Sponsors
who approve the overall strategy

Casual
Casual interest groups who will wait and see

Advocates
Strong supporters of the strategy who lend their weight/influence

Blockers
People or groups who can effectively prevent change from happening

Impacted
People indirectly impacted by the change process

Change agents
People instrumental in introducing change

Targets
Those affected directly by the process

bad influence on the success of the intended organisation change. Figure 4.4 illustrates the major groups of stakeholders typically found in organisation design projects. Mapping stakeholders at the start of the design process is essential in order to track their engagement during the project. The process of stakeholder engagement is discussed in Chapter 6.

The goal of stakeholder engagement is to:

◪ identify individuals or groups affected by and capable of influencing the design;
◪ explain the initiative to the key stakeholders;
◪ assess their interests and areas of resistance, and how they might help or hinder progress;
◪ agree their roles and responsibilities within the programme.

Note that although this activity is initiated in the assess phase of the blueprint, it is one that is continued throughout the life cycle of the organisation design programme (as stakeholders can rapidly change their views and positions).

People/internal context
The amount of activity in this category depends on the scope and scale of the organisation design project. In launching the low-cost subsidiary Ted, United Airlines carried out a significant amount of people and internal context assessment because it faced vast challenges in getting internal support for the new airline:[4]

> The expectations for employees were high. They had to achieve quick "turn times" (the time it takes to park the plane, clean it, board it and push it back from the gate); present a relaxed, fun and friendly customer experience on board the plane; and maintain the operational integrity of a fleet of aircraft while upholding United's commitment to safety.
>
> Compounding this challenge was that the launch took place three months after it was announced to the public, and was planned during the company's bankruptcy proceedings. To succeed, Ted had to change the opinions of many of United's 56,000 domestic employees from apprehension about launching a new product during bankruptcy, to the realization that Ted was a necessary part of United's future.

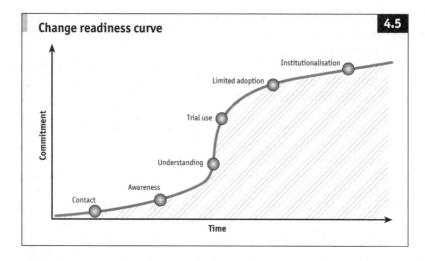

Change readiness curve

4.5

Change readiness

This is one of the change enablers shown in the fifth row of Figure 4.1; it also appears as an area of activity in the blueprint. The change readiness curve shown in Figure 4.5 illustrates where people typically are in relation to a new product, service, or system. The example of the BlackBerry illustrates the change readiness curve. Only a few years ago most people had little contact with a BlackBerry beyond reading about the product. But it did not take long for readers to become aware of other people using it and for their curiosity to be aroused. Visits to websites and retailers, and conversations with users of the product, led to an increased understanding of its capabilities and uses and people were tempted to trial use it. Limited adoption of the product quickly followed, and it was only a short time later that use of a BlackBerry or equivalent was widespread even to the state of dependency. This is the stage of institutionalisation.

It is the same with change associated with a new organisation design. People affected by a change have to reach the top of the change curve before the change is successfully embedded. Assessing how change ready they are in principle – will they be early adopters or will they only slowly or perhaps never adapt – helps get the design and implementation phases of the programme right for those it will have an impact on, using tactics and strategies to move them up the change curve. Corrado Passera, CEO of Banca Intesa, a leading Italian bank, comments on change readiness:

At the beginning, it is better to remain as quiet as possible while the plan is being prepared. When you present it externally for the first time, which will involve a lot of publicity, you should accept that the reaction will be sceptical and that this may last for some time, even for years in extreme cases. You shouldn't expect people's minds to change until you have some facts to persuade them – a number of high-profile projects, for instance, which you can roll out and will thereby demonstrate that you are delivering on your promises.

The extent to which stakeholders recognise and accept the need for change is determined by assessing aspects such as leaders' ability to manage change, levels of commitment to change, and the strength and extent of barriers to changes in the organisation's culture and processes. Change readiness assessments are valuable because they help clarify where a design programme might run into problems and they enable plans to be developed to make people ready for change. They identify possible barriers, enablers and risks, which in turn helps identify where to focus change implementation management activities and resources.

Depending on which is used these assessments will highlight, for example:

- how far people subscribe to the organisation design vision;
- how much commitment to the planned initiative needs to be built;
- what impact people's current performance and skill levels are likely to have on the success of the initiative;
- the need for any changes in leadership behaviour and activity;
- the degree of support for the proposed changes throughout the organisation and from other stakeholders;
- the barriers to and drivers of change;
- the issues that must be tackled to facilitate the change process.

With this information to hand, recommendations can be made on reducing the risk of failure, and the implications for achieving a successful design, given the current organisational conditions, can be set out. Figure 4.6 illustrates the results of a change readiness assessment, from which insight into what needs to be addressed can be gained.

In the assessment phase of an organisation design programme, the usual form of change readiness assessment is a survey combined with face-to-face interviews of individuals or groups, with follow-up interviews

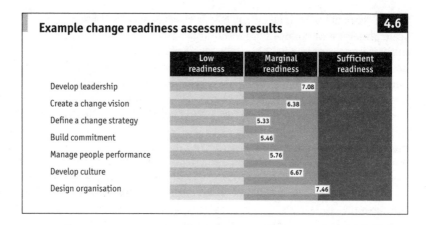

Example change readiness assessment results — 4.6

	Low readiness	Marginal readiness	Sufficient readiness
Develop leadership		7.08	
Create a change vision		6.38	
Define a change strategy	5.33		
Build commitment	5.46		
Manage people performance	5.76		
Develop culture		6.67	
Design organisation		7.46	

as appropriate. Assessing change readiness is not a one-off process and it must be monitored as the design phases proceed. To avoid survey fatigue a range of assessment tools can be used, including:

- cross-section of individual interviews by stakeholder, function and level;
- electronic groupware sessions with small groups of employees and other stakeholders (see Useful sources of information);
- review of any existing survey data and other appropriate existing studies or documentation;
- targeted e-surveys;
- Future Search conferences (see Chapter 2);
- organisational culture inventory (see Useful sources of information);
- team effectiveness inventory (see Useful sources of information);
- change readiness questionnaire (see Useful sources of information);
- risk assessment of change;
- change history assessment;
- change readiness workshops;
- storytelling (see Chapter 2)

Phase 2: Design
Organisation design programme office/team
This is row 2 in Figure 4.1 and an element of activity in the blueprint. Aspects of a formal programme management office for organisation

design work are described earlier in this chapter and in Chapter 7. Small-scale projects will not need the formality of a programme office, but note that it is important to have more than one person working on organisation designs. Whatever their size design projects have a degree of complexity, and it is useful to get a range of perspectives on progress towards objectives. At a minimum a design team should comprise a representative cross-section of the organisation under review. The approaches advocated in Chapter 2 give insight to ways of inviting participation and involvement from people who will be affected by the new design. To design and implement a transition, the programme team members must have a clear picture of the processes managed at each level in the organisation and be capable of influencing others, negotiating and lobbying effectively on behalf of the project.

The role of the programme team in the design phase is to plan the implementation path, aligning all the various stakeholder interests and components (see Figure 1.2 on page 5) of the organisation to support the new design. Monitoring, evaluation, risk management and quality assurance are essential programme management activities. Together they create an environment that keeps people motivated and involved during the transition while continuing to do their normal day-to-day work.

The design team's composition may change as the implementation proceeds. Choosing the right people is crucial as they must not only be capable but also be seen to be capable, they must have sufficient experience and, of course, they must be fully committed champions of the project.

Processes, structures, systems, human resource policies

The design phase task is to plan the alignment of processes, structures, systems and human resource (HR) policies with each other and with the objectives and vision of the design work. The important thing to remember is that changes in one area have repercussions, intended or not, in another area. Depending on the objectives of the organisation design programme, there will be work on the following:

- Business processes, including internal work flows, such as recruitment, and work flows between companies, such as procurement of products.
- Structures. Structural options are discussed in Chapter 3, but where the organisation design demands structural change the work must be planned and carried out by the design team(s) in close

liaison with relevant stakeholders. Structural work may include major or minor changes to the main structure, reporting structures, management layers, spans, communication and decision-making between different parts of the enterprise, workforce profile, and so on.

◪ Systems, including financial systems, management information systems, and other IT dependent systems.

◪ HR policies, including reward and recognition, job designs, headcount, career progression and training. One of the reasons for lack of success in many new organisation designs is that HR systems and processes fail to keep pace with the scale and implications of the change. All human resources plans, policies and systems must support the intended design outcomes as the Netflix example suggests.

Netflix's HR policies

Netflix, an online DVD subscription service, designed its HR policies to respond innovatively to customer demands and to keep employees happy to do this.

Netflix could be called an employee innovator, too. Warehouse workers – those closest to the customer – get free Netflix subscriptions and DVD players in order to understand what customers go through when "Finding Nemo" doesn't arrive in time for their kid's birthday party. Corporate employees stay happy – and therefore eager to solve tough engineering problems to improve the user experience – with perks like no hard limits on vacation time and free trips to Sundance each January. "Tomorrow when you come to work, if it doesn't make the customer happy, move the business forward, and save us money, don't [do it]," recalls chief talent officer Patty McCord. "Anything we're doing has to meet all three criteria."

Source: McGregor, J., "High Tech Achiever: Netflix", *Fast Company*, October 2005

Change leadership

Leadership support (discussed earlier) is a requirement through the life cycle of the programme. Leaders of design change can never afford to take their eye off the ball or become complacent. The unpredictable is always lurking on the sidelines and if the context changes it is likely that the strategy will need to change too. Leaders need to be active and visible, to reinforce and communicate the reasons for the change, demonstrate and build commitment for the change, act as a role model for any new skills and behaviours the change requires, and accept accountability for progress of the design work. Corrado Passera of Banca Intesa describes the role of the top team and of leaders throughout the organisation during the design process:[5]

> Change initiatives only take root through a well-functioning top team and committed leadership across the organisation. That means having a credible organisation and model in the first place. It has to be clear to everyone who is doing what. ... People in the company must understand that you are part of a group that works well together. The way to fail in a transformation is to have managers at the top who are fundamentally reluctant to push through change. If that is the case, people will try to exploit the situation and to get between you, as the leader, and your colleagues.

Stakeholder engagement/communication and involvement
A communication plan should be developed and put into effect during the assessment phase. Early and adept communications stall the rumour mill and pave the way for building trust that people will be kept informed as the design is shaped. Using a variety of media and techniques to communicate with the various categories of stakeholders is more successful than a one-size-fits-all approach.

Passera talks about communicating Banca Intesa's transformation plan to refocus the organisation on retail banking:[6]

> I devoted a lot of time to the communication effort, which, after all, had to reach 60,000 people at Intesa. For example, I personally wrote what amounted to a short book – not like an analyst's presentation with figures and graphs, but a book written in human language, telling people where we were, where we wanted to go, and how we were going to get there.
>
> Each individual received a personal copy and could access it via a website, and the text also became the foundation for an extensive training programme. ... I travelled round the country myself, directly explaining the mission to groups of managers and employees. It's a long process but you have to put your face in front of the people if you want them to follow you.

Different communication and involvement approaches should be adopted for internal and external audiences. Typically, there are four types of information to communicate to both groups:

- ◪ Why the organisation design is necessary.
- ◪ What progress is being made with the plan.
- ◪ Specific examples of success, failure, and people's responses.
- ◪ General related information – for example, what is being reported in the press, comments from the leadership team, or suggestions.

Communication experts typically describe the change curve in terms of four steps – awareness and understanding, buy-in, adoption and use – and talk of stakeholders as "audiences". In the awareness step, the organisation design programme is marketed to the appropriate audiences, highlighting the specific benefits to those audiences. The objectives of the awareness and understanding step are to educate the audiences on the features of the programme and to solicit their input on the programme's use. The buy-in step requires communications strategies and tactics that encourage and support embracing the programme. The adoption step reinforces and rewards the use of the organisation design programme with persuasive communication (without which negative concerns can solidify into active opposition). The use step involves consistently and regularly communicating messages that embed the work of the organisation design, for example reporting on successes, reviews, lessons learned and the milestones.

Take the example of Tyco (a global diversified company comprising four business segments: electronics, fire and security, healthcare, engineered products and services), where CEO Ed Breen considered a radical new design for the organisation but met a negative response from a group of external stakeholders – the analysts.

Tyco: a negative response

To hear Ed Breen tell it, splitting his company in three is the most natural thing in the world.

On this late February day, the CEO of Tyco International (Research) is sitting in a conference room in the company's New York outpost, two blocks from the regal former seat of his disgraced predecessor, Dennis Kozlowski. The 50-year-old Breen, who comes across more like a friendly dad in a 1950s TV series than an imperial chief executive, cheerfully ticks off reasons it makes sense to rend the $40 billion conglomerate into pieces. "Flexibility" is one that he cites; also "clarity", "focus", and giving the units "their own currency".

[But] coming with the earnings miss, the announcement of the breakup plan has led some Wall Street analysts – most of whom endorse the proposal – to conclude that management doesn't have any better ideas for fixing the company. "They did a terrific job of recapitalizing the balance sheet and paying off a substantial amount of debt, improving the cash flows, and improving the overall profitability," says Merrill Lynch analyst John Inch. "They picked off some low-hanging fruit. But the question now becomes, Have they run into a wall?"

Source: Varchaver, N., "What is Ed Breen Thinking?", *Fortune*, March 15th 2006

When this book went to press, Tyco was in the process of splitting into three and, given the range of interested parties, the use of a mix of customised communications tactics with each audience was in the plan. Table 4.1 gives some examples of the type of mix and tactics commonly used.

Table 4.1 **Communications tactics to support change adoption**

Stages of change adoption	Communications activities
Awareness and understanding	Familiarisation through regular information flow: meetings, e-mails, blogs, print, earned and/or paid media
Buy-in	Persuasion through personal and group meetings, demonstrations, training, continuing information flow
Adoption	Training and support, continued information support
Use	Information sharing, development of more sophisticated messages that encourage people to identify with and advocate the new organisation design

In the early stages of a design project, communication has a strong change management purpose, as in the Tyco example where Breen is suggesting the idea rather than implementing it. As the project continues, communication provides more of a front-end to knowledge management. Thus affected audiences know where to get more information on continuing strategy and plans, training programmes, or other resources that can help them understand the organisation design programme, its impacts and their role in its success. It is good practice to prepare procedures and templates for crisis communications, should there be a need for a fast response to an emerging issue.

Culture
Questions about culture usually centre on how to design to break down the silo mentality (see Glossary) in the organisation. Simon London notes why this mentality is a liability and suggests that ultimately "the tone is set from the top":[7]

> If silos are such a liability, why do they persist? Because, like viruses, they occur naturally. Ask any large group of normally defensive, insecure people to work together on a project. Then stand back and watch the silos emerge. Our society of large, complex organisations is a perfect breeding ground.
>
> This is not to say that managers are powerless to combat them. The experience of General Electric suggests that concerted effort to encourage cross-company co-operation can yield results. Jack Welch's "boundarylessness" initiative of the mid-1990s got the message out in no uncertain terms. GE's subsequent adoption of Six Sigma, the process improvement methodology, is credited with further breaking down barriers by giving managers from across the organisation a common language.
>
> Like so much of what goes on within organisations, however, the kind of defensive, political behaviour that encourages silos is a function of corporate culture. A quick flirtation with Six Sigma or any other management technique is unlikely to change the tacit "way we do things around here". More important is the steady flow of signals about the types of people who will do well in an organisation and the attitudes that are frowned upon.
>
> Ultimately, then, the tone is set from the top. Chief executives who demonstrate an uncompromising all-or-nothing management style can hardly complain when their subordinates are reluctant to co-operate with one another.

Like leaders sending "the steady flow of signals" about acceptable behaviour, designs can also reinforce cultures of collaboration, knowledge sharing, innovation, or whatever is thought to be a desirable culture by aligning other organisational components in support. After leadership signals, reward and recognition systems have the most significant effect on changing or maintaining the culture. Beyond these aligned value sets, job designs and organisational structures all bolster the desired culture. Take the approach of Nordstrom, a US department store, where all the organisational components are focused on helping staff to stick to the rules.

WELCOME TO NORDSTROM
We're glad to have you with our Company.
Our number one goal is to provide
outstanding customer service.
Set both your personal and
professional goals high.
We have great confidence in your
ability to achieve them.

Nordstrom Rules:
Rule 1. Use your good
judgment in all situations.
There will be no additional rules.
Please feel free to ask
your department manager,
store manager or division general
manager any question at any time.

The result was that in April 2006 comparable store sales increased 7.3% compared with a year earlier, easily exceeding analysts' expectations. (The consensus opinion of all analysts who cover the Seattle-based retailer was an increase of 4.8%.) This success is part of a trend that Nordstrom has enjoyed over many years – a notable one in the harsh world of retailing.

Training
As the new design is developed and implemented new skills (soft and hard) required for successful outcomes will be teased out. Obviously, training people in the right things and in good time is crucial (but does not always happen) and appropriate methods of developing staff must be instituted. Change management skills development should be included

as part of the overall skills and training programme. Organisation design initiative training is usually related to the following:

- Going through the change process itself. Employees affected by the new design will be in the front line of the change process and therefore must know how to contribute to the change as effectively as possible and how to work within changing circumstances.
- New systems, technologies, or processes – the way new systems operate and the technical aspects of doing work with different equipment or different interfaces.
- The work of the business when it has been "re-engineered". If the nature of employees' activities and responsibilities changes, the employees are likely to have to acquire new expertise in the way they fulfil their role or do their jobs.

Within these three areas the training should be tailored to specific stakeholder groups and provided in appropriate ways (for example, coaching, e-learning, face-to-face instruction, self-paced learning and on-the-job training).

Tailoring the training related to change, new ways of working, new systems and processes and new job roles requires careful thought and sensitivity. For example:

- Develop training that is linked to the overall business strategy, that positions the new organisation design as a business benefit, and that is delivered at appropriate points in the project life cycle.
- Establish collaborative relationships that pool resources in order to train employees in a time- and cost-efficient way. (Often training and development costs are discretionary, so training efforts may be limited as a result of budget constraints.)
- Make training available in a variety of formats, acknowledging different learning styles and access to training programmes.
- Recognise that training related to a new design puts an added burden on staff. This limits time that can be spent on activities that are not essential to day-to-day productivity.
- Build training content from employees' current strengths (for example, knowledge of their customers, insights into organisation culture, history of how work gets done), giving them the capability

and motivation to be high-performing in new roles, to do their work in new ways, and equipping them to be more fully able to provide effective customer service.

Phase 3: Implement
Performance measures

As the organisation design is implemented all the elements that contribute to it – systems, processes, technology, structures, capabilities, and so on – must be monitored and measured, as must risks, successes, milestones, small wins and lessons learned. Without adequate tracking it is impossible to keep the project heading in the right direction. Powerful business intelligence and the use of analytics will help achieve the necessary momentum.

As an example of the power of analytical information, Thomas Davenport suggests that "business processes are among the last remaining points of [organisation] differentiation" and that the power of analytics is to "wring every drop of value from these processes".[8] He cites several organisations which are closely analysing the performance of their processes, making organisation design changes as appropriate, and continuing to monitor and follow up. He makes the point that:[9]

> Companies just now embracing such strategies, however, will find that they take several years to come to fruition. The organizations in our study described a long, sometimes arduous journey. The UK Consumer Cards and Loans business within Barclays Bank, for example, spent five years executing its plan to apply analytics to the marketing of credit cards and other financial products. The company had to make process changes in virtually every aspect of its consumer business: underwriting risk, setting credit limits, servicing accounts, controlling fraud, cross selling, and so on. On the technical side, it had to integrate data on 10 million Barclaycard customers, improve the quality of the data, and build systems to step up data collection and analysis. In addition, the company embarked on a long series of small tests to begin learning how to attract and retain the best customers at the lowest price. And it had to hire new people with top-drawer quantitative skills.

Note that this example encapsulates the principles of alignment of all organisational elements to achieve an intended outcome.

Beyond the quantitative monitoring and because organisation design activities inevitably involve people's emotional reactions to change, these qualitative aspects must be monitored too. Failure to "take the temperature" of the people constitutes a significant risk to organisation design success. Other more qualitative aspects include looking for signs that:

- transition to the new state is disrupting normal business operation;
- relationships are being fractured or broken;
- things are not going well.

Chapter 5 discusses measures and monitoring in more detail.

Job design/role changes

Organisational change inevitably brings with it changes in job descriptions and the creation of new jobs. This is sensitive, and so requires the close involvement of the organisation's HR managers, whose knowledge of timing, content and impact of any suggested changes in job descriptions, career paths and succession planning should help ensure a smooth transition.

Generally, approaches to job design should result in:

- logical entrance levels and career patterns for employees to move to more skilled and higher graded positions;
- strategies to enable suitably qualified personnel to occupy new or continuing positions (sometimes this means staff having to reapply for their jobs or apply for new ones);
- the identification of training and development needs to meet future staffing requirements.

Phase 4: Embed

Planning and implementing the embedding of a new organisation design often takes a back seat to the work that goes on in the earlier three phases. It is as if all energy has been expended in assessing, designing and implementing, so actually living the new design becomes "Ho hum, we're there now", rather than an energetic exploration of what is working well and what is not.

If there has been a true alignment of all the various components during the earlier phases, embedding should be a straightforward matter of a thorough post-implementation review or reviews, listening attentively to feedback and making adjustments in the light of any areas found wanting.

In a complex design, if embedding is to be successful a series of further steps and stages is likely to be necessary. Nike's design for sustainability provides a good example of an organisation implementing an ambitious programme, reviewing it, learning and seeking ways to embed it more deeply over time.

Making sustainability real

CHALLENGE: Move a large and global organization into organizational learning and sustainable practices.

ACTION: Launch the organization's sustainable learning initiative through a program that touches all corners of the company.

OUR GOAL: Spread the understanding of sustainability throughout the company and demonstrate its value to the business.

Global Reporting Initiative (GRI; see Glossary) CATEGORY: 5. Management Systems

In Fall 1998, Nike adopted its first Corporate Environmental Policy. This formal commitment to sustainability was a major step, but how were we going to ensure that we could "walk the talk?" Sustainability principles and application were foreign to the majority of Nike employees. There was a need to communicate that this is everyone's job, but also to educate people on sustainability issues. It became a matter of starting somewhere.

That somewhere began when Laila Kaiser and Jill Zanger of our NEAT department set out to affect systemic change amongst 22,658 people. They enlisted the help of external consultants with expertise in organizational change, sustainability knowledge, and leadership. (Many thanks to SEED Systems, Polaris Learning, Wood and Associates and The Natural Step.) Together, we developed an organizational learning program focused on "action learning" around environmental principles and application. Selected Nike employees from around the world were engaged to review case studies and attend 3–4 training sessions over nine months. These employees were also challenged to apply what they learned to specific business projects already under-way or growing out of the learning.

The program included about 35 "champions" (mainly senior managers, vice-presidents, general managers and directors), who were tasked with providing support for 65 "captains," or employees in the trenches designing products, running logistics and sourcing materials. Sustainability experts spoke at the training sessions to broaden the horizons of the group as it sought solutions to environmental challenges in our business.

The goal of the program was to create a critical mass of change agents who might individually and collectively lead the transition to sustainability for Nike. Did we achieve this goal? No. Do we think it was successful? Yes.

In retrospect, it was the wrong goal. A group of 100 people alone cannot lead the transition to sustainability at a large organization like Nike. They can certainly be a critical group in that change, and pave the way for others. We learned the hard way that if you don't have 100 percent of senior management actively engaged in systemic change, then you are only chipping away at the iceberg's edge. We also erred in that the majority of the participants were from the product and supply chain side of our business. The more consumer-oriented parts of our business – marketing, sales and retail – were not as well represented. While this mix allowed a definite focus on areas where environmental impact is more obvious, we have a long way to go with truly effecting systemic change in the rest of the business.

We were successful in other ways. We created a strong network of people who learned how to think of Nike as a complex system rather than just a group of distinct departments. The value of that changed perspective is immeasurable. Also, each captain convened a team of their peers to identify sustainability goals against business issues. Real business objectives are being achieved with a sustainability return. Sixty-five projects were initiated or affected by this process, with environmental sustainability as a key consideration. Six of those projects are highlighted here. Many of these projects saved the company money, some innovated new processes and product ideas, and a few might even revolutionize the way we do business in the future.

Source: www.nike.com/nikebiz/gc/r/pdf/environment.pdf (page 6)

CASE STUDY: sequencing a new design

On March 21st 2006 Susan Lamb, chief operating officer of Alder Park (one of the largest and historically most successful not-for-profit organisations in the Eastern Atlantic region, with over 1600 employees), presented her team's recommendations for a radically different organisational form to the board.

When she joined a year previously Lamb inherited a reversal of Alder Park's fortunes:

- Donations revenues had shrunk by 20%.
- Revenue had declined (from £41.5m to £40m).
- There was to be no new government funding.
- The government funding they had was to be decreased.

This presentation marked a watershed for Alder Park. With a cash shortfall of over £1m and funding hard to come by, the organisation was facing a difficult future.

Lamb was convinced that bold steps were needed, and she was confident that as a result of her dealings with the board, Alder Park's employees and other stakeholders over the year her proposals would be accepted.

Lamb had joined an organisation with an admirable track record. For more than 40 years it had provided job training and support, employment opportunities, residential services and recreational activities for people with developmental disabilities at seven sites steered by the CEO who was also the founder. But times had changed and Alder Park was not in good shape.

Lamb's first task on joining had been to persuade the board that it was time to revisit Alder Park's vision, mission, values, strategies and goals for the next five to ten years. Having got their support, she brought in a small management consulting company to advise on the next steps and to work with Alder Park in taking them.

At a three-day offsite session (only 12 weeks after her start date) involving all 17 board members and all Alder Park's managers the work began. The agenda was to assess Alder Park's current condition, explore future possibilities and draw up an outline plan for change. Out of the three-day session came a new vision and mission (Table 4.2) and the setting up of a strategy task force made up of board and staff members.

Table 4.2 **Alder Park's old and new vision and mission**

Vision old	Vision new
Alder Park will be a recognised leader in providing resources to promote and provide full economic and social empowerment for people with disabilities in integrated environments, increasing vocational, employment, residential and recreational services locally and worldwide.	A world where people with disabilities are fully included.
Mission old	*Mission new*
To effect the best, most far-reaching opportunities for people with disabilities, working with them as individuals with their own talents, abilities, and personal goals.	Empowering people with developmental disabilities to enrich their own lives through our services.

Lamb was adamant about involving the board and the staff from the start. To develop their skills for handling the radical changes that the new vision and mission implied, she endorsed a programme of internal education, development, communication and on-the-job practice in strategic thinking, planning and scenario testing.

Six months after the first offsite meeting the strategy task force presented their report and recommendations on the way forward to Lamb. Driven by the requirements

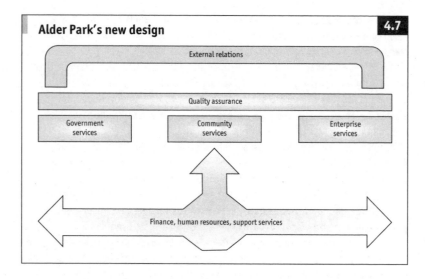

to embrace a customer focus, target efficiencies for improved effectiveness and integrate the service delivery model, the task force presented a design (Figure 4.7) that significantly streamlined Alder Park. It would be effective in facilitating the sharing of information, building and leveraging organisational capability, eliminating silos and reducing operational overlaps, duplication and costs.

Accompanying the model were seven recommended goals developed by small teams, each headed by one of the task force members. One of these goals is shown in Table 4.3.

Lamb was impressed by the detail and the thought that had gone into this piece of work. It built on Alder Park's history and strengths yet took it in new directions. She felt that the range of collaborative, participative and involving organisation design and development techniques, tools and approaches used by the teams had produced a report that would have a good chance of being adopted by all the stakeholders.

However, she was not yet ready to present the report to the full board for approval. There was still a lot of detailed work that she wanted completed, in particular:

- a proposal on a governance structure that would handle the design and implementation phases;
- a more rigorous stakeholder analysis – she had heard rumblings about the founder, and some of the stakeholder groups;
- an organisation-wide change readiness assessment to give her information on whether work had to be done to bring people on board before starting the implementation phase;

Table 4.3 **One of Alder Park's seven goals**

Goal 7 – Finance, Human Resource and Services will deliver best in class results in quality, innovation, and cost.
By January (two years out), we will implement a management information system (MIS) to provide participant and financial information across all departments and real-time access to current and historical data. The objective is to enhance programme effectiveness and be cost neutral with investments repaid by savings in operating expenses. This MIS will provide all reporting and inquiry capabilities for tracking progress against our five-year goals. By January (one year out), a business plan for accomplishing this goal will be presented to the strategy task force/board with specific details and goals with a timeline for implementation.

7.1 Implement management information systems that provide programs, business, HR, and financial information across the three service areas with real-time access to historical and current data.	7.1a Identify and address immediate opportunities to improve systems and use of systems. 7.1b Conduct comprehensive assessment of existing MIS with recommendations for current and future needs (FY1); implement recommendations (FY2).
7.2 Align management to support planned expansion in services and programmes.	7.2a Address short-terms needs to standardise processes and integrate systems. 7.2b Develop management plan for expected growth in programmes and services.

▰ a comprehensive communications plan related to the findings of the stakeholder analysis and the change readiness assessment (there was already an awareness-raising communication plan being implemented);

▰ a timeline for implementation with recommended milestones, success factors, measures and quality-assurance processes.

At this point Lamb felt that the consultants had done a good job. They had helped create the vision and the strategic planning process, and they had transferred sufficient skills to Alder Park employees and other stakeholders to enable them to continue with the organisation design themselves. It was therefore time for them to bow out.

The governance structure proposed was simple (basically that shown in the lower half of Figure 4.2 on page 85), establishing straightforward but robust controls and decision points. The team members were wary of recommending a governance process that was top heavy or time and resource intensive. The project board (or steering group), which had evolved from the strategy task force, comprised six board members with the chairman as sponsor. The project manager was Lamb, to whom eight work stream leaders reported.

The stakeholder analysis highlighted a number of issues. The managers and staff, faced with the reality of implementation and a radical new way of operating Alder Park, met to consider their nervousness and anxiety about change. They realised that they would have to manage the day-to-day business while making the transition to the new design. They would have to commit even more time, effort and resources to put new structures in place than they had in drawing up the plan.

Additionally, the founder was beginning to feel pushed out as he saw the proposed future of Alder Park come into sharp focus. He felt disenfranchised and unappreciated. He began to withdraw his support for the plan and started to lobby those board members closest to him to do the same.

The change readiness assessment suggested that although the new vision and mission were well accepted, the business case for change was not fully understood. People felt things were fine as they were. It also highlighted the fact that people were not, in general, change ready or capable.

Over the following four months Lamb worked with her teams to set up the governance structure and address the issues raised by the stakeholder analysis and the change readiness assessment. They also worked on the implementation timeline and plans. At monthly intervals they reviewed progress. By the date of the board meeting all participants in these first two phases of the organisation design process felt confident that they would gain approval to move forward.

Lamb and the work stream leaders emerged from the board meeting with big smiles on their faces. They had unanimous endorsement from members to proceed into the implementation phase. Although they were jubilant that all the work to date had borne fruit, they also understood that the journey through implementation and into embedding the new design would be a substantial challenge. However, it was one that they felt they would collectively and successfully rise to.

Reflections on this case

In her previous organisation Lamb had participated in large-scale organisation design work, and had learned from this experience. In starting the design work at Alder Park she knew she had to pay close attention to five aspects of the organisation design process.

1 Leadership support

Without the support of the CEO, the board and Alder Park's senior managers, Lamb would not have been able to carry through the new design. Although new to the role she had done a significant amount of due diligence before she joined and knew she would have to tread carefully through the minefield of politics in the organisation. She had been appointed by the board, with the CEO's unenthusiastic blessing, so her first tactic was to enlist support for her proposals from board members whom the CEO respected and listened to.

Lamb also started a conscious process of developing rapport with her senior management team. She was determined to build from what was working well at Alder Park (an appreciative inquiry approach) as she knew only too well how workforces respond to newly appointed slash-and-burn executives.

Throughout the year it took to get to the point of approval to implement her plan for change, Lamb worked on maintaining and developing commitment. With hindsight (and evidence from the detailed stakeholder analysis she commissioned six months in) Lamb acknowledged that she had spent too little time working with the CEO, and sought to remedy this in the second phase.

2 Carefully planned phase-in

A year to get to the implementation stage may seem long but it was time well spent. The stakeholders' education, development and skills had to be built. Alder Park had not seen much change in its 40-year history, and to introduce sudden change would not have been right for its culture. Lamb ran workshops with staff and other stakeholders discussing approaches to strategic planning, the sequencing of an organisation design project, what elements would be involved and how the process would play out (see Figures 4.1 and 4.3 and pages 82 and 86).

Because her approach was participative, she was able to gauge how things were going. She was sensitive to the needs of most stakeholders, and was able to push them when they needed it and stand back when appropriate.

3 Focus on the details of implementation

Some people found Lamb's insistence on detailed planning tiresome. They wanted to get on and do something and baulked at meetings to go over Microsoft project plans that had hundreds of lines of sequenced and interdependent actions. However, when the point of implementation came people were aware that Alder Park was going to operate radically differently – they had no illusions that this was going to be old wine in new bottles. They also knew that a range of implementation activities would be going on simultaneously in different work streams and that life would feel chaotic and uncomfortable during the process.

They knew this partly because timelines, critical milestones and decision points were published on the organisation's intranet for staff to react to and comment on; partly because the principle of "no surprises" was one that was embraced by the design teams (for example, they enlisted the support of HR staff and others in having conversations with staff whose roles were going to change); and partly because there was continuous and consistent communication that kept people informed at all stages (see Table 4.1 on page 99).

4 Working collaboratively to remove silos and instil customer focus

From past work Lamb knew that cross-functional teams (whose members represented all levels at Alder Park) working on specific aspects of the design would not only get the design work done but also start to develop new, informal social networks that would help break down the silos. Over the course of the year teams were established to conduct specific pieces of work, for example to identify areas of obvious efficiencies and cost savings, and to determine new business opportunities. Teams were encouraged to focus all their suggestions and recommendations on actions that would support the new vision and mission – clearly putting the customers (people with developmental disabilities) at centre stage. This was a big change for many staff, who were of the view that their customers were passive recipients of what was offered to them, rather than individuals who could make their own choices and decisions.

5 Flexibility to make refinements

An aspect that the design teams found difficult to handle was distinguishing "noise" (see Glossary) from important information in the operating environment. For example, was the announcement that government funding would be cut extremely significant or of marginal significance? Once they understood how to ask the right questions, they were able to make adjustments to their plans (or in some cases almost start over again).

As a way of helping the teams manage this constant contextual change, Lamb discussed with them Nadler's Updated Congruence Model (see Table 2.2 on page 24), demonstrating how operating conditions affected the organisational components and noting that the challenge was to keep the components aligned and in balance in order to deliver the strategy.

With the understanding that being responsive to changes was essential, the teams began to build flexibility into their plans. For example, they started to present options and to give relative weightings to suggestions

Table 4.4 **Checklist of the steps in the strategic planning process**

Environmental scan	Examine the outside environment surrounding the organisation (societal/task environments).
Environmental forecast	Predict how the environment is changing in order to determine implications for the future of the organisation.
Customer/market/ competitor analysis	Establish a stronger understanding of why the organisation exists by determining how the market is changing, understanding who the future customers are, and analyzing organisation competition.
Strategic planning premises	Develop strategic planning premises that reflect the assumptions about the future (based on the environmental forecast).
Internal assessment	Management determines the strengths and weaknesses of the organisation as it currently exists in order to establish a planning base using a SWOT analysis (strengths, weaknesses, opportunities and threats). By maximising strengths and minimising weaknesses an organisation exploits opportunities and avoids threats.
Mission/vision development	The mission and vision of the organisation are outlined. The mission is the basic purpose of the organisation. The vision describes what the organisation will look like in the future.
Strategic thrusts	The three or four key goals on which the organisation focuses it efforts over the next 5 years.
Plan operationalisation	It is best to follow these steps in this order. However, sometimes it may be necessary to revisit various steps as the organisation moves along through the strategic planning process.

Source: Anthony, W.P., Perrewe, P.L. and Kacmar, K.M., *Strategic Human Resource Management*, Harcourt Brace, 1996

and recommendations. This developing openness to adaptability became a valuable organisational capability as the implementation process got under way.

A year after the board had given Lamb approval to go ahead with the proposed changes, Alder Park was enjoying the benefits of the new design. Customers were happy, revenue forecasts were on track, staff were motivated and working productively, and after a difficult series of discussions the founder was using his skills to fund-raise rather than lead and manage the enterprise.

Tools for this case

Of the tools that were used in this case, two were particularly helpful for staff new to the process of organisation design. The first was a checklist of steps in the strategic planning process (see Table 4.4). This formed the basis for activity in the first three-day workshop, and subsequently at town hall meetings and work stream skills development sessions.

The second tool was a clarification of the role of the project board (see Figure 4.2 on page 85). In this case the project board (or project steering group) comprised some of Alder Park's executive board. For most of them this was their first time working as members of such a group. They had a tendency to try to manage the day-to-day running of the project rather than take an oversight role. Initially, this led to friction between them and the project sponsor (the chair of the board) and the project manager (Susan Lamb).

Table 4.5 **Role of project board (steering group)**

Overview
- ☑ Effective business change programmes and projects require clear, active and visible leadership from the top.
- ☑ The project board is responsible for ensuring that the programme meets its overall objectives and delivers the benefits outlined in the business case.
- ☑ Realisation of benefits should be included in the project board's objectives. The project board has accountability to stop or realign the project if the original benefits case is not likely to be realised.
- ☑ The project board should comprise those who have the most interest, and the most to gain from, the successful implementation of the project.

Specific accountabilities of the project board

Gatekeeper	☑ Ensure only projects that support the business strategy are initiated.
	☑ Ensure those which no longer support the business strategy, or where the risks of achieving the outcomes and benefits are judged to be too great, are cancelled.
	☑ Ensure the project has clear terms of reference and business case.
	☑ Sign off the terms of reference and business case before they are submitted for review.
	☑ At key milestones (quality gates) through the life of the project, ensure that they are satisfied before the project is put forward for approval to progress to the next stage.
	☑ Ensure any corporate programme management and project management processes are followed.
	☑ At the closure of the project, see that the benefits are realised and a post-implementation review is carried out.

Monitor	▨ Validate the plan.
	▨ Hold regular reviews of progress against plan at a high level (at an operational level, this is the responsibility of a project manager).
	▨ Ensure the business case (terms of reference for smaller projects) is reviewed regularly and any proposed changes of scope, cost or timescale are checked against their possible effects on the business case.
	▨ Ensure risks have been identified, and are being tracked and mitigated as far as possible.
	▨ Give overall guidance on policy, direction and scope.
	▨ Approve and monitor projects with an IT element against the project charter.
Support and coach	▨ Give support to the project manager as required by him or her.
	▨ Support may be in the form of direction, guidance, lobbying for additional resources and resolving serious problems.
Decision-maker	▨ If decisions are required that are outside the scope of the project, these should be referred to the project board.
Champion/ communicator	▨ Champion the project internally and externally.
	▨ Hold regular project board meetings.
	▨ Maintain a senior-level relationship with key external suppliers to ensure they give their full support to the project.
Problem solver	▨ Resolve the more difficult problems that the project team does not have the skills or experience to resolve.
Resource negotiator	▨ Ensure that adequate and appropriate resources are available to ensure the delivery of project benefits on time.

Summary

It is evident from the description of the organisation design process that it is not one that can be prescribed accurately. Rather it is a sequenced process that emerges from information about a specific organisation in its operating context.

The important things to remember are that:

▨ the process is based on a progression of activities that may iterate several times through the project life cycle;

▨ good organisation design work seeks to find the best methods of delivering a business strategy through aligning the various components of the organisation;

▨ well-designed projects are implemented through a combination of good governance, clear communication and meticulous planning.

5 Measurement

MEASUREMENT OF ORGANISATION design is a thorny topic. At different stages of the process, people want to know with a high degree of certainty the answers to four questions:

1 What analysis and assessment need to be done to give a reliable diagnosis of whether or not to initiate a new design?
2 Will the design achieve what it is intended to achieve: fix the business issue and at the same time develop the culture and behaviours for continuing success?
3 Is the gap closing effectively and smoothly between the original state (old design) and the future state (new design)?
4 Are the desired benefits and outcomes being realised in the new design?

People also want to be able to measure what they are losing as well as what they are gaining as the new design comes into play. For example, they may be losing existing organisational knowledge if key people leave. However, they may be gaining new and valuable organisational knowledge as new networks and connections are established.

High levels of certainty may be desired, but because organisations are in a constant state of flux and not in laboratory-controlled conditions, most organisational measures are no more than "dipsticks" at a point in time. By the time of the next measuring round the context has changed and the sets of measures are not directly comparable. Also any outliers in the measures (for example, in a customer satisfaction survey) are often removed and decisions made based on the average. But there is always the possibility that one of the outliers is the "black swan" – the rare event that brings large consequences that cannot be ignored.[1]

The value of measures lies in giving a sense of comfort (albeit perhaps false) and in helping make sense of the situation and determining what to do next. This apparently true story, which took place during military manoeuvres in Switzerland, is instructive:[2]

> The young lieutenant of a small Hungarian detachment in the Alps
> sent a reconnaissance unit into the icy wilderness. It began to snow
> immediately, snowed for two days, and the unit did not return. The
> lieutenant suffered, fearing that he had dispatched his own people
> to death. But on the third day the unit came back. Where had they
> been? How had they made their way? Yes, they said, we considered
> ourselves lost and waited for the end. And then one of us found a map
> in his pocket. That calmed us down. We pitched camp, lasted out the
> snowstorm, and then with the map we discovered our bearings. And
> here we are. The lieutenant borrowed this remarkable map and had a
> good look at it. He discovered to his astonishment that it was not a map
> of the Alps, but a map of the Pyrenees.

The map in the story served as a yardstick (measure) to orient the soldiers,
but it was acting on the map that got them back. They were able to get a
good outcome from the wrong map because:[3]

> They had a purpose, and they had an image of where they were and
> where they were going. They kept moving, they kept noticing cues and
> they kept updating their sense of where they were.

Similarly, using measures as general indicators and sources of feedback
to spur action is sensible. But believing that they will point to the right
answer to any of the four questions listed above is a mistake.

In almost all situations, if good enough answers to the questions are
available, they are sufficient for success. This chapter discusses ways
of using measures to achieve organisation design objectives. It does
not consider measures from the perspectives of statistics, mathematics,
economics or academic research design; rather, it takes a pragmatic and
largely practical look at measurement tools and their applications. So
measurement in this context means formalised activity (assessing, monitoring, gauging, ascertaining, surveying, and so on) aimed at producing
structured data. The data are then interpreted and, if appropriate, applied
in the process of making judgments, decisions and choices.

Choosing measurement tools

There is a bewildering range of quantitative and qualitative tools available
to gather and produce structured data, so a systematic approach must be
adopted to decide which ones should be used:

1 Decide the purpose of the measurement. In most cases, measurement of an organisation design has two purposes:

- to measure an organisation design's impact on achieving the business objectives – this can be an existing design or progress of a new design;
- to monitor the programme or project management aspects of designing, implementing, and embedding a new organisation design.

These are high-level purposes and because each organisation design is unique, the measurement activity must be selected for that particular design.

2 Choose the measurement method. There are three types: quantitative (numbers), qualitative (words), or mixed (numbers and words). Again, the choice depends on the individual design as each type has advantages and disadvantages, and none is perfect.

3 Get a suitable tool for the job. Some tools will be better than others for particular jobs. For example, a screwdriver is most suitable for driving a screw into wood, but at a pinch a knife blade or other instrument that fits into the slot on the screw head will do.

4 Agree how the tool will be applied. Almost any tool, quantitative or qualitative, can be applied in a number of ways. For example, the choice of a quantitative survey raises a number of questions: Should it be paper-based or web-based? Should it be administered to a sample of the population (what type/size of sample) or to the whole population? Should it be at one time point or several time points?

5 Prepare the ground for success. In applying a tool there can be unexpected consequences, as the context is usually complex. For example, deciding to do a skills level analysis could result in labour union intervention if it was felt the results would be used to select individuals to lay off. To manage the risk of things going wrong:

- test the instrument or method chosen;
- prioritise the objectives of the measurement (often the list is too long), reducing it to a chosen few – no more than five;

- think where uncertainty will come from and use schemes to reduce it, for example focusing on a sub-population rather than the whole target population;
- agree the protocol for the collection of measures (if the collection is by interview, for example, train all interviewers to use the same approaches and questions).

The following sections elaborate on each of these five steps.

Decide the purpose of the measurement

As stated earlier, the first purpose of measurement is to gauge the impact of the organisation design on the achievement of business objectives. So going back a step, the purpose of any organisation design is to make the enterprise high performing – that is it must satisfy its customers profitably and sustain its competitive advantage.

Much has been written about high-performance organisations and the practices they have in common that appear to keep them leading their sectors. Although there are minor variations, there is remarkable commonality across industries and countries. Both the US Government Accountability Office and the UK Department of Trade and Industry have published reports (with case studies) on what makes for organisational high performance in their respective countries as an encouragement to enterprises to adopt high-performance practices. Some of the findings are reproduced in Table 5.1.

Thus the early organisation design challenge – met in the assess phase – is determining what future high performance looks like in terms of carrying out the business strategy, deciding which of the characteristics of high performance are most likely to deliver it (or are currently doing so), and then agreeing what to measure and how to measure it. Of course, for these activities to produce useful results there must be expressed clarity on the business strategy (see Chapter 2).

Timpson, a UK retailer, is a good example of a high-performance organisation where the vision, mission and strategy are clear and where the organisation is designed to respond rapidly to the environmental context by adjusting the products and services it produces.

Table 5.1 **US and UK government findings on high-performing organisations**

US Government Accountability Office

High-performing organisations have a focus on achieving results and outcomes and a results-oriented organisational culture is fostered to reinforce this focus. Key characteristics and capabilities of high-performing organisations that support this results-oriented focus include having a clear, well-articulated, and compelling mission, strategically using partnerships, focusing on the needs of clients and customers, and strategically managing people. High-performing organisations have a coherent mission, the strategic goals for achieving it, and a performance management system that aligns with these goals to show employees how their performance can contribute to overall organisational results.

To manage people strategically, most high-performing organisations have strong, charismatic, visionary, and sustained leadership, the capability to identify what skills and competencies employees and the organisation need, and other key characteristics including effective recruiting, comprehensive training and development, retention of high-performing employees, and a streamlined hiring process.

UK Department of Trade and Industry

A widely accepted definition of High Performance Work Practices (HPWPs)is that they are a set of complementary work practices covering three broad areas.
1. High employee involvement practices, eg, self-directed teams, quality circles and sharing/access to company information.
2. Human resource practices, eg, sophisticated recruitment processes, performance appraisals, work redesign and mentoring.
3. Reward and commitment practices, eg, various financial rewards, family friendly policies, job rotation and flexi hours.

These broad areas are sometimes referred to as "bundles" of practices and cover 35 work practices.

The range and manner in which HPWPs are used by the companies depends on the specific performance goals of the organisation, the industrial context, and how the relevant product strategy in a particular organisation is employed to achieve results ... different HPWPs or "bundles" of practices are likely to be used in different sectors to achieve different business outcomes.

Central to the effective implementation of HPWPs is organisational leadership and the culture this creates.

Sources: *High-Performing Organizations: Metrics, Means, and Mechanisms for Achieving High Performance in the 21st Century Public Management Environment*, February 2004. GAO-04-343SP High-Performing Organizations Forum (www.gao.gov); *High Performance Work Practices: linking strategy and skills to performance outcomes*, Department of Trade and Industry, URN 05/665, 02/05 (www.dti.gov.uk)

Timpson's approach to building a successful business

Timpson is one of the few British high-street businesses with a long family history – stretching back to 1868 when the first shop was opened in Manchester. The current chairman, John Timpson, is the fourth generation of the family who transformed Timpson from the original shoe business to a multi-product high-street shop.

Having made a successful transformation from selling shoes to shoe repairs in the 1980s, the business environment for Timpson continued to change. In the early days, shoe repairs represented 95% of Timpson's turnover but this business has since steadily declined. The shoe repairs market is now [2004] 10% of its former size. Timpson's strategy to address this has been to diversify into complementary services that it can deliver from its existing high-street shops and to constantly seek new services to replace declining demand. Key-cutting, engraving and watch repairs are examples of successful replacement services that have been developed. New services such as locksmiths and jewellery repairs are currently being put into place.

Interestingly, despite the continuous change in the variety of services provided, Timpson has not altered its approach to building a successful business, namely: a customer focused/quality service strategy. The Timpson strategy is built on motivating and empowering staff to maximise sales while working without the constraint of many rules. "Firstly, we invest total authority in our shop staff to do what they think is best, no company rule must get in the way. Secondly, we have to 'amaze' our customers. If we can do that with every customer, things will start to change." The aim of its quality service and empowerment approach is to harness the power of their customers and get them to do their advertising. This means that if there are 250,000 customers a week, the target is 250,000 word-of-mouth recommendations for Timpson.

Source: Department of Trade and Industry (see Table 5.1)

Timpson's two-pronged strategy is to diversify into complementary services that can be offered from its high-street shops and to grow through customer recommendation. The strategy informs the design of the organisation in that the organisational components are aligned to deliver the strategy. For example, Timpson uses a range of supporting high-performance work practices (HPWPs). Measures are focused on three areas: the continuing effectiveness of the HPWPs, the customer recommendation targets and the diversification strategy. This example illustrates the two points that measures of design are organisation specific and that there has to be a clear purpose, related to the business strategy, for the measurement. Nordstrom (see Chapter 4, page 101) has a remarkably similar strategy of putting the customer first and a similar focus on empowering staff to act in the interests of customers with the minimum of rules.

The second purpose of measurement in an organisation design project

Table 5.2 **Documents for measuring progress on programmes and projects**

Document title	What the document is used for
Benefit Profile	To define each benefit and track its delivery and realisation
Benefit Realisation Plan	To track delivery of benefits across the programme
Benefits Management Strategy	To define and set up the approach to managing benefits
Communications Plan	To plan and monitor the communication activities during the programme
Highlight Report or Status Report/ Progress Report	To summarise project progress and highlight areas requiring management intervention
Issues Log	To capture and actively manage programme issues
Lessons Learned Report	To disseminate useful lessons for future projects and programmes
Programme Brief	To initiate the programme and provide the basis for the programme's business case
Programme Business Case	To approve investment and assess the ongoing viability of the programme
Programme Plan	To design the overall programme and then monitor and control progress
Project Initiation Document (PID)	The basis for management and control of the project
Quality Management Strategy	To define and set up the necessary activities for managing quality across the programme
Risk Log	To capture and actively manage the programme risks
Risk Management Strategy	To define and set up the required activities and responsibilities for managing risks
Stakeholder Management Strategy and Plan	To define, implement and track the activities and responsibilities for managing stakeholders

Source: Adapted from OGC Successful Delivery Toolkit (www.ogc.gov.uk/sdtoolkit)

(or programme) is to monitor project progress against agreed criteria – for example, to determine whether or not the project is running to time and within budget, whether stakeholders are adequately engaged and whether the communications are having the intended effect.

Projects or programmes set up conforming to Association for Project Management (www.apm.org.uk) or Project Management Institute (www.pmi.org) guidelines have specific frameworks and templates on project measurement. Table 5.2 provides an overview of a typical set of measurement documents for a project.

Choose the measurement method

Given the two purposes of measuring an organisation design project (gauging the impact of the design on organisation performance and monitoring project progress), the choice of measurement method (quantitative, qualitative, or mixed) is governed by the following:

- ◪ What is to be measured.
- ◪ The audience/market for the findings.
- ◪ The resources of the investigator (or investigation team), such as experience, cost, time available.

The first factor in measurement choice, knowing what to measure, involves identifying specifics that will give meaningful information in relation to the two measurement purposes. In the British Airways (BA) example (see Table 5.3), the indications were that sales through retail shops were decreasing and online sales were increasing. The organisation design had to change to meet new customer demands and deliver sufficient sales revenue through the new channel. A project was initiated to implement a new design.

BA chose quantitative measures in situations that were regular, precise, countable, objective and comparable within each data item: for example, the number of sales made each month and the number of phone calls taken per hour. Qualitative measures were chosen in situations involving behaviour that was situational, dynamic, uncountable and subjective and had a range of perspectives: for example, the feelings of staff about closure and progress with labour union consultations. Mixed methods were chosen in situations that were amenable to both quantitative and qualitative data collection and where results from one method supported results from the other: for example, customer satisfaction, measured by comparing the number of sales made in each channel and by interviewing customers about their purchase choices.

The audience or market for the information gathered is the second factor in measurement choice. Qualitative information is presented in narrative form, often with contextual information and quotes from people. Quantitative information is usually presented in one of three simple forms: a table, a line or bar chart, or a pie chart, that is, a statistical report sometimes with brief commentary. (Remember, though, that there

Table 5.3 **BA's redesign of sales channels**

Press release	Measurement example (to aid decisions)	Choice of method
British Airways is to restructure parts of its UK direct sales operations in response to changing customer behaviour and increased sales on its ba.com website.	Channel sales (for comparison purposes) Customer satisfaction	Quantitative Quantitative or mixed
The restructure will see the proposed closure by August 2006 of British Airways' Travel Shops business as well as the airline's Belfast based customer call centre.	Project progress against plan. (Is restructuring and closure running to time, within budget, with good business continuity?)	Mixed (using project tracking documentation)
The proposed changes will affect around 300 staff who work in the 17 high-street travel shops, corporate travel agency Worldlink based at Heathrow and its back-office support areas. A further 100 staff currently work in the Belfast call centre.	Feelings of staff about closures.	Qualitative
The airline will consult with its trade unions about the proposed closures.	Progress of consultation with unions Effectiveness of communications and involvement plan	Qualitative Mixed
Martin George, British Airways' commercial director, said: "It is clear that an increasing number of our customers want to book and organise their travel plans with British Airways via the Internet. This is a travel industry wide trend and we have to ensure that our business reflects this."	Customer satisfaction Travel industry trends	Quantitative or mixed Quantitative
"Our UK call centres have seen the number of telephone calls fall by more than 60% since 2001 from 15m to 6m calls today and we have reduced our headcount in this area of the business by similar amounts from 2,200 to 800 people."	Call volume Productivity	Quantitative Quantitative

Source: www.britishairways.com/travel/bapress/public/en_us (March 15th 2006) are other forms of presentation, such as scatterplots.) As Table 5.4 shows, tables and line or bar charts present two data elements, but a pie chart presents only one.

Table 5.4 **Data presentation methods**

Numeric presentation	Data element 1	Data element 2
Table	Row	Column
Line and bar charts	y-axis	x-axis
Pie chart	A slice of the pie (eg, one element of HR activity)	The whole pie (eg, all HR activity)

Note that the styles of information presentation – use of colour, shading, highlighting, tone, supporting graphics/illustrations, numbers or words, and so on – have an impact on the way the audience perceive and interpret the data. When choosing a measurement method it is important to think about how the data might best match the needs of its target audience.

Marks & Spencer, under CEO Roger Holmes, measured project progress against plan in a "dashboard" (see Figure 5.1). The audience was the steering group members of the HR organisation design programme who met monthly. With the dashboard, steering group members got a visual and comparative month-by-month synopsis with specifics of interest or concern being "called out", usually by the project manager, and discussed during the meeting.

The presentation of data is not something to be taken lightly. For provocative views on the hazards of presentation and how to avoid them, see the work of Edward Tufte, a writer on and teacher of analytical design (www.edwardtufte.com/tufte). Figure 5.2 shows a commentary he gave on the purchase of Enron stock as the company's fortunes started to fail.

The third factor that helps determine the choice of method is the resources available for measurement. Briefly, time, cost and expertise are instrumental in shaping measurement choices, and generally there is a trade off between these (Figure 5.3).

- ◪ **Time** is involved at all stages of the measurement process: selecting or designing the tool, testing it, running the full measurement process, analysing the results and preparing a

Marks & Spencer's programme dashboard

KEY PROGRAMME ISSUES

Issue no.	Workstream/description	Actions	Date to be complete	Owner
1	PIU ▪ 1 full-time equivalent resource shortfall	▪ Rescope project if resource issue unresolvable	15/01	DK
2	Grand Union ▪ project scope ▪ resource	▪ Clarify HR accountabilities within WOW ▪ Agree resource for remaining milestones	31/01	DK
3	Performance management: ▪ HOHR to define approach	▪ Plan delivery ▪ Agree measures	15/01	JW
4	Resourcing: ▪ overlapping work streams ▪ dual process owner	▪ Complete recommendations paper	31/12	CM
5	Reward: ▪ currently behind plan with budget	▪ Complete business case for F&GOC9/01	9/01	HP
6	SSR ▪ changes of behaviour from HRSS customers still to be agreed	▪ Maria to meet with stakeholders to agree action & engagement	31/01	ML
7	Career paths: ▪ no scope defined for phase 2 ▪ no resource currently in place	▪ Scope phase 2 following TSK outcome ▪ Commit resource to deliver	31/01	PV

KEY PROGRAMME RISKS

Risk	Description	Date	Owner
1	Grand Union-WOW still to be initiated leading to incomplete delivery of work due to shortened timescales	End January	1
2	Lack of clarity around Grand Union-WOW culture resulting in HR being unable to deliver its part	End January	2
3	IT roadmap is unable to secure necessary funds to deliver HR IT strategy particularly affecting P&Ss not currently agreed in op plan	End January	3
4	Incomplete delivery plans & HR ownership for embedding performance management could lead to failure to embed	End January	4
5	Reward securing of next FY budget could affect delivery in S&PS	9/01	5
6			
7			

Source: Author's archives

5.1

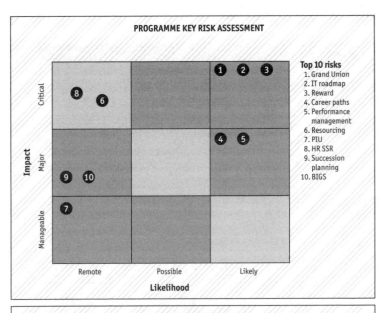

PROGRAMME KEY RISK ASSESSMENT

Top 10 risks
1. Grand Union
2. IT roadmap
3. Reward
4. Career paths
5. Performance management
6. Resourcing
7. PIU
8. HR SSR
9. Succession planning
10. BIGS

Impact: Critical / Major / Manageable

Likelihood: Remote / Possible / Likely

NEXT KEY MILESTONES

Milestone	Baseline date	Revised date	Owner
Launch career paths booklet & agree scope for phase 2	31/10	January	TBC
Complete definition of M&S world & LBS behavioural analysis	December	January	NS
Complete reward paper for submission to F&GOC	12/12	9/01	DK
Complete recommendations paper for resourcing	31/12	31/12	CM
Agree measures for management information pack – PIU	31/12	31/12	LS
Begin engagement of HR in SSR – changing the way we behave	January	January	ML

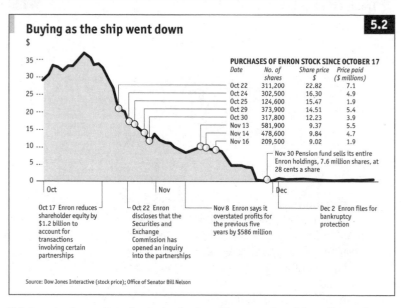

Buying as the ship went down

5.2

$

PURCHASES OF ENRON STOCK SINCE OCTOBER 17

Date	No. of shares	Share price $	Price paid ($ millions)
Oct 22	311,200	22.82	7.1
Oct 24	302,500	16.30	4.9
Oct 25	124,600	15.47	1.9
Oct 29	373,900	14.51	5.4
Oct 30	317,800	12.23	3.9
Nov 13	581,900	9.37	5.5
Nov 14	478,600	9.84	4.7
Nov 16	209,500	9.02	1.9

Nov 30 Pension fund sells its entire Enron holdings, 7.6 million shares, at 28 cents a share

Oct 17 Enron reduces shareholder equity by $1.2 billion to account for transactions involving certain partnerships

Oct 22 Enron discloses that the Securities and Exchange Commission has opened an inquiry into the partnerships

Nov 8 Enron says it overstated profits for the previous five years by $586 million

Dec 2 Enron files for bankruptcy protection

Source: Dow Jones Interactive (stock price); Office of Senator Bill Nelson

This is a superb narrative of a stock price (graph), a narrative of the collapse of Enron (words annotating a time scale), and a narrative of lousy investments by the Florida state pension fund (table). The graph, table, and words are linked together very nicely. The caption at the top suggests a possible cause of the lousy investments. (The Florida state pension fund behaved like someone who left a jacket on the airplane; they were trying to get back on while everyone else was getting out.) Data sources are also indicated.

The major defect is that no designer is named. Someone did this good work and they should get credit for it. The *Times* gives the names of reporters and photographers; this graphic is a substantial piece of journalism, as valuable as a photograph or news story. Who did it?

It would be useful to have a longer time-horizon, perhaps reaching back a full year. Maybe the Florida pension fund was buying Enron stock every week for a year on automatic pilot or something. Or maybe not; a longer time-horizon will tell us that and thereby strengthen or weaken the evidence for mischief with regard to stock purchases during the collapse.

This is an excellent, first-rate news graphic. And it was done under deadline pressure at a daily newspaper!

Source: Edward Tufte, February 6th 2002

Trade-off decisions

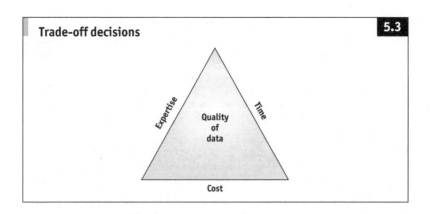

presentation. Clearly, buying an off-the-shelf online quantitative instrument that produces immediate reports brings a quicker result than designing a qualitative process that, for example, requires designing a participative event or focus groups, analysing narrative and developing a report. Quantitative methods of measurement are usually quicker and easier to administer than qualitative. For example, a "quick and dirty" internally constructed web survey may yield good enough information for the purpose. Qualitative measures involving focus groups, workshops or interviews take longer to set up (as they involve people and schedules) and analyse. They can be labour intensive, but they are useful for digging deeper into an issue.

◪ **Cost** comes into play when making build-or-buy decisions. Balance the cost of buying a software licence to use a survey tool, or the hardware to run one, against a price per user with the cost of labour and expertise to design and administer an in-house process. It may be possible to piggy-back on existing organisational measures such as balanced business scorecards and thus negate the need for additional measures related to the success of the design in meeting business objectives. But measuring progress of the design project against plan will probably need specific measures.

◪ **Expertise** is critical when it comes to designing measures. Asking a few questions may appear to be an easy task, but getting valid, reliable, comparable, valuable, high-quality information is not easy. All sorts of design decisions have to be made: for example, on quantitative versus qualitative methods, survey questions, ratings scales, sample or whole population. When making trade-offs between time, cost and expertise it is better to compromise on the time and cost. Measurement design expertise is essential in order to avoid junk information. The next section discusses this further.

Get a suitable tool for the job

Boundaries to both resource availability and intended audience may help narrow measurement choices, but not by much. Expertise is required to help determine what to measure and why it is being measured – that is, what information the measure yields that contributes to one or both of the two purposes of measuring an organisation design and design project (see page 118). In BA's decision to change its focus from "brick" sales to "click" sales (Table 5.3 on page 124), one of the elements being measured was customer satisfaction. Measurement showed decreasing levels of satisfaction with retail shop purchases and an increasing desire for better online purchase availability. Designing an organisation to respond to this meant, among other things, bringing better co-ordination between business units, more sharing of customer data and improved internal flexibility.

Table 5.5 shows that in this instance there are potentially valid measurement points which will indicate whether the new design is developing customer satisfaction in at least four areas: customer service, business process, human capital and financial. If all were measured, there would be nine sets of data – and this is for only one aspect of the design. Additionally, all nine points could be measured quantitatively and qualitatively either as sole methods or as a mixed method.

Clearly, measuring all of these would be resource intensive so the challenge is to get the most valid and usable information from the minimum amount of measurement, to get actionable information rather than noise. This challenge can be met in three ways.

1 Narrowing the field. Identify one or two measures that will provide good enough information to trigger action or provide information in a number of areas: a couple of measures that act as surrogates for a much greater number of measures. The following extract from Frederick Reichheld's article "The One Number You Need to Grow" tells how US car rental company Enterprise did this:[3]

> Taylor and his senior team had figured out a way to measure and
> manage customer loyalty without the complexity of traditional
> customer surveys. Every month, Enterprise polled its customers
> using just two simple questions, one about the quality of their rental

Table 5.5 **Improve levels of customer satisfaction**

Design aims	Example measures (mixed method)	Customer services	Business process	Human capital	Financial
Better integration and co-ordination across business units (service centres, sales, IT, finance, HR)	Communication and interaction patterns Customer satisfaction	X	X	X	
More sharing of customer knowledge and insights	Transfer of information between business units (network analysis, stories) Customer satisfaction surveys	X X	X		
Improved internal flexibility to respond to changes in buying patterns and trends	Adaptability of organisational elements (change readiness assessments, leadership behaviour observation)		X	X	X

Source: Adapted from Heerwagen, J., *Designing for Organisational Effectiveness*, US General Services Administration (www.wbdg.org/design/design_orgeff.php?print=1)

experience and the other about the likelihood that they would rent from the company again. Because the process was so simple, it was fast. That allowed the company to publish ranked results for its 5,000 US branches within days, giving the offices real-time feedback on how they were doing and the opportunity to learn from successful peers.

2 Agreeing criteria and boundaries for choice. In the first instance this means identifying tools that:

- ◪ lie within resource boundaries (time, cost, expertise);
- ◪ measure the narrowed field that will inform the wider action;
- ◪ recognise the audience/market;
- ◪ adhere to the KISS principle (keep it simple stupid).

Enterprise, for example, used a short online survey[4] that met these criteria. The survey lay within resource boundaries as it was quick to generate reports, was appropriately priced and was reliable. It measured a narrow field through a small number of questions, but the answers encouraged managers to seek more information, for example: What has changed? Why? What can be done about it? Thus from the regular flow of data returned by routine administration of the survey Enterprise was able to inform action, tailored to the organisation, in all the cells shown in Table 5.5. Furthermore, the design and administration of the survey recognised that the people completing the survey and the people using the results had little time to spend on lengthy form completion or inter-pretation of results; in other words, it recognised the audience.

3 **Deciding the measurement tool.** There are three choices: buy a tool off the shelf; customise an existing tool; design a tool for a specific situation. Generally, a tool bought off the shelf is more likely to be valid, reliable, current and generalisable (that is, the sample results can be universally applied or extended to the population from which the sample was taken – though this should be checked because, for example, a tool for an American audience may not work for a British one). Customisation takes time, is often expensive and there is the possibility of losing the rigour of the results. Designing for a specific situation is also costly and brings added risks if people inexpert in measurement design are charged with developing the instrument.

An ideal scenario is one where a organisation designer partners with a measurement expert, possibly from an external third party independent organisation, to quickly scan the market for suitable off-the-shelf tools. If no off-the-shelf tool is available, the next best option is customisation and the last recourse is developing a measurement tool from scratch. The American Society for Quality, www.asq.org, and the Chartered Quality Institute (UK), www.thecqi.org, are both good sources of advice and infor-mation on measurement issues.

Agree how the tool will be applied

What to measure, why to measure it and the audience for it inform the choice of tool. Thinking about how to apply the tools is also part of the choice process. In either qualitative or quantitative data gathering there are two possibilities: census data gathering and sample data gathering.

Census data gathering draws information from every individual entity. So, for example, in the case of an employee satisfaction survey every employee would be asked to respond. Or in the case of financial reporting every department or business unit would be asked to supply information (usually automatically generated by financial software).

Sample data gathering draws information from a smaller group of the targeted population in a way that represents as closely as possible the whole population. Airlines, for example, on every flight ask a small percentage of passengers to complete customer satisfaction surveys. The sample is identified by using a randomised selection of seat numbers. (This method is known as probability sampling where the selection of the units, in this case passengers, is left to chance to minimise bias in the study.)

Sample size depends on the level of certainty required from the data. The bigger the sample size the more likelihood there is of certainty and the less of error. (Assuming the measurement tool design is good.)

However, in identifying the right sample even a randomised method is not necessarily perfect. A vivid example is given in Jenny Diski's novel *Rainforest*, where the protagonist is a researcher studying the ecology of the forest using a sampling method. One of the other characters comments:

> "There's one thing that occurred to me though, about your grids and your search for the ultimate truth about rainforests. Supposing they're in the wrong places, your squares? Supposing they're in the one place that doesn't give you a representative sample of the whole forest? Supposing," he concluded with a sudden laugh as the thought came to him, "the truth you're searching for is between your squares, or concealed by the lines that make the framework of the grid? All those bits of paper would be meaningless, wouldn't they?"

Prepare the ground for success

To get good results from measurement processes, first make sure that the use of the measurement tool will not cause problems and then maximise the response rate.

Use and implementation issues can be avoided by investing in a pilot of the full-scale study. Piloting may be seen as adding time and cost, but it mitigates the risk of things going wrong and is well worth the investment. In the example below, which comes from an internal audit of the fourth employee opinion survey run by Marks & Spencer, the decision was taken not to pilot the study. However, a post-implementation review highlighted a number of issues that could have been spotted and worked out before the full roll-out.

Summary Employee Opinion Survey

The Employee Opinion Survey (EOS) is not being used effectively to address employee concerns.

88% of staff completed this fourth survey and HR management believes that it is a valuable tool to measure employee attitudes; however, there are weaknesses throughout the survey process:

- The EOS product is not fully meeting organisational requirements. A significant number of staff interviewed found questions irrelevant and did not fully understand the results.
- The EOS team has taken the survey from concept to delivery but improvements to management control have been identified to improve the efficiency and effectiveness of the process.
- The EOS has not been sufficiently embedded into the organisation design. Line management is not communicating results or action plans to staff and action is not consistently taken to address low survey scores.

In this example the problems highlighted stem from the mechanics of designing and implementing the survey – a pilot would have helped prevent the product failing to meet requirements and inadequacies of management control. Even where measurement tools are bought off the shelf it is worth piloting the process. It highlights the good and the bad not only of the use but also of the design of the measurement tool, saves money and time in the long run, and helps improve survey results.

Maximising the response rate is not an issue when the output is generated automatically, for example on number of units sold. But where the measurement involves people participating in a workshop or focus group, or completing a survey, participation can be problematic. A low response rate affects the accuracy of the results. It may be, for example, that people who do not provide information differ systematically from people who do provide information.

One of the principle factors in maximising participation and returns is effective communication with all stakeholders, not only the targeted participants but also those people who have to communicate or act on results. Learning from the Employee Opinion Survey experience, Marks & Spencer planned a subsequent survey differently. In an organisation design project that aimed to measure (map) the gap between the current capabilities of the workforce and the ability to deliver the business strategy, two things were built into the plan: a pilot and a highly detailed communications process. The example below is an extract from the pilot phase communications plan.

Map the Gap Communications Plan

The main aim/outcome of this project (including theme)
- To communicate to key stakeholders the purpose of Map the Gap project
- To produce a timetable of key milestones to communicate to Project Team
- To provide a briefing tool for team members when communicating to external parties, eg, Management team, Trade Unions, BIG on Division 5 & Division West
- To produce Workshop material for Division 5 & Division West
- To support the delivery of a clear consistent message on the project throughout the organisation by providing briefing tools for Section Managers for Division 5 and Commercial/Performance Managers for Division West.

The scope of this project (how wide is it?)
It includes:

- Timetable of events
- Communication plan for stakeholders
- Briefing notes for Project Team to communicate to relevant audience
- Producing training material for Map the Gap workshops
- Producing a tool to communicate to all employees on Division5 & Division West the purpose of Map the Gap project

It does not include:

- Technology platform to capture the data
- Identifying criteria to measure ways of working
- Producing tools to bridge skills gaps
- Budget Planning
- Ways of Working/Job profile communication

Key project objectives and outcomes
All stakeholders and employees on Division 5 & Division West to understand and commit to the "Map the Gap" project

Communication Workshop Outcomes of the Day
So that everyone

- **Understands** the project objectives and how they will help stores to deliver the commercial objective which in turn will increase sales
- **Understands** how their roles are important to the business vision and what part they have to play
- Is **clear** about their skills and competences and knows where their development needs are
- Feels **informed**, involved and confident in completing the Survey and sees the link of being able to take the business forward and improve overall business performance and productivity

The plan also included steps to encourage participation: a personalised invitation from a high-level sponsor to attend a workshop, a prize for completing a questionnaire, and so on.

Preparing the ground for success involves supporting people in taking actions suggested by the findings of the measurement. Word quickly gets around if nothing happens as a result of a survey, and when this occurs it is difficult to get support and participation in further data gathering. Follow-up action is often neglected, as the EOS example shows. In some cases this is because management and staff do not know what their responsibilities are in relation to action planning and action taking; in other cases the results of measurement are unpalatable or deemed unbelievable and thus ignored.

Remember that part of preparing the ground for success includes thinking about follow up. This frequently falls by the wayside when other organisational events overtake the organisation design work or the costs of taking action appear to outweigh the benefits.

Measurement principles

As highlighted above, effective measurement is not as precise an art as people might like to believe. There are no right measures. For any given organisation, measures of organisation design success and programme progress vary, depending on its mission, its environmental context, the nature of its work, the product or service it produces and customer demands. However, there are two principles that must always underpin any form of measurement: respect for people and respect for quality of output.

Respect for people

This involves the principle of getting informed consent, which means that participants have voluntarily agreed to give the information, understand what they are agreeing to and have been informed of the purposes of the request for information, why it is being sought and how it will be used. Applying the principle means communicating effectively with participants (as discussed in the previous section), maintaining confidentiality throughout the measurement process and securing measurement data.

Maintaining confidentiality is crucial to measurement activity. Response rates are lower when people feel their views may be exposed. It is important to take active steps, regardless of whether the measure is quantitative or qualitative, to ensure participants are clear that the information they provide is kept both confidential and secure. This is more easily done with print, web-based or computer-generated quantitative information, when forms can be printed with information about the purposes of the survey together with a statement that responses are anonymous and/or confidential. Participants then tick a box agreeing that they have read and understood the purposes of the survey and agree to information being used on the terms stated.

In workshops and focus groups where qualitative information is sought, maintaining confidentiality either becomes part of the participants' contract with each other, or can be structured using web-based groupware that allows people to record views anonymously. Where technology is unavailable and confidentiality may be an issue, the Chatham House Rule can be invoked.

The Chatham House Rule

"When a meeting, or part thereof, is held under the Chatham House Rule, participants are free to use the information received, but neither the identity nor the affiliation of the speaker(s), nor that of any other participant, may be revealed."

The world-famous Chatham House Rule may be invoked at meetings to encourage openness and the sharing of information. The value of this rule is that it allows people to speak as individuals, and to express views that may not be those of their organisations, and therefore it encourages free discussion. People usually feel more relaxed if they don't have to worry about their reputation or the implications if they are publicly quoted.

Chatham House can take disciplinary action against one of its members who breaks the rule. Not all organisations that use the rule have sanctions. The rule then depends for its success on being seen as morally binding.

Source: www.chathamhouse.org.uk

Reassure participants that where quotes or attributions are made in any reports, names will not be mentioned without gaining the express permission of the participant. When using cameras, there is a risk that participants' identities may be revealed and that their privacy may be affected in unanticipated ways. Inform participants if you intend to show videos or use photos in seminars or conference presentations. To maintain confidentiality, secure data carefully and allow only authorised personnel access to it.

Respect for quality of output

This means taking the steps outlined in this chapter to ensure that the data gained are valid, reliable and current and reflect conditions accurately. It also means ethical, careful and objective reporting of the findings. Threats to objective reporting come from several directions and can be related to self-interest, self-review, advocacy, familiarity or trust and intimidation.[6]

Unfortunately, the quality of output is often determined retrospectively through reviews or investigations. When measurement is found to be of low quality, fabricated, misleading, or misreported (either internally or externally) there is usually deep damage done to the reputation of the responsible party, as the example of Shell's measurement of oil reserves illustrates.

Shell's overstatement of oil reserves

By way of illustrating how aggressively reserves had been overbooked when Sir Philip Watts, the now-deposed Shell chairman, was chief executive of EP [Exploration and Production], consider Shell's treatment of its Gorgon project in Australia.

Shell had booked 500 million barrels of oil equivalent (boe) as of 31 December 1997. But as one City oil analyst pointed out to *Financial Director*, no gas has yet been produced from the project, and by 2004 none of Shell's other partners in this project had booked a cubic foot of gas from this field as part of their proven reserves.

This same analyst made the further point that the SEC guidelines require companies not simply to discover oil in order to book reserves as proven but to have concrete projects in place and ready to run: oil that cannot be extracted is simply an interesting statistic, not a valued commodity.

Having this 500 million boe on the books undoubtedly did good things for the market's perception of Shell as a solid competitor to BP and Exxon.

As Philip Nichol, global sector director for oil at investment bank ABN Amro, says:

> What we now discover is that, where we all thought Shell was a great company, the company has basically been in decline for a decade.
> Management have been focusing on profitability and allowing the reserves to wind down without that fact becoming visible to the market.

Source: www.accountancyage.com/financial-director/features/2049846/stringing-along.
Harrington, A., *Financial Director*, June 4th 2004

Robust measurement reporting requires a mindset of scepticism, detachment and neutrality. With these qualities there is less likelihood of stating, conveying, suggesting, or omitting results in order to present a rosy view.

CASE STUDY: measuring a turnaround

Four months into the project Matthew Davis was anxious. He had been charged with turning round a whole new division in the company and things were not looking good at this stage.

The turnaround project had been glossy and well publicised internally. Zed, as it was named, was to be a bold and innovative venture in the notoriously difficult children's wear market. Its vision was "to be a clothing company where heroes are made and fantasies come true", and its mission was "to put clear blue water between Zed children's wear and the competition and become the best children's wear retailer in the world".

From the start, there were rumblings in the parent company about the vision – people did not seem to understand the heroes and fantasies language even though Davis explained it:

> We believe the experience we need to offer is analogous with the cinema experience. We're developing a sense of anticipation in the kids – much as

film trailers do. We want them to feel that the shopping experience is going to be fun and exciting, that they're seeing a "great film" with product stories that are relevant and motivating so that when they leave the shop they'll have a sense of fulfilment or reward.

He presented the vision with passion and vigour:

Think of your own kids – wouldn't they want to live out their fantasies or meet their heroes? Our plan is to drive kids' footfall into the stores, through our promotions tied to spend thresholds. The younger kids will live their fantasies say by visiting Disneyland or Tussaud's Theme parks, and the older ones will meet their heroes by, for example, winning a place at Manchester United's Summer Soccer School.

Along with the vision and mission, Davis's team developed three performance goals for the first year of the project. The first was hard and measurable, and no one could disagree with the notion of supplying better targeted (more fashionable) product, delivered faster and cheaper to market. The second was more qualitative, and Davis's team had a harder job presenting this to a sometimes sceptical audience:

Imagine that, through improvements to the store environment, we will make the shopping experience attractive to adults and children alike. We're planning to design a place where children WANT to shop – one that's cool and aspirational – using a theatrical approach. We'll communicate [what the] key themes [are] to be each month, and have linked event zones, new ranges and collections in store, promotions and advertising, news and information.

The third goal was also qualitative and as Davis admitted to himself, perhaps the hardest to achieve: he was to turn around children's wear but with staff who had been with the company for years and who had strong views on the way things should be. New to the organisation himself, he strongly believed that the only way he would get things on track was by establishing a culture of ownership and accountability among colleagues. In his meetings with them he repeated the point that: "I want you all to be individually responsive, to take measured risks and be capable of swift delivery of our goals."

Davis's team chose four measures for the three goals:

- ☑ Restoration of clear market leadership for children's wear with a target of 7.5% market share (current 6.2%) by the end of the second year and the achievement of P&L objectives.

- Zed having "what kid's want" up from 14% to 35% by the end of the second year.
- A supply chain capable of delivery from concept to store in 12 weeks.
- A culture change tracked by an organisational culture inventory administered at regular intervals.

But even with these measures Davis couldn't get the organisational support he wanted, as he reported to his team:

> We've got the green light on some aspects of the stores revamp – mainly small scale stuff, but we can't go forward on making things "child friendly" in the way we wanted – there are funding problems so that's been put on hold for a year. Also I've just had word that our advertising is delayed until we have proved that our business model works (ie, next Spring all being well – it's imperative that we get the model to deliver!) – we've been held to ransom on the serious slip in sales in the previous two months that we've had largely because we took our eye off keeping the business running in favour of the organisation design work. We must recover our sales.

Staff were demoralised by the spring delivery being off by £6m and the resignation of a senior member of the team as a result. Davis, working flat out himself, acknowledged that overall his people's workload and stress were high and resources were stretched. That weekend he talked to his friend, Andrew Collet:

> Here's the story. As you know I was hired to turn around the failing children's wear division of the clothing retailer. Those who hired me were clear that they wanted a new, innovative, and competitive business model to regain lost ground. I think I've got that but I'm now facing the requirement to produce results long before it's possible to do so. I've got to keep the business running – not as usual, but better than that – and simultaneously the transition into the new model. The measures that I've got don't seem to be giving me the right information to make changes to the plan, and I seem to have an impossible number of priorities to juggle.
>
> Communication isn't working – not just with our suppliers, but among ourselves, there's no teamwork and we don't seem to trust each other. Then there's the relationship, or lack of it, that we've got with the supplier – communication and trust are rock-bottom there too, and look at the size of the mountain ahead.

Davis gloomily sketched his view (see Figure 5.4).

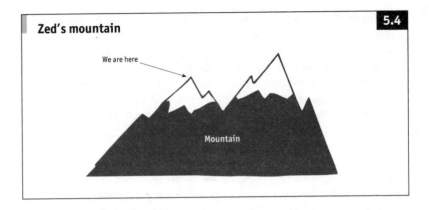

Almost desperately he listed the priorities he saw in the immediate three months, grouping them by functional team:

Look, IT, HR, Finance, Marketing, Selling, Category, Design, Commercial and Technical, and Transition all have at least four and some have five priorities to work on – it's just crazy!

Collet, recognising the edge of panic, responded:

Matthew, step back and take a calm look – having 38 priorities, and you haven't mentioned tackling culture and communication issues across the whole division, is simply not doable. You're not one of the heroes in Zed's vision. You're a hard pressed executive trying to do the right thing under pressure.

Further discussion made it clear that if Zed was to get back on track, a totally different approach would be needed for Davis to demonstrate his turnaround capability to the parent organisation in the given timescale. "You're right," said Davis, pulling himself together, "I'm remembering that I know a couple of people who've faced similar situations. Maybe I could learn from their experiences." On Monday morning, with Collet's encouragement, he picked up the phone and made some calls.

It was a surprise to Davis that one of the most thought-provoking conversations he had was with Nigel Trant, a bond trader and mathematician whom someone had suggested he call. Trant said:

Take a close look at the measures you're using to track progress. Most traditional measures view organisations as predictable mechanisms. They look at issues one-by-one – just as you've outlined each of your functional areas having four or five priorities. Not only that, they often measure short-term which leads to short-sighted decisions. In your case you're in an unpredictable situation. The problems are complex and contingent but your measurement approach is gravitating to the more obvious parts of the challenge and steering clear of the rest. Try taking a whole organisation view and measuring only a few aspects, common to all, but that will enable concerted action across the piece.

Davis pondered this and then remembered the five enablers of organisation design success: leadership support, stakeholder engagement, change readiness, communication and training (see Chapter 4). It dawned on him that the common theme was lack of stakeholder engagement. The parent organisation's leaders said they were supportive but acted differently, his own staff and staff in the supplier organisations lacked motivation and energy, and customers were voting with their feet.

At the next meeting with his team Davis outlined his thoughts:

Things aren't going as well as we expected and hoped at this stage. I'm wondering if we're focusing energy on the wrong things. Let's discuss the possibility of tracking stakeholder engagement and taking collaborative and aligned actions to develop and sustain this. I think that doing so would significantly reduce the number of priorities we've got on the table and at the same time direct our actions towards more efficiently achieving our business strategy. I don't want to change the goals but I do want to change the way we're approaching them.

There was a pause as people took in this new idea. Then the finance officer spoke:

I don't know if this will work, but there's a Stakeholder Engagement Standard[7] – it may not exactly match our needs but I think we could adapt the approach. It's comprehensive with tools and templates, and the standard is recognised in the marketplace.[8]

Four months later, with the entire team focused on the strategic objective of engaging stakeholders in mustering behind helping Zed achieve its three performance goals, there had been a significant shift in Zed's fortunes. By focusing on one question, asked weekly – How engaged are our stakeholders? – closely measuring the results, ensuring appropriate action, and communicating clearly and frequently with stakeholders, Davis had built trust in his capability to take the division to success. This led to relationships all round improving, motivation and productivity increasing, and, not coincidentally, business results changing for the better.

By the end of the year, Davis and his team felt confident they were on track and had won support not only from the staff but also from the customers. As Davis reported to Collet:

> It's been a tough period and one that began badly. I'm glad to say that things are looking good – it had never dawned on me that choice of measure could have such a dramatic knock on effect on outcomes. Take a look at this.

Davis pushed the current issue of a trade newspaper across the table to Collet:

> A great report, don't you think? "Zed is showing signs of regaining share in the children's wear market and has made good progress in a difficult environment. It still has much to do to ensure sustained growth in the long term but the new design of the division along with better value, better buying, and better styling resulted in better performance as the year progressed, the company said."

Reflections on this case

This case highlights the complex relationship between business goals and performance measures. Davis had business goals and started off by measuring each of these both directly and discretely. This had the effect of fragmenting effort and alienating stakeholders. Realising this he started to do several things right:

- ◪ He took the brave step of looking for a different approach and seeking support to do this. Some leaders find it difficult to admit to themselves, let alone others, that they are in a quandary or in over their heads. However, in stressful times leaders who are able to admit fallibility and find support and guidance to help rethink their approach are more likely to be winners than losers (for more on this see Chapter 7). People coming new to an organisation at a senior level often have a tendency to either try to drive performance or build social networks of influence. Davis was more inclined to do the former, but he realised before it was too late that to succeed he also had to do the latter. In his mind he had been focused on getting on rather than fitting in. The nature of the company required him to do both if he was to be effective and successful.

◪ He looked for a measure that was important and durable (rather than something easy to measure). The Enterprise example on page 130 suggests that one question skilfully used can generate a range of actions that together drive the business goals. The Gallup Organisation has found similar strength in fewer focused measures, making a powerful case for gaining employee engagement by asking 12 questions using the Gallup Q^{12} (see Useful sources of information). Careful choice of a few overarching measures that lead to action towards the goals is a better route than direct measurement of the gap between current state and end-goal state. It also changes the focus from fire-fighting on priorities to concentrating on adjusting as the context changes (moving from addressing urgent items to addressing important ones). As Davis learned, the measures chosen must also be adaptable to changing circumstances – in his case the reduction in funding meant a change of plans related to store layout. His first measure on this – Are we on track for delivering new store layouts? – did not stay the course. His new measure – How well are we engaging stakeholders in our store layout plans? – was adaptable as circumstances changed.

◪ He involved his team in the development of a common measurement process. Recognising that members of his management team were focused on their individual priorities and thus fighting with each other for resources, Davis used the approach of involving them in his thinking. This led to a more collegial and then productive approach to achieving the goals. With a common measure rather than individual priorities, team members started to align their functional and operational decisions, sharing ideas and insights as they went along. Parallel with this they started to use the collaborative approach with their own teams. The result was that the mindset of all staff gradually changed from one of working at Zed to one of working for Zed.

◪ He monitored consistently and regularly, thus inculcating a culture of measurement throughout. In the weekly meeting, Davis and his team reviewed the latest responses to the question: How engaged are our stakeholders? Data were gathered through several means (focus groups, one-to-one meetings, a sample survey, and so on) but in a systematic way, so that the team was seeing an evolving but reliable picture each week. The approach was carefully implemented to avoid over-surveying the same stakeholders and to keep response rates high. As people saw the effectiveness of the approach they became advocates for it, thus strengthening the process.

◪ He communicated progress with stakeholders. Davis was quick to admit that he had neglected targeted and frequent communication with stakeholders (there is more on this in Chapter 6). With his head down among the weeds, he had missed opportunities to involve them in progress and assure them that he was looking after their interests, the interests of Zed and the interests of the company as a whole. As he started to learn more about stakeholder engagement, Davis continued to ramp up communication flows, encouraging feedback and taking ideas on board. By becoming more visible and approachable and acting on what he heard Davis showed stakeholders that he was a person they could get to like and be happy to work for. A culture of "we're all in this together – let's make it work" started to develop.

Tools for this case

The acronym FABRIC provides a useful checklist for making decisions about measurement tools and methods.[9]

A FABRIC measure should be:

Focused on the organisation's aims and objectives; exclude measures that are interesting but not directly relevant. Make sure everyone involved agrees that the measurements are going to be useful and relevant to what the organisation is aiming to achieve.

Appropriate to, and useful for, the stakeholders who are likely to use it. Remember that measurements and analysis have resource implications – the benefit of each measure must be in proportion to the effort required to take it. Existing information sources should be considered before new ones are created.

Balanced, giving a picture of what the organisation is doing, covering all significant areas of work; choose measures for all important areas, and at all levels – costs, output volumes, efficiency, quality, progress towards strategic aims – even if the measures have to be subjective.

Robust in order to withstand organisational changes or individuals leaving; the information gathered must be accurate enough for its intended use as management decisions will be based upon it. Additionally, it must be verifiable, with clear documentation behind it, so that the processes which produce the measure can be validated. Further the measures should be responsive to change; measures that are relevant both before and after a radical change are useful in judging its success; those that focus on temporary aspects, or those that may change, are less useful.

Integrated into the organisation, being part of the business planning and management processes; the activity measured must be capable of being influenced by actions which can be attributed to the organisation; and it should be clear where accountability lies. With this, measures should be timely, producing data regularly enough to track progress and quickly enough for the data to still be useful.

Cost effective. This means that the measures balance the benefits of the information against the costs of collecting it. This can be facilitated by ensuring they are:

▱ clearly and unambiguously defined so that data will be collected consistently, and the measure is easy to understand and use;
▱ comparable with either past periods or similar programmes elsewhere;
▱ avoiding perverse incentives, ie, they do not encourage behaviours to meet a target rather than to improve. (For example, measuring the quantity of calls answered but not the usefulness and quality of the responses may not produce a better service.)

One of the issues with various measurement approaches and frameworks is that they remain at too high a level to be of practical benefit. They do not help with specifying the measure, discussing what methodology should be used, or how often measurement should take place. Useful practical guidance is provided in a short document from the National Oceanic and Atmospheric Administration (NOAA – an agency within the US Department of Commerce) called *Performance Measurement Guidelines*.[10] Davis's team found the flow chart (Figure 5.5) and accompanying narrative a helpful tool in defining the performance indicators under the main measurement question: How engaged are our stakeholders?

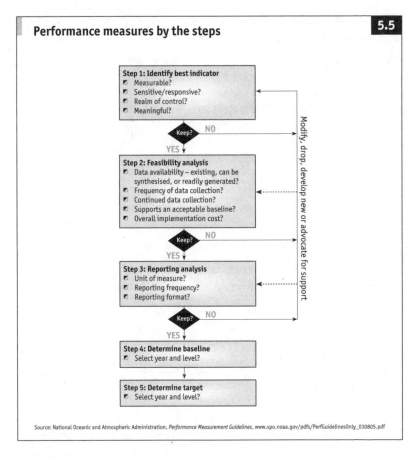

Performance measures by the steps — 5.5

Source: National Oceanic and Atmospheric Administration, *Performance Measurement Guidelines*, www.spo.noaa.gov/pdfs/PerfGuidelinesOnly_030805.pdf

Summary

Measurement is a slippery fish: difficult to catch and difficult to hold on to. Like fish it suffers from the angler's story: "I caught one this big ...." People can choose to believe or disbelieve the results of the measurement.

Nevertheless, from two perspectives it is an important and necessary part of a successful organisation design implementation. Good measurement:

- indicates whether the movement from current design to intended design is working to achieve business goals and strategies; and
- tracks the progress of the organisation design project.

The focus of this chapter has been more on the former because it is more complex – unlike programme or project management no standard methodologies exist.

There are many methodological approaches and tools available, and a systematic and reflective approach to deciding which to use works in favour of a robust outcome and usable results. Deciding on a small number of things to measure is a good option and taking an ethical approach to measurement guards against charges of misreporting and bias.

6 Stakeholder engagement

How do you get happy shareholders? Start with satisfied customers. How do you get satisfied customers? Start with happy employees. How do you please employees? Try not to wreck the community they live in.

John Mayberry, former CEO, Dofasco Inc

STAKEHOLDER ENGAGEMENT IS an intentional process of interacting with individuals and groups who have the power to affect (positively or negatively) an organisation's financial, social responsibility and environmental performance (known as the triple bottom line). The outcome of effective stakeholder engagement is an alignment of mutual interests, reduced risks to the organisation and improved results in the triple bottom line. J. Sainsbury, a UK retailer, explains:[1]

> We recognise that our engagement with stakeholders goes beyond our 16m customers, 153,000 colleagues and our many suppliers and investors. The organisations we seek to engage actively with range from those that can have an impact on our business, such as government, politicians and regulators, to those whose views are relevant to the way we run our business, such as non-governmental organisations, charities, trade unions and trade associations. Developing and building relationships with a range of stakeholders helps us to understand issues, develop our business and manage risks better.

As discussed in Chapter 4, organisation design work begins with being clear about the business case for change. This frames the reasons for devoting time and energy to engaging stakeholders, raising questions such as:

- How knowledgeable are stakeholders about the current state of affairs?
- How much do they understand and believe that a new design is necessary?
- How can we balance what stakeholders might want in a new design with what is best for the business?

- How and when will stakeholder needs be considered as the design progresses?
- What is the best way of communicating and working with stakeholders during the design process to ensure that they have a sense of ownership of the design?
- What resources (time, money, expertise, and so on) is it reasonable to budget for stakeholder engagement work?
- What outcomes will a successful stakeholder engagement strategy achieve?

To answer these questions this chapter first considers the five steps of a stakeholder engagement process:

1 Clarifying objectives for engaging stakeholders
2 Identifying the stakeholders
3 Mapping (categorising) the stakeholders
4 Determining what will engage them
5 Planning precisely how to engage them

It then looks at three specific factors – trust, loyalty and advocacy – that, if evident, indicate stakeholder engagement. If they are not obvious, stakeholders may not be engaged in the new design, which is a real risk to its success.

Five steps of the stakeholder engagement process
Step 1: Clarifying objectives for engaging stakeholders
In organisation design work the objectives of engagement are specifically to get support for and buy-in to the new design. The ultimate objective is to have employees performing highly in the new design, and customers, shareholders, and other stakeholders showing enthusiastic support for it. Thus the objectives for engaging them relate to the four phases of the design sequence as illustrated in Table 6.1.

Step 2: Identifying the stakeholders
Most organisations have a wide range of stakeholders, and it is significant that organisation design projects frequently cast too tight a net around those that they consider will be affected by the new design. When identifying stakeholders it is important to cast widely to begin with. Look at stakeholders not just inside but also outside the organisation. Figure 6.1 overleaf shows a fairly detailed identification of stakeholders in nine

Table 6.1 **Stakeholder engagement objectives**

Phase of organisation design project	Example high-level objectives	A successful outcome
Assess phase	To educate stakeholders about the business case for change in a way that grabs their interest	Stakeholders act as advocates for the business case
	To listen to the issues and needs of stakeholders as the business case for change is communicated	Stakeholders trust that their views are taken seriously and inform the progress of the design
Design phase	To demonstrate the commitment to balance the needs of the stakeholders with what is best for the business in the new design	Stakeholders retain loyalty to the organisation, demonstrate trust that the new design meets mutual interests, and act as advocates for the new design
Implement phase	To work closely with stakeholders in the implementation to develop their sense of ownership of the new design	Stakeholders transfer loyalty from the old design to the new design
Embed phase	To assess levels of commitment to the new design, and act on feedback	Stakeholders act as advocates for the new design

different sectors at ANZ, an Australian financial institution. Note how the identification also includes potential employees, customers, partners and thought leaders.

To aid identification of stakeholders, adapt the STEEPLE tool (see Table 1.1 on page 9) slightly to provide a template. A completed example at a high level is shown in Table 6.2.

Step 3: Mapping (categorising) the stakeholders

Mapping the stakeholders means taking each of those identified and placing them in relative positions on a matrix which has two axes of influence and impact as shown in Figure 6.2 on page 154. The map enables an at-a-glance overview of where stakeholder engagement work needs to be focused.

Stakeholders judged to be highly impacted by the new design but who have low influence on its success or failure are mapped into the lower right-hand segment (supervisors are the example in this instance). Stakeholders who have high influence on its success but are only somewhat impacted by the new design are mapped into the top left-hand segment (analysts are the example in this instance), and so on.

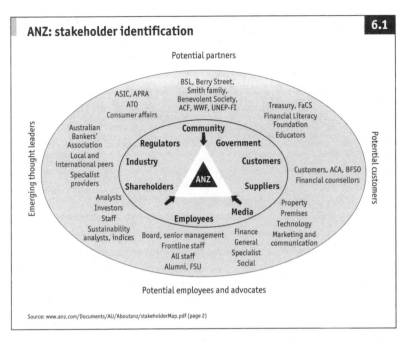

Table 6.2 **Tool to aid identification of stakeholders**

	Internal stakeholders	*External stakeholders*
Social	Employees Leaders Board members	Shareholders
Technological	IT system owners IT departments	Software and hardware suppliers
Environmental	Facilities departments	Lobbying groups
Economic	Financial system owners Business intelligence departments	Financial analysts
Political	In-group and out-group leaders	Government agencies and departments
Legal	Compliance owners HR managers General counsel departments	Industry-specific regulators
Extras	The organisational sacred cows, eg, everyone must have his/her own car parking space (precluding building on a site)	Trade associations Procurement pools

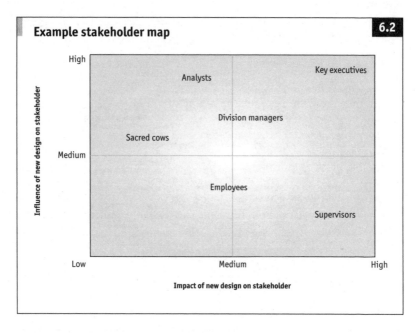

Example stakeholder map | 6.2

Before mapping it is important to:

◪ develop assumptions about each stakeholder's power, support and importance to project success;
◪ determine the current and desired levels of trust, loyalty and advocacy of each stakeholder (there is more on trust, loyalty and advocacy later in this chapter);
◪ validate these assumptions through, for example, one-to-one interviews with key individual stakeholders or facilitated sessions, focus groups and surveys of larger, aggregated groups.

Areas to probe in this sort of assumption testing include the following:

◪ Knowledge of new design programme – who knows and who cares?
◪ Perceptions – relevance of new design to "what's really important around here".
◪ Levels of commitment to new design – will the level of commitment last through the rough spots?

- Beliefs and fears – who will gain and who will lose?
- Conventional wisdom – why is this new design just like the last one (ie, this has been done before)?

The engagement work involves moving stakeholders into a segment where they are committed to and advocating the new design. Be aware that the work of stakeholder engagement continues through the life cycle of the project as any individual or group can swiftly move from one position on the matrix to another. Treating a stakeholder map as a static and stable piece of information is highly risky.

Step 4 Determining what will engage them
Briefly, there are five methods available to engage stakeholders as summarised in Table 6.3.

Table 6.3 **Engagement methods**

Method	Why use it?
Communication	Telling and selling are powerful tools
Education	Informing choices helps people make good choices
Involvement	Encouraging participation builds ownership and commitment
Incentives	Tapping into personal or financial goals and showing "what's in it for me" work to bring people on board
Power	Using power in the right circumstances and in the right way is an effective tool

Use these on a pick-and-mix basis customised to address the concerns of each individual or group of stakeholders. Christoph Brunner, chief operating officer of Credit Suisse's private banking unit, notes the power of encouraging customer involvement in redesigning his organisation when he participated in "Experience Immersion", a programme that gets executives out to bank branches, talking to customers, doing banking transactions and observing the customers as they interact with bank staff. Each session brings about reflection on the organisation design:[2]

> In some cases, we actually make it hard for customers to do business with us. [I saw] that little things make a big difference. For example,

just having signage that people understand. Having friendly and helpful employees. As a bank, we often think that only the financial products themselves matter – but there is so much more that goes around that.

Step 5 Planning precisely how to engage them

Engagement requires a strategic, systematic yet flexible approach to creating buy-in, minimising opposition and developing ownership and continuing commitment. A good measurable plan establishes key input for communications, training and compensation action.

The stakeholder map (an example is shown in Figure 6.2 on page 154) can be used as a basis for determining the engagement plan and activity level. Put simply, stakeholders in the top left quadrant should be kept satisfied, those in the top right should be managed closely, those in the bottom left can be monitored and those in the bottom right should be kept informed (see Figure 6.3).

With the stakeholders in mind, and knowing whether the task is to move them from one quadrant to another or to keep them in the current quadrant, devise a detailed and customised plan for each individual or group. Table 6.4 is an example from an organisation design initiative

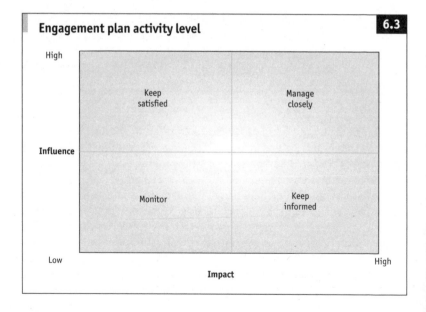

Table 6.4 **Example of stakeholder engagement plan detail**

Area of change	Impact	Stakeholder	Anticipated reaction/issues	Activity
Increased budget accountability	High	J. Smith	a) Want more control over spending b) May not want to encumber product managers c) May not want added visibility to their spending d) May not want visibility of past failures	Develop and review process vision, including anticipated benefits to the labels Gain support through his line managers Gain support through FD Present vision at conference
		Product managers	e) Most won't want added controls f) Don't want added visibility to their activities	Gain support through XY and YZ Investigate changes to compensation structure to support budgetary control Ensure that new process is easy to work with
		Finance manager	g) Says historically has never worked h) Personally in favour of cost control i) How will this impact on his job?	Develop and review process vision, including anticipated benefits Gain support through FD if hit roadblock Constant reinforcement of how they will maintain control of process after changes Develop presentation and push for their participation (secure AB and BC support as well) Focus on one-to-one communication
		P. Brown	j) Wants more control over spending k) Level of commitment/action unclear	Create and present simplified target environment document with "Group of 4" assistance, including anticipated benefits to the labels Use target environment document as strawman

undertaken at Xerox. Note that there may be budget or other constraints on the plan and these should be taken into account.

Factors indicating stakeholder engagement

Conscious stakeholder engagement is essential not only in an organisation design project but also in the day-to-day running of an enterprise. If it is done effectively, it encourages, develops and maintains a sense of commitment and common purpose that creates value. Triodos Bank, for example, has a well-conceived approach to employee engagement, as a statement on its website illustrates:[3]

> Triodos Bank could not achieve its mission without the whole-hearted support, effort and commitment of all its staff. It will only be able to make a name for itself as a pioneering force in sustainable banking if its staff continue to be able to identify with, and make a real contribution towards, the Bank's mission.

Triodos's engagement strategy is not limited to employees. It also embraces customer engagement, for example by inviting individual customers to see how business customers benefit from their relationship with the bank.

The result of this form of day-to-day engagement with employees and customers is demonstrated in the bank's annual results, as this extract from a Triodos press release shows.

Triodos shows symptoms of real health

While the UK's high-street's banking behemoths report multibillion pound profits, a much smaller bank is showing (2005) increasingly significant signs of health. With growth in returns of 41% for its shareholders and a 25% increase in funds under management to £1.6 billion, the Triodos Group's best results in its 25-year history have come from a radically different approach to money, which puts people and the environment alongside profit.

Source: www.triodos.co.uk/uk/whats_new/latest_news/press_releases/222367?lang=

Results like this owe a lot to the earning and maintaining of staff and customer commitment. Companies which foster commitment do so in various ways, for example by:

- learning from feedback on products or services;
- collaborating to solve problems or address opportunities;
- improving the quality of life in their local communities;
- operating in a responsible and ethical way;
- seeking to contribute more than simple bottom-line profit.

The resulting "face" of commitment is stakeholder trust in the company, loyalty to it and advocacy of it to others. These three stakeholder attributes are also fundamental to organisation design project success. Design projects that can build on methods, techniques and approaches already in use in the organisation enjoy a head start in stakeholder engagement activity.

The following sections consider trust, loyalty and advocacy in the wider organisational context and indicate where organisation design projects benefit in developing these qualities in their specific stakeholder populations.

Trust

Trust is the willingness to be vulnerable to (or rely on) another party when that party cannot be controlled or monitored.[4] Trust involves risk. For example, when customers buy a product they put their trust in the manufacturer that it is safe to use. When they buy a service they trust that they are getting value for money and that the service will conform to their expectations. It takes constant investment to maintain trust at a level at which customers feel that they can believe what the company says and will be treated well. Many companies explicitly recognise this. Vodafone, which like many telecoms companies faces a number of market challenges, recognises that investing in trust maintenance is a stakeholder activity critical to its survival:[5]

> Several issues are key to maintaining the trust of our customers. These are the clarity of our pricing, the way we handle customer privacy and the responsibility of our advertising and marketing material. Underpinning this is the need for our communications with customers and potential customers always to be clear, transparent and fair. Responsible marketing and the clear pricing of our services are key to maintaining consumer trust.

Companies have to work hard at maintaining trust. It is an attribute that is easy to lose if something goes wrong and the organisation's response is poor. Even though it happened more than 25 years ago, the way that Johnson & Johnson managed the 1982 Tylenol disaster is still cited as an exemplary way of responding to a crisis. The decision taken at the time was to use the company's Credo as a guide to taking the correct actions. Knowing that "We believe our first responsibility is to the doctors, nurses and patients, to mothers and fathers and all others who use our products and services", leaders were able to act swiftly and with integrity to the situation (cyanide being found in some Tylenol products). Following the immediate withdrawal of all Tylenol products, Johnson & Johnson designed a new packaging process that customers trusted. As a result of its open and clear communications, which were in perfect alignment with its actions during the crisis, the company succeeded in maintaining its customers' trust.

In contrast, Dell has experienced problems with trust. On its website (www.dell.com) it states:

> Dell's success is based on maintaining direct relationships built on trust. To sustain this trust with our employees, customers, suppliers and investors, we must hold ourselves to the highest standards of business.

But press reports and customer dissatisfaction during late 2005 and early 2006 indicated a gap between what Dell was saying and the way it acted. Two of the many negative comments posted on the blog site www.consumeraffairs.com illustrate this:

> In summary, the laptop I bought was shoddy and their technical support was not helpful. I'll NEVER buy from Dell again, ever. (Posted 06/26/06)

> I did not get the software that I purchased with my computer. It would be easier to go to the moon than get help from Dell technical support who sent me to customer service who sent me back to tech. (Posted 04/14/06)

Customer feedback of this type was reinforced by media comment also implying that the business model mitigated against developing customer trust. As *The Economist* noted:[6]

Increasing sales to consumers is difficult for Dell because individuals tend to want to see and touch computers before buying them. They also like to be able to return the machine easily if it breaks. Dell's lack of retail presence, once ballyhooed as a benefit, has turned into a grave disadvantage. Likewise, sales in countries outside America are often based on the advice of sales staff, which places Dell's "direct-only" business model at a disadvantage.

Dell's response (in May 2006) was to unveil a turnaround plan "to improve customer service and product quality while shaving billions of dollars in costs". Dell's spokesman Jess Blackburn admitted:[7]

> In the consumer space, we shipped a lot of systems and grew very quickly and we have acknowledged that we did not increase our service and support to meet the demands of a lot of new computer users.

The organisation design work involved in Dell's turnaround plan is significant. It involves bringing in new executive talent from outside the company; re-evaluating suppliers; improving customer service (spending more than $100m) by hiring new support workers and retraining existing ones; expanding new offerings such as a remote-repair service; pricing products better; and changing chip supplier from Intel to AMD. Note that these activities relate to every component of the organisation model shown in Figure 1.2 (see page 5).

Table 6.5 **Link between organisation design model and Dell turnaround activity**

Organisational design model component	Related Dell activity
Systems	Hiring new support workers (HR systems)
Structure	Expanding remote-repair service
People	Bringing in new executive talent from outside the company, hiring new support workers, retraining existing ones
Performance measures	Re-evaluating suppliers
Processes	Changing chip supplier (procurement processes)
Culture	Focusing on customer service

The scale of the organisation design work implied in the turnaround, aimed at improving customer service and support, presents a significant stakeholder trust-building challenge for Dell, as Table 6.6 illustrates.

Table 6.6 **Dell turnaround activity linked to trust-building challenges**

Organisation design activity	Examples of trust-building challenges
Hiring new support workers (HR systems)	Dell gaining the new employees' trust as a good employer to work for.
	Customers trusting that new employees have the skills and experience to provide accurate responses to service issues.
Expanding remote-repair service	Customers trusting that remote-repair services are as efficient as more local repair services.
	Employees trusting that expansion will open opportunities for career development.
Bringing in new executive talent from outside the company, hiring new support workers, retraining existing ones	Employees trusting that new executive talent will have the skills and capabilities to handle the turnaround.
	New executive talent trusting that their efforts will not be undermined by too early (or pre) judgments on their capability.
Re-evaluating suppliers	Existing suppliers trusting that they will be treated fairly in the re-evaluation process.
Changing chip supplier (procurement processes)	Analysts trusting that selling more AMD-based machines will not bring more complexity and cost to Dell's business.
Focusing on customer service	Shareholders trusting that the reputational damage can be restored resulting in improved business performance.

In Dell's favour is the recognition that however welcome the turnaround moves are, their impact will not be felt for some time. As Jason Maxwell, analyst at TCW, a large Dell shareholder, said:[8]

> It'll take a while to repair the reputational damage. It's a longer-term fix. In the short term, it doesn't help Dell make its quarterly targets.

This implies that Dell has some time available to move through the four phases of an organisation design (assess, design, implement and embed) in a considered way, to align all the components with its stated mission

– "To be the most successful computer company in the world at delivering the best customer experience in markets we serve" – and simultaneously to build and rebuild stakeholder trust.

Engaging stakeholders by building and maintaining their trust is a wise investment, as the Edelman Trust Barometer, an annual survey, points out:[9]

> Trust has important bottom-line consequences. In most markets, more than 80% say they would refuse to buy goods or services from a company they do not trust, and more than 70% will "criticize them to people they know," with one-third sharing their opinions and experiences of a distrusted company on the Web. (2006 survey)

Employee trust – which can be won or lost in similar ways to customer trust – is necessary for a new organisation design to succeed. In the workplace, if employees trust management and leaders they will focus on the job (and thus remain productive), rather than spend time and focus attention on various forms of defensive and self-defensive (covering their backs) risk-mitigation behaviour. Research studies[10] show that employees' trust in all levels of management, particularly their immediate supervisor, improves organisational performance, openness in communication and information sharing, and acceptance of organisational decisions.

In conditions of change and uncertainty there is a greater need for trust because people feel vulnerable. The more trust employees have in management the more smoothly things will go. This is partly because employees will be less concerned with how the new organisation design affects their jobs than with the way the transition process is designed and implemented and the types of decisions that are made by management during this period. Organisational design changes can produce or destroy employee trust depending on how the implementation is structured and managed.

When organisation design work involves employees, levels of trust in management rise. Researchers in this field conclude that this is because participation gives employees a voice in the way the change process is planned and carried out. Employees develop trust in the design objectives and methods when they see that "their interests and values are understood and taken seriously".[11]

An organisation design project based on maintaining or developing trust is one where managers, design leaders and project team members demonstrate enough self-confidence and trust in the employees to:[12]

◪ speak openly about the design work and their own feelings and responses to it, including voicing doubts and fears as well as hopes and aspirations;

◪ demonstrate willingness to listen, learn about and respect employees' views of the organisation, and appreciate how they think and feel about their workplace, in the way that Sam Palmisano, chairman, president and CEO of IBM, suggests:[13]

> So, for 72 hours last summer [2004], we invited all 319,000 IBMers around the world to engage in an open "values jam" on our global intranet. IBMers by the tens of thousands weighed in. They were thoughtful and passionate about the company they want to be a part of. They were also brutally honest. Some of what they wrote was painful to read, because they pointed out all the bureaucratic and dysfunctional things that get in the way of serving clients, working as a team or implementing new ideas. But we were resolute in keeping the dialog free-flowing and candid. And I don't think what resulted – broad, enthusiastic, grass-roots consensus – could have been obtained in any other way.

◪ demonstrate their belief in employees and the business, pointing out how the design work is trying to help employees accomplish their work goals more effectively and reminding them regularly that all parties are working for the same thing;

◪ highlight risky situations and help employees deal with them by modelling risk taking, thus showing employees that they too are willing to risk to serve the ends of the design project;

◪ relate to employees in the way they themselves would want to be related to, including demonstrating that they are not fearless, just as employees are not;

◪ follow through on all their promises and commitments, and share responsibility for getting work done;

◪ put into practice lessons learned from previous projects – including encouraging employees in the current project to discuss approaches with employees involved in earlier projects.

Remember that people easily lose trust in periods of instability and change.

Loyalty

Loyalty is the emotional and functional state of being unswerving in allegiance, or faithful to an institution or product. It is not the same as trust

– people can trust others but this does not need to involve loyalty. So, for example, air travellers can trust that almost any airline will be safe to travel with, but they may have no loyalty to a particular airline, purchase choices being made on the basis of cost, schedule, or whatever.

Loyalty is a functional, emotional and enthusiastic dedication to a relationship that people believe will improve their lives in the long run. Functional loyalty is quantitative and trackable. Emotional loyalty is qualitative and indicated by statements about the feel or experience of the organisation. Table 6.7 shows some types of measures of each in relation to two important stakeholder groups: staff and customers.

Table 6.7 **Examples of measures of staff and customer loyalty**

	Functional tracked by:	*Emotional indicated by:*
Customer	Loyalty programmes, eg, frequent flier Number of visits to store or website Total spend	Going out of their way to purchase, eg, at shop where they know the staff Talking about repeat buying from places where they are treated well
Staff	Retention rates Intention to quit Turnover rates	Going the extra distance Speaking up and recommending changes in a positive, confident way Recommending their company to others

Measures of functional aspects of loyalty can be misleading. Functional loyalty is vulnerable to a better offer: a valued employee may enjoy working for an organisation but still be lured away by a competitor; a customer who moves to a different town may have no choice or may find it more convenient to shop in a different supermarket chain than the one they had been shopping in.

Building and maintaining emotional loyalty – which transcends functional loyalty and is less vulnerable to changing circumstances – requires developing a relationship over the long term that stakeholders care about and want to maintain.

In many organisation design projects, unless actions to maintain or increase both functional and emotional loyalty are planned into the project, stakeholders become more likely to move on because uncertainty affects their relationship with the organisation. Thus when mapping stakeholders it is helpful to label their current and aimed for levels of loyalty.

Within organisation design work, project loyalty development and maintenance activity will be focused on two stakeholder groups: staff and customers (there is less need to build loyalty in other groups although their trust is still required). Building staff loyalty includes making them feel that they are treated fairly, that they are cared for, that they are trusted to do a good job, that their contribution is valued and that their needs will be met. American Apparel is a good example of an organisation that currently commands employee loyalty and is carefully aligned in all its components (see Figure 1.2 on page 5) to maintain it.

American Apparel: achieving employee loyalty

American Apparel is a vertically integrated manufacturer and retailer of clothing for men, women, kids and dogs. This means that we've consolidated all stages of production under one roof at our Downtown Los Angeles factory – from the cutting and sewing of the garment, right through to the photography and marketing.

Ultimately, it is vertical integration, an efficient system that cuts out the middlemen, that enables the company to be sweatshop free. Because we do not outsource to local or developing-nation sweatshops, the entire process is time-efficient and the company can respond at breakneck speed to demand. This enables us to be competitive within the global market.

For American Apparel, being sweatshop free means offering all of our employees, sewers and administrators alike, basic benefits. We provide affordable health care for workers and their families, company-subsidised lunches, bus passes, free ESL classes, on-site masseurs, free parking, proper lighting and ventilation, and the most up-to-date equipment (be it the latest cutting machine or software). We offer these as a matter of policy, not only because we care about our employees, but also because we understand that a positive work environment is a more productive one.

Most importantly, we pay the highest wages in the garment industry (the average sewer at American Apparel earns $13 an hour but this can be as high as $27 an hour), we offer year-round employment and job security, with the goal of lifetime employment. There is virtually no turnover when it comes to our garment workers, and their loyalty to the company is a huge source of pride.

Source: www.americanapparel.net/mission/vertical.html

Investing in developing emotionally (not just functionally) loyal staff is good for business results. Conversely, when staff are not loyal and the result is high turnover, it can be costly for organisations, as the example below illustrates.

The cost of high staff turnover

David Russo, formerly in HR at the SAS Institute (a business intelligence company), did a calculation in my class one day. A student asked him why SAS does so much family-friendly stuff. He said, "We have something like 5,000 employees. Our turnover rate last year was 3%. What's the industry average?" Somebody said 20%. Russo replied, "Actually, 20% is low, but I don't care. We'll use 20%. The difference between 20% and 3% is 17%. Multiply 17% by 5,000 people, and that's 850 people. What does turnover cost per person? Calculate it in terms of salary." The students estimated that the cost is one year's salary and that the average salary is $60,000. Russo said, "Both of those figures are low, but that doesn't matter. I'll use them. Multiply $60,000 by 850 people, and that's more than $50 million in savings."

Source: Webber, A.M., "Danger: Toxic Company", *Fast Company*, October 1998

Building customer loyalty is similar to building staff loyalty. Customers too want to feel that they are human beings and not simply a source of revenue. Customers who feel they are valued, that their custom matters to the organisation, that they are treated well and fairly by the staff, and that their needs will be met are more likely to be emotionally, not just functionally, loyal to the company. Again this translates into good business results. Frederick Reichheld of Bain & Company, a management consultancy, notes:[14]

> Seemingly insignificant changes in customer retention rates in several of our clients' businesses resulted in eye-popping improvements in profits. Then, we studied a wide array of industries, and found that a 5 percentage point shift in customer retention results in 25–100% profit swings.

The message is clear for an organisation design project: developing and/or maintaining staff and customer functional, and especially emotional, loyalty will pay dividends both quantitatively and qualitatively. Remember that losing loyalty costs more than money, so use the design process as an opportunity to develop and retain it.

Advocacy

It is not enough simply to develop, retain, maintain or grow stakeholder trust and loyalty if these stakeholders are not then active advocates of the organisation, promoting, supporting and enthusiastically recommending it to others.

To initiate a design that promotes advocacy, the most powerful first step is to see the organisation through the eyes of stakeholders. A popular BBC/OPB TV co-production, *Back to the Floor*, highlights the power of this experience and the organisation design changes that frequently come about as a result. Wedgwood is one company featured.

A stakeholder's view

The chief executive is in for a shock when he joins the production line of his largest factory in Stoke-on-Trent. Disillusioned workers are living in fear of redundancy. Forty of Yvonne Morrall's colleagues have already lost their jobs and she is nervous and unhappy with the threat of more robots that don't work. "Less people, more machines, more profits," is how Yvonne thinks the top management view things. She tells [Brian] Patterson:

> We see another machine and think, "How many jobs is that going to cost?" People on the shop floor feel that people like yourself are all about profits. They feel as if they are not worth anything any more. Why bother, because my job's probably going to be taken over by a machine anyway. You drive off in your BMWs and that's it, you don't care.

Her candour is a breakthrough for Patterson, who is so deeply affected that it keeps him awake that night for hours. The next morning he acts immediately, calling a meeting with 20 workers to find out what they think of the new Wedgwood.

For Patterson, this has been a truly revelatory week that has made him think again on every reform and every aspect of his company:

> I've had my eyes opened in an amazing way into what people ... think and feel. I would never have known that really through the normal systems of management communication.

Source: www.pbs.org/opb/backtothefloor/wedgwood/index.htm

Active word-of-mouth advocacy is a major contributor to high perform-ance. A three-year study carried out by the London School of Economics found that net promoter scores (NPS – an industry measurement estab-lished by Bain & Company in 2003) are a statistically significant predictor of sales and growth. Specifically, the authors of the report note:[15]

- A 7% increase in word-of-mouth advocacy unlocks 1% additional company growth.
- A 2% reduction in negative word-of-mouth boosts sales growth by 1%.
- In monetary terms, for the average company in the analysis, a 1% increase in word-of-mouth advocacy equated to £8.82m extra sales.
- A 1% reduction in negative word-of-mouth for the average company in the study resulted in £24.84m in additional sales.
- Companies with above average positive word-of-mouth and below average negative word-of-mouth grow four times as fast as those with below average positive word-of-mouth and above average negative word-of-mouth.

It goes without saying that to recommend or praise an organisation stakeholders have to trust it (although they may not have to feel any func-tional or emotional loyalty towards it). Again, two groups of stakeholders that have great power in affecting the success of an organisation by acting as positive or negative advocates for it are staff and customers.

Staff advocacy is important in maintaining turnover at cost-effective levels, contributing to motivation and also to performance. Relief Resources, a US-based temporary staffing agency, is committed to devel-oping relationships with their staff based on honesty and inclusion:[16]

> What's important to us is that you be connected to our mission and have an opportunity to contribute in meaningful ways. You'll feel supported and guided, respected and trusted, and truly appreciated.

This in turn inspires trust and loyalty, as exemplified by this comment by Patrick S. Sempala, Relief Resources Field Staff, Wellesley Hills, MA:[17]

> You have all done such a great job supporting me with work. I am thankful to be involved with Relief Resources. Everyone there shares the same commitment to doing our best for all the programs we serve.

The results are twofold (as with American Apparel): first, the company has a much lower turnover rate than the industry standard; and second, staff become advocates of the organisation, recommending it to others as a good place to work:[18]

> Most of our workers come from referrals from other employees or from people in the community. That means we hardly have to do any advertising, which is the biggest expense for most temp agencies. Our investment in relationships has yielded incredible bottom line benefits in terms of cost savings.
>
> Doug Hammond, president and founder, Relief Resources

A new organisation design is the ideal moment to consider developing positive advocates among staff. The design challenge is to recognise that social and technological changes are bringing rapid shifts in power, and that this is having a considerable impact on the relationships between staff and organisations. This requires designs flexible enough to respond quickly to new demands. For example, *The Economist* notes:[19]

> For some time to come, talented people in the West will demand more from employers, and clever employers will create new gewgaws to entice them to join. Those employers should note that for a growing number of these workers the most appealing gewgaw of all is the freedom to work as and when they please.

Organisations that are unable to respond to this type of thing will find that staff will not advocate on their behalf, turnover will increase and it will be difficult to recruit new talent into the organisation.

Customer advocacy is somewhat different from staff advocacy as there is no contractual bond between customer and organisation. Customers form judgments based on their experience of the organisation, the trust they put in it and the loyalty they feel towards it. Customers are much less likely to be loyal now than they were in the past, partly because they have easy access to extensive sources of web-based information that enable them to make informed judgments on products and services. They no longer rely on companies' feeding them information. The result is:[20]

> [Some companies] are providing customers with open, honest and complete information – and then finding the best products for them, even if those offerings are from competitors. They are truly expressing their customers' best interests, essentially becoming advocates for

them. The strategy is this: if a company advocates for its customers, they will reciprocate with their trust, loyalty and purchases – either now or in the future. The firm might then command higher prices for its products and services, as many customers will be willing to pay for the extra value. And when people trust a company, they will often tell others about it, helping to reduce the organisation's costs for acquiring new customers.

With this in mind, each component of the new organisation needs to be designed to align with concepts of making customers successful, in essence providing a design answer to the question: How can this organisation be designed to support customers and advocate for them? This requires a profound change in thinking for most organisations.

It can, however, be done successfully. Pampers, a firm that makes diapers (nappies), is an example. Rather than focusing on the product, the organisation presents itself as:[21]

The Pampers Parenting Institute committed to providing parents with the best in information and support from the world's leading experts in child health and development.

More than presenting itself as a diaper manufacturing and sales operation, Pampers suggests it is a reliable source of information on each stage of child development from pregnancy through new baby, baby, toddler and pre-schooler. Parents thus start to trust the brand less for the diapers and more for the way the company acts on their behalf as an information provider. The lure to the products is through relatively subtle placement in side-bars and through promotions and competitions. Instead of being persuaded to buy products, customers are "invited" to join Pampers.com. One result of this is that they act as advocates for the products on non-Pampers websites:[22]

I have twin boys and these Pampers are the best. To attach the Pamper is extremely easy. I will not mention another well known name brand but nothing compares to these.

As a new design is being planned and implemented, a focus on what will make it work for staff and customers creates the conditions in which they will become advocates for the organisation. So the design work needs to be done with this in mind, aligned and reinforced through such things as:

- Buzz techniques "that use the trendsetters in each community and subtly push them into talking up your brand to their friends and admirers".[23]
- Referral programmes that reward staff or customers for recommending the organisation to others.
- Comparisons of products, services, employment conditions with those of competitors.
- Investment in quality products, services, employee benefits – the baseline things that ensure a certain level of satisfaction.
- Reliable and effective service levels – for example in responding to customer or staff enquiries or support needs.
- Loyalty and trust building activity (see previous sections) that encourages advocacy, as implemented by Chris Benham, a retail project manager at J. Sainsbury:[24]

   39% of customer awareness came from the activity and advocacy of in-store employees … that was completely unprecedented for us.

- Communication that is open, clear and honest so that staff and customers know what the deal is and what they can expect from it.

CASE STUDY: developing stakeholder trust, loyalty and advocacy

The date for the spin off of High Mark Finance as an independent company from its parent, a global credit card and business services organisation, was fast approaching. It would be one of the largest financial advice firms in the country with over 12,000 financial advisers and 2.8m clients. In the preceding two years High Mark had had a patchy record in client satisfaction, as measured by J.D. Power & Associates, and there were worries about how both advisers and customers would react to the change. Employees and customers were blogging away and their posts were not friendly.

The view of Jon Peacock, regional manager for the north-west, was that High Mark's focus on "reinventing retirement" aimed at relatively wealthy people could be a difficult new area for his employed advisers to engage in as most of them were under 30 and were not confident in advising people older than themselves. Equally, he was uncertain that his self-employed advisers, franchised under High Mark (and in his management portfolio), would be able to refocus their businesses. For many it would mean dropping some clients because they did not have the profile High Mark wanted to invest resources in for others who did have the right profile.

Furthermore, the region for which Peacock was responsible was largely a young commuter area which did not have the more affluent segments of the population or people who were old enough to start worrying about their financial well-being in retirement. To meet this challenge High Mark advisers, both employed and self-employed, would have to focus on getting high-earning people in their 30s and 40s to recognise that now was the time to start to prepare for their financial comfort against the day when they stopped working.

Peacock was also worried that even those in the current client base who could be retained in the new target base would not act as advocates for High Mark. He asked a colleague:

> Would they recommend us to their friends, either when we were the old company or as we become the new High Mark? There's a certain amount of inertia around financial services clients that makes sticking with a company look like loyalty. But loyalty does not make a recommendation. Maybe some clients are getting the impression that we're not interested in them. Last year we had 93% client retention, but the most recent quarter showed a dramatic drop – to 88%. If it drops further following the spin-off date we'll have a very hard time recovering ground. It's the same picture with our franchisee adviser retention – last year it was 91% and now it's 87%. Turnover among our employees is on the increase too. The main reason for this seems to be that their trust in management is dropping and they have become much more likely to leave.. Dangerous rocks are looming and we need to take action now before we hit them.

Realising that Peacock needed guidance and support in leading his region of High Mark through the transition from being a business unit in a large organisation to being an independent entity, Peacock's colleague recommended that he take up the offer of business coaching from the parent company. A week later Peacock met the coach, who said:

> What kinds of things could be done in the north-west region to reinforce adviser trust, loyalty and advocacy beyond the head office mandated ones of optimising compensation, incentives and awards, rolling out enhanced training, having the right tools on advisers' desktops, strengthening recruitment processes, and keeping an even keel between productivity and growth in the network?

Peacock had been the north-west regional manager for a number of years, and his region had always been the benchmark for others in terms of meeting goals and targets. His people were licensed and well trained and he felt distressed about the current situation. Thinking of it in terms of trust, loyalty and advocacy put a different slant on things. He thought back over the past year or so from the time the spin-off was first mooted. After mulling over the coach's comments for some time, Peacock said:

> Those are good questions. I wonder if I've taken my eye off the things that make people committed and motivated – relationships, responsibility and autonomy, encouragement, a voice in the change, a quality of working life. The things that you've just mentioned I've seen countless times in corporate presentations and it's just struck me that they're about processes, systems and numbers. They're not about what we're doing to keep people feeling that they're valuable assets rather than simply productivity units, or profitability generators. Yes we need some of that but we've developed an organisation design targeted on trying to make the business successful rather than trying to make the advisers and the customers successful.
>
> I've felt it myself but tried to ignore my own feelings of increasing pressure to perform with too little conversation and discussion about the values and practices of the new High Mark, where I stand in it, what I can expect from it, what is happening. The spin-off has put a great stress on everyone to design an organisation that convinced shareholders that High Mark was the right thing to do. Maybe worrying too much about the analysts and too little about our advisers and customers is showing in what's happening now.

So when asked what he was going to do, Peacock responded:

> I'm going to clear my calendar and spend part of next week alongside an employed adviser, and part of it alongside a franchisee. When I get back I'll call my management team together and describe what I see going on, and how I feel about it. Then I'm going to offer some explanations for why things seem to be going downhill. I'll suggest some ways forward from my perspective but before I do that I'm going to invite them to describe and explain from their viewpoints. I'm hoping that together we can suggest a range of ways forward for designing into the new organisation the committed, motivated advocates we want our advisers and customers to be. I don't know if my approach will work but I hope it will start things rolling in the right direction.

Over the next six months Peacock and the coach worked on developing an organisation design that would create the conditions for trust, loyalty and advocacy in the north-west region. They gave particular attention to getting better alignment between the systems, structures, people, performance measures, processes and the culture, involving employees and staff in the discussions about how best to do this. Because a large proportion of revenue came from self-employed advisers running franchises, there had to be a single overarching vision that they all subscribed to, but this had to be combined with the flexibility to operate competing strategies (see Nadler's Updated Congruence Model, Table 2.2, page 24).

Peacock set up a project team comprising a cross-section of the organisation. He tasked team members with assessing the current situation, evaluating the change readiness of the advisers (employed and self-employed), conducting a stakeholder analysis and mapping exercise, preparing a high-level communications plan that focused on the specific needs of the north-west region's stakeholders, and determining the level of managerial support needed to make the north-west region high performing. He also asked them to gauge the level of training that would be required to give advisers the confidence to work with the targeted customer group.

The findings of this exercise convinced Peacock that he had to focus on building and rebuilding the trust and loyalty of his stakeholders, in particular the advisers and existing customers who were in the segment High Mark was focusing on. Having got to that point, Peacock felt that he would start to see advocates emerging. It was hard work. Trust and loyalty lost are not easily regained, so it was particularly gratifying when the phone rang one day while Peacock and his coach were discussing the outcomes of that week's "listening post" with customers. It was the manager of the neighbouring division, who said:

Hey, Jon, what's going on over there? I've just seen your adviser and customer satisfaction rates, and they're way ahead of mine and back to the level they were when we were all part of the larger organisation. Tell me how you're doing it.

Jon laughed and replied:

I've designed in some processes for looking through the eyes of the advisers and customers rather than through the eyes of the shareholders and analysts. It's working – listen to what one of the participants in the listening group just said:

"I am a client of High Mark, the other day I called their free phone number and was shocked. The person I talked to was very nice and helpful. He walked me through the options that I had for when my certificate came up for renewal. He did not try to sell me anything, just gave me the facts. It's nice to know even in today's day and age that one can call and get someone who is genuine and kind. From my experience they are a very down-to-earth company. I've just recommended them to a friend at work."

Comments like that are on the increase and with them are coming better financial results. So not only are our customers benefiting, the new design focus is bringing shareholder satisfaction too.

Reflections on this case

A major change, such as a spin-off, acquisition or start-up of a new product or service line, brings with it huge upheaval and more than usually close scrutiny from shareholders anxious about the value of their stock. An example was when Volkswagen recruited Wolfgang Bernhard to cut costs and bring in 5–10 new vehicles within five years:[25]

> Investor confidence in him ran so high that Volkswagen's market value rose nearly $1.25 billion on the day his appointment was announced in October 2004.

With all types of organisation there is a tendency to focus on designing the "hard" aspects of the new state – the systems, processes, structures and technologies – and to neglect the design of the "soft" aspects – behaviours, culture and relationships. This is a mistake, but an easy one to make because the hard aspects are easier to quantify, measure and do something about. It is best to take the view that although the soft stuff is the hard stuff to design, being successful at it brings results that more than repay the work involved.

In the case of High Mark, Peacock did several things once he recognised the design was going wrong:

- He went on field trips to see what was happening with customers and staff day-to-day. It is easy for managers to lose touch with the frontline operation and therefore not to experience it as customers and staff do. Recognising this, some organisations have introduced programmes that encourage contact with parts of the business from which managers are normally remote. The programmes take different forms: shadowing staff, becoming a staff member for a short period, buying the company's goods through the channels that the customers use and variations on these themes. The idea is to help managers identify and understand what the blockage is and what needs to happen to encourage staff and customers to trust the organisation, develop an active loyalty to it and speak highly of it to others.

- He established listening groups. These are forums where stakeholders participate in facilitated discussions to air their views on particular topics or respond to questions asked by managers. Usually a senior manager is present or may be conducting the group. Groups are generally made up of no more than 15 people representing a cross-section of the targeted population: that is, those people who have the profile of the group the organisation is interested in. In the case of staff it might be a supervisor group; in the case of customers it might be men between the ages of 30 and 40. Roger Holmes, former CEO at Marks & Spencer, started his report on some listening groups he attended as follows:

> I have just completed a series of colleague listening groups in Head Office and stores in the Midlands and North West regions. Participants represented a good cross-section of responsibilities from store to office and from sales adviser to "head of".
>
> Overall, the atmosphere is, not surprisingly, much more positive. The key concerns expressed in the early groups have been addressed, ie, we're proud of what we're offering our customers in stores, pleased that customers and the press are more positive, and when in outside company are much more likely to volunteer that they work for us. There are, however, a number of significant concerns related to how we work internally, and I was struck at the number of groups relating poor morale as a consequence. With the challenges of an increased business agenda and a more demanding external environment, I sense that there are some important issues that we must address if we are to be equipped to succeed.

Of course, listening groups are not the only way to listen to customers and staff, as Table 6.8 overleaf shows.

- He went back to some basic design models to diagnose where he had missed pieces. Peacock had adopted Nadler's Updated Congruence Model (see Table 2.2 on page 24) for his design. This comprises four organisational elements: people, culture, formal organisation and critical tasks. He recognised that the main focus of his High Mark design was on the systems, processes and structures (that is, the formal organisation and the critical tasks), and that he had neglected the people and culture elements. This

Table 6.8 **Ways of listening to customers and staff**

Stakeholders	How to listen
Customers	Sales information Weekly and monthly monitoring of views Surveying customers who have visited new and refurbished stores Customer panels Annual independent surveys Communications to head office Communications to specific business groups
Staff	Company-wide local, regional and national employee representation forums Confidential helpline Regular employee surveys Internal communications, including employee magazines, regular business updates and team briefings Focused consultation programmes Listening groups conducted by senior management

meant that High Mark was out of alignment. The result was poor morale bringing with it a lowering of loyalty, trust and advocacy. Using a model to help identify and highlight any lack of alignment is helpful, as is doing some straightforward alignment tests (see Tools for this case below).

◪ He recognised the power of designing the "soft stuff" to create conditions of loyalty, trust and advocacy. The people and culture aspects of an organisation are the more difficult ones to design, so it is tempting to pay less attention to them and hope things will work out. However, a quick scan of employee blogs or customer report sites often reveals the power and influence that these stakeholders have and the numerous ways they can wield this power. In *The Power of Alignment*, George Labovitz and Victor Rosansky present guidelines for vertically and horizontally aligning an organisation's design to deliver its strategy.[26] In High Mark's case, the strategy was centred on the vision of "reinventing retirement financial planning". Peacock's decision to involve customers and staff in discussions on this resulted in not only organisational alignment decisions but also the restoration of trust, loyalty and advocacy. Once these stakeholders felt that they had a voice and that their views would be translated into actions they started to trust High Mark and rally behind it.

Tools for this case

In this case it was not always possible to bring appropriate stakeholders to workshops and focus groups. High Mark made use of technology-based collaborative software and groupware to get optimum attendance at meetings. Many different technologies exist for this and they are rapidly developing in sophistication and ease of use. Good practice seems to suggest that people meet face-to-face in the first instance to establish rapport, develop a sense of each other and feel comfortable working together. However, it seems that after an initial meeting people are happy to use technology to support their collaboration and discussion. A good forum for finding out more about collaborative technologies is www.ctcevents.com which describes the annual Collaborative Technologies Conference.

People usually need to remind themselves of the option to listen but rarely of the option to talk. Attentively listening is a skill to learn. In this case executives attended a skills workshop and received the checklist in Table 6.9 overleaf as a reminder.

Lastly, Peacock worked with his coach on an alignment diagnosis profile (see Table 6.10 on page 181). He scored the statements on the profile, totalled the score for each section, and then plotted and connected the four scores on the diamond in Figure 6.4. This allowed him to see that High Mark was weak in some areas and strong in others.

Summary

Stakeholder engagement is a crucial activity in the organisation design process. Analysing and mapping stakeholders reveals what to build into a detailed and flexible engagement plan that builds trust, loyalty and advocacy.

Staff and customers are two stakeholder groups with which it is critical to develop trusting and loyal relationships. Generating either or both of these attributes does not necessarily lead to advocacy. However, organisations that have staff and customers who are trusting and loyal are more likely to be advocates of that enterprise.

Trust and loyalty are developed by taking steps to design the organisation from the perspective of those stakeholders, the objective being to answer the question: What design will lead to our staff and customers being successful? Encouraging staff and customers to participate and collaborate in the design process is a recipe for success.

Table 6.9 **Keys to effective and active listening**

Listening is wanting to hear. It requires a degree of concentration that involves mental receptiveness coupled with physical alertness

Keys to effective and active listening include	Being intent on hearing what is said
	Detecting any underlying or hidden meaning that accompanies a speaker's words
	Separating out the speaker's facts from their feelings to get the meaning
	Preventing emotional reactions to the speaker from conflicting with accurate perceptions of meanings
	Withholding the tendency to be thinking of a response before the speaker has finished
	Reviewing and summarising the speaker's message content
	Asking clarification questions of the speaker
	Wanting to hear so not filling silences but waiting
	Focusing on key points
	Taking notes, when possible, to express interest and to improve retention of the message.

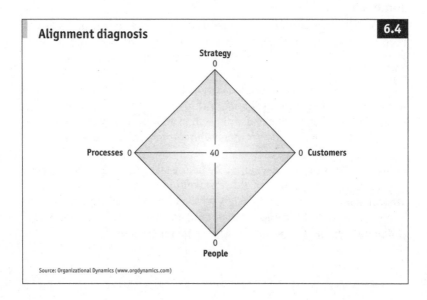

Alignment diagnosis 6.4

Source: Organizational Dynamics (www.orgdynamics.com)

Table 6.10 **Alignment diagnostic profile (short version)**

Strategy	Strongly agree									Strongly disagree
Organisational strategies are clearly communicated to me	1	2	3	4	5	6	7	8	9	10
Organisational strategies guide the identification of skills and knowledge I need to have	1	2	3	4	5	6	7	8	9	10
People here are willing to change when new organisational strategies require it	1	2	3	4	5	6	7	8	9	10
Our senior managers agree on the organisational strategy	1	2	3	4	5	6	7	8	9	10
Total										
Customers										
For each service our organisation provides, there is an agreed upon, prioritised list of what customers care about	1	2	3	4	5	6	7	8	9	10
People in this organisation are provided with useful information about customer complaints	1	2	3	4	5	6	7	8	9	10
Strategies are periodically reviewed to ensure the satisfaction of critical customer needs	1	2	3	4	5	6	7	8	9	10
Processes are reviewed regularly to ensure that they contribute to the attainment of customer satisfaction	1	2	3	4	5	6	7	8	9	10
Total										
People										
Our organisation collects information from employees about how well things work	1	2	3	4	5	6	7	8	9	10
My work unit or team is rewarded for its performance as a team	1	2	3	4	5	6	7	8	9	10
Groups within the organisation co-operate to achieve customer satisfaction	1	2	3	4	5	6	7	8	9	10

	Strongly agree							Strongly disagree		
When processes are changed, the impact on employee satisfaction is measured	1	2	3	4	5	6	7	8	9	10
Total										
Processes										
Our managers care about how work gets done as well as about the results	1	2	3	4	5	6	7	8	9	10
We review our work processes regularly to see how well they are functioning	1	2	3	4	5	6	7	8	9	10
When something goes wrong, we correct the underlying reasons so that the problem will not happen again	1	2	3	4	5	6	7	8	9	10
Processes are reviewed to ensure they contribute to the achievement of strategic goals	1	2	3	4	5	6	7	8	9	10
Total										

Source: Organizational Dynamics (www.orgdynamics.com)

7 Leadership and organisation design

Hard it is to learn the mind of any mortal, or the heart, 'til he be tried in chief authority. Power shows the man.

Sophocles, *Antigone*

FORMAL LEADERSHIP OF an organisation design project may lie with one person in the hierarchy, but in practice designs are developed, implemented and led by many. Typically, depending on the size of the organisation and the design project, an individual will sponsor a business plan for the design but the day-to-day operational leadership will be delegated to a steering group and then on to programme directors, project managers, team leaders, and so on. Figure 7.1 (also shown in Chapter 4 as Figure 4.2) illustrates the project leadership roles, who is accountable to whom, and who is to lead whom in order for the project to succeed.

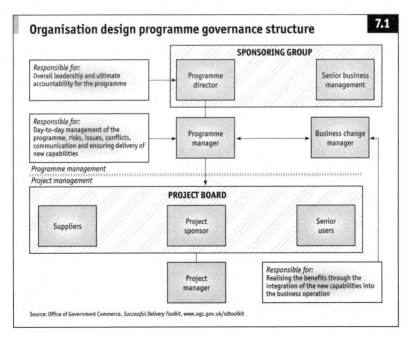

Organisation design programme governance structure `7.1`

SPONSORING GROUP

Responsible for:
Overall leadership and ultimate accountability for the programme

Programme director

Senior business management

Responsible for:
Day-to-day management of the programme, risks, issues, conflicts, communication and ensuring delivery of new capabilities

Programme manager

Business change manager

Programme management
Project management

PROJECT BOARD

Suppliers

Project sponsor

Senior users

Project manager

Responsible for:
Realising the benefits through the integration of the new capabilities into the business operation

Source: Office of Government Commerce, *Successful Delivery Toolkit*, www.ogc.gov.uk/sdtoolkit

Note that some of the roles shown in Figure 7.1 include the word "manager". This does not mean that people in these positions are not leading – they are both leading and managing. This might seem obvious but, given the many perspectives on leadership versus management, it is worth making the point (taking fairly standard definitions) that if leaders set and spearhead a new direction or vision for a group, and if managers control or direct people and resources in the group to realise the new direction or vision, then as far as an organisation design project goes the individuals shown on the chart are in both roles. With this perspective in mind there is no reason why a person cannot be simultaneously a leader and a manager. Inevitably, within an organisation design project, this is what many of the players are.

Combining leading with doing is crucial, as Phil Evans and Bob Wolf explain in a *Harvard Business Review* article that looks at the way Linux and Toyota Production Systems ensure it happens:[1]

> At every level, Linux and TPS leaders play three critical roles. They instruct community members – often by example – in the disciplines we've just described. They articulate clear and simple goals for each project based on their strategic vision. And they connect people, by merit of being very well connected themselves. The top Linux programmers process upwards of 300 or 400 e-mails daily. Fujio Cho, the president of Toyota, manages by similarly numerous daily interactions that transcend the normal chain of command. Neither community treats leading as a discipline distinct from doing. Rather, the credibility and, therefore, authority of leaders derives from their proficiency as practitioners. The content of leaders' staccato communications is less about work than it is work. (When Linux creator Linus Torvalds dashes off his scores of daily e-mails, he writes almost as much in the C programming language as he does in English.) Occasionally, leaders do have to perform traditional leadership acts, such as arbitrating conflicts. That, however, is the exception and is viewed as a bit of a system failure.

What Evans and Wolf are implying is that leadership is not only about position but also about use of various other sources of power, in this instance proficiency as practitioners. Considering formal leaders of organisation design work in terms of their ability to wield power (defined as having the means to influence the behaviour of others) is helpful because there are many sources of power that leaders can draw on. Some of these are as follows:[2]

- Formal authority
- Control of scarce resources
- Use of organisational structure, rules and regulations
- Control of decision processes
- Control of knowledge and information
- Control of boundaries
- Ability to cope with uncertainty
- Control of technology
- Interpersonal alliances, networks and control of informal organisation
- Control of counter organisations
- Symbolism and the management of meaning
- Structural factors that affect the stage of action
- The power one already has (personal power)
- "Ownership" of a contract vehicle
- Reputation, credibility, or charisma (sometimes called referent power[3])
- Control of definition of certain situations, for example the difference between terrorism and freedom fighting

Typically, designated organisational leaders draw on formal authority, control of resources and use of organisational structure, rules and regulations. But they have to draw on other sources depending on the situation. In many organisation design projects formal leadership is vested in consultants or contractors who are not directly employed by the enterprise. These leaders have to use different sources of power – while they may have formal authority, they may not control resources or the use of organisational structures. If these "outsider" leaders are not skilled at identifying and using the power sources at their disposal, they are often sidelined for not being "one of us".

As well as the organisation design leaders – those in the formal designated roles shown in Figure 7.1 on page 183 – there will be others inside the organisation who can wield power to influence or control organisation design work. These may be people with positional power (in other leadership roles but not directly involved with the organisation design project) or people who do not have any formal leadership position but can influence the behaviour of people by wielding other types of power. These informal leaders may have more impact on an organisation design than the formal leaders. Take this example of trying to unionise Wal-Mart, where Wal-Mart changed design as a result of the action:[4]

The Service Employees International Union (SEIU) funded group "Wal-Mart Watch" also kicked off its campaign in April with full-page ads in major newspapers that focused on what it called low-level wages the retailer pays to its workers. Chris Kofinis, a spokesman for the United Food and Commercial Workers union (UFCW) campaign, said the shift from traditional organizing to a grass-roots public campaign was necessary because of Wal-Mart's ability to block union efforts. In April, for example, the company closed a store in Quebec, Canada, after its workers voted to join the UFCW. In 2000, it eliminated all US meatpacking positions after meatpackers in Texas voted to unionize.

Determined not to recognise labour unions, Wal-Mart took the decision to close a store, leading to a shake-up of the organisational design in Canada. And in eliminating all meat-packing positions it had to find other methods of doing this work, again changing the design of the organisation.

Beyond the organisation itself there are external formal leaders who have the power to affect the success of the current or new design. Many British Airways employees still recall the disastrous launch of their new airplane tailfin while Bob Ayling was chief executive:[5]

During that period [January 1996 to March 2000] BA shares underperformed the market by 40% as Mr Ayling battled with low staff morale, rising fuel prices, the Asian economic crisis, competition from low-cost airlines – and, inevitably, falling profits. Mr Ayling tried to be innovative, in 1997 even introducing funky tailfin designs for BA's aircraft based on Chinese calligraphy, Polish tower blocks, the Kalahari desert and Delft pottery. The exercise, however, proved a public relations disaster. At the launch Lady Thatcher draped her handkerchief over an offending model. Mr Eddington [has since] announced a return to British livery, reintroducing the Union Flag on each tailfin.

External audiences saw this tailfin project as the failure of a market repositioning of the airline. What they did not see was the internal repercussions of this failure which led to significant organisation redesign work in the business units involved. In this instance the UK's former prime minister used her personal power to influence the way the media and others perceived what could have been seen as a bold and imaginative move. (Imagine the difference if Thatcher had heaped praise on the tailfins for their creative way of showing that British Airways was a truly global airline welcoming a diversity of people and acknowledging "one world").

More recently NASA, the US space agency, felt the sting of the US Office of Management and Budget redirecting its work in the budget allocated in 2007. Here a body using the power of its control of scarce resources directed the agency in a particular way: the funding cut forced NASA into a new organisation design.

Restructuring to improve results

In support of the president's goal to make government spending more effective, some NASA programmes that are not directly relevant to the exploration mission or other agency priorities, have underperformed, or are financially unsustainable, will be reformulated or terminated to allow for greater focus on the agency's high-priority programmes.

Commenting on this, NASA administrator Michael Griffin said that the agency had to take a "couple billion out of science and a billion and a half out of the exploration line" to fund the spaceflight programmes. "I wish we hadn't had to do it. I didn't want to, but that's what we needed to do," he added.[6]

Funding cuts of any scale have a direct impact on the size and shape of the organisations affected. Look again at Figure 1.2 (page 5) and imagine how taking out a "couple of billion" would affect each one of the components (systems, processes, people, performance measures, structure, culture).

External informal leaders can also use their power to good or bad effect (depending on point of view). An example of an informal external leader is shareholder activist Michael Messmore. According to an article in *Business Week:*[7]

> Delta Air Lines pilot Michael H. Messmore was incensed at the $28m golden parachute handed to former Delta Chief Executive Ronald W. Allen when he resigned in 1997. To stop such excesses, Messmore, with the backing of the Air Line Pilots Association, submitted a proxy resolution in 2000 demanding shareholder approval of such deals.

> The initiative was rejected three years in a row. But at Delta's annual meeting on April 25 [2003], widespread shareholder anger over revelations of bankruptcy-proof retirement packages for current executives put Messmore's resolution over the top, with a 54% majority. Another pilot-sponsored proposal calling for the cost of stock options to be deducted from earnings racked up a 60% majority. "Executive compensation is out of whack," says Messmore.

His type of activism promotes change, as the article goes on to point out:

> The current spate of shareholder votes is likely to spur a fair amount of reform. For example, both companies that lost proxy battles over executive pay last year, Bank of America and Norfolk Southern Corp., eventually adopted the measures. "Everyone's a lot more sensitive to majority votes now," says Rosanna Landis Weaver, an analyst at the Investor Responsibility Research Center in Washington ... and just days before the April 29 annual meeting at Exelon Corp., labor withdrew a similar resolution after the electric company pledged to stop giving executives pension credit for more years than they have worked. "It is better for us to be viewed as proactive," says an Exelon executive. "It became clear that a number of shareholders were interested in changing the policy."

From these examples it is evident that organisation design success depends on the complex interactions of four broad leadership groups: internal formal leaders, internal informal leaders, external formal leaders and external informal leaders. Each of these groups has at their disposal various sources of power (listed on page 185), and although formal leaders may have access to more of these than informal leaders, the way the power is wielded is an important determinant of the outcome. As martial arts practitioners know, soft as cotton can be as hard as steel.

Access to and use of power is one of several variables determining ability to lead. Others include style of attracting and holding on to followers; stability of circumstances; personal motivation; and the organisation's political landscape. The efficacy of a leader changes as the context changes, and someone who cannot adjust their style of leadership or draw on a different source of power is opening the door for someone else to seize the leadership role.

This chapter now examines the internal formal and informal leadership of organisation design work, focusing on the formal leaders within the enterprise charged with delivering the new design and the internal informal leaders who can act to support or stymie it.

Formal leadership in organisation design

Figure 7.1 on page 183 shows the formal organisation of typical large-scale projects and programmes. The names of the formal leaders of an organisation design project appear in the boxes. Smaller projects will not have the same number of people involved: in some cases, a line manager will lead a project single-handedly. Whatever the number of designated leaders they all have, by virtue of their position, three specific power sources: formal authority; control of scarce resources; and use of organisational structure, rules and regulations. They may have additional sources of power, but it is these three that are usually associated with hierarchical position. How well they use or are able to use their power depends on the context and on their leadership style and behaviour.

The context for organisation design typically presents formal leaders with seven challenges. In essence, they must simultaneously:

- balance the demands of the day job with the demands of the project;
- manage a range of competing important and urgent priorities, tasks, and activities;
- help staff cope with what is inevitably seen as yet another change (in some organisations this is called managing "change fatigue");
- satisfy the need of the business for a fast change that also gets things right;
- get the timing right on leadership issues – know when to push and when to let go;
- motivate stakeholders who do not report to them but whose input is critical to the project;
- work effectively with other leaders both inside and outside the project.

This is difficult to accomplish but it can be done. One leader who appears to have succeeded in meeting these seven challenges is Aaron Schwartz, who joined Bruno Magli, a high-end shoe company, in 2004 as president North America. He had a mandate to redesign the organisation and the leadership skills to do it effectively. His report on the experience is shown in Table 7.1.

Table 7.1 **The leadership challenges in organisation design work**

Report	*Challenge*
"North America had always been a precarious market for Bruno Magli, and it was especially so after September 11th. The business was under siege. We had treacherous retail leases and currency pressure from the euro, and were undergoing management changes as the Bruno Magli family retired. By 2004 we needed to clean up the business. Frankly, the fastest, most effective way to do that in the States was to file for Chapter 11 bankruptcy.	1 Balance the demands of the day job with the demands of the project 2 Manage multiple competing important and urgent priorities, tasks, and activities. 3 Satisfy the need of the business for a fast change that also gets things right.
"Even though we were using it as a strategic tool, the very word 'bankruptcy' can cause heart palpitations. The parent company in Italy was dumbfounded – they pictured us closing the business and selling the furniture. But this was all very carefully planned.	4 Motivate stakeholders who do not report to them but whose input is critical to the project.
"Still, I was anxious. In fact, I was a nervous wreck. No matter how much expert advice you get from lawyers and PR firms, it's still bankruptcy. I kept thinking, I'm plunging this 74-year-old company into ruin. But it was such a release to be able to tell employees that I was nervous, too. Don't hide it. You absolutely have to be honest with people. We said, 'We're not going to tell you that nobody's going to lose their job.' Although we had to lay off about 50 people, there were no surprises.	5 Work effectively with other leaders both inside and outside the project. 6 Get the timing right on leadership issues – know when to push and when to let go.
"I know this doesn't sound right, but the bankruptcy was like a gift. Everyone knew we were changing, so a buzz built around what our future might be. It was like a start-up with the safety net of an established brand and a strong corporate parent. And the results showed. By this spring, we couldn't deliver enough products to meet demand. That was a real vindication."	7 Help staff cope with what, inevitably, is seen as yet another change (in some organisations this is called managing "change fatigue").
Bruno Magli North America emerged from bankruptcy in January 2005. After closing its retail stores in the United States as part of the restructuring, the luxury shoemaker opened its first shop-within-a-shop concept in May at the Arthur Beren shoe store in Beverly Hills.	

Source: Underwood, R., "Leading Through Limbo", *Fast Company*, September 2005

The company's newly designed US arm started doing well – annual sales in 2005 were \$35.8m, about 50% of worldwide sales – and after two years with Bruno Magli Schwartz moved on to Polo Ralph Lauren.

Although there are some roles in organisation design work that are dedicated to the project, for example the programme manager, much of the work is led by people holding dual roles. Schwartz typifies a leader who simultaneously spearheaded an organisation design programme and led the day-to-day operation of an enterprise. Whatever the leadership level in the business, to lead project work and day-job work successfully – meaning managing the seven challenges listed on page 189 – it is necessary to determine the demands of the role in the project and develop an appropriate leadership style.

Determine the demands of the role in the project

Have a clear grasp of the vision, mission and purpose of the project
This may sound obvious but when someone is given a leadership role in a project that is already under way, it is easy to leap into action without properly understanding the project's objectives. To understand what is being taken on:

- identify and assess what is going on behind the scenes;
- meet at least some of the stakeholders and get their views;
- make certain there is high-level agreement (sponsor or accountable executive) on outcomes and deliverables;
- agree and document the context and boundaries of the leadership role;
- assess and get a realistic view of the project in the context of all the other work that makes time demands.

Determine whether work needs to be reprioritised or resources reallocated
This will involve discussions within the business and may involve renegotiating personal performance objectives and balanced business scorecard measures and taking steps to reset performance expectations. Leaders who try to take on large pieces of project work on top of their normal workload without making agreed adjustments are not doing anyone a favour.

Clarify and establish the boundaries of the role
Usually it is up to the leader to get some statements from stakeholders about the boundaries of the role so that people are not going into the organisation project with untested assumptions. Consultants and contractors coming into project leadership roles must be diligent in

deducing how consistent the view is that insiders hold about the role and its deliverables.

Establish levels of accountability and responsibility
Accountability and responsibility are not the same thing. A team leader may be responsible for the effective performance of team members and may be accountable for ensuring that they deliver a 10% increase in product sales in the next quarter. Alternatively, the team leader may be accountable for the 10% increase in product sales but it is someone else's team members who are the prime agents. Check that there are clear linkages between accountabilities and responsibilities and/or clear methods of resolving issues that may arise in trying to deliver outcomes using resources for which the leader is not responsible.

Secure resources
Securing resources includes appointing an effective deputy who is fully briefed and engaged in both the project and the day-to-day work and is able to stand in for the leader as the situation demands. It also means leaders making sure they have enough time in which to plan, eliminate duplication of activities, and communicate consistently and regularly with stakeholders (in both the project and day-to-day work).

Develop an appropriate leadership style
Mobilise the formal and informal leaders to work together
This is a hard trick to pull off, particularly for people brought in specifically to turn around a project in trouble. It is a matter of achieving the right balance of getting on with colleagues and staff and getting on with achieving the objectives of the project – both within a short period of time.[8]

Build trust quickly by being both credible and competent
Beyond leadership style people look for certain behaviours before they start to trust their leaders (see Chapter 6 for more on trust). Staff observe what leaders pay attention to, measure and control on a regular basis; for example:

- how they react to critical incidents and organisational crises;
- how they allocate scarce resources;
- instances of deliberate modelling, teaching and coaching;
- criteria for allocating rewards and status and recruiting, selecting, promoting, retiring and excommunicating organisation members.[9]

Leaders who are unpredictable, volatile or eccentric, or who are micro-managers or have other characteristics known as "derailers" (see Glossary), cannot build trust. Derailers can have devastating effects on the lives of their followers and their organisations. "Chainsaw" Al Dunlap, fired from his role as CEO of Sunbeam in 1998 after just less than two years in post, is one example of a tyrannical leader whose methods destroyed morale in the company and almost destroyed the company itself:[10]

> Rarely does anyone express joy at another's misfortune, but Dunlap's ouster elicited unrestrained glee from many quarters. Former employees who had been victims of his legendary chainsaw nearly danced in the streets of Coshatta, La., where Dunlap shuttered a plant. Says David M. Friedson, CEO of Windmere-Durable Holdings Inc., a competitor of Sunbeam: "He is the logical extreme of an executive who has no values, no honor, no loyalty, and no ethics. And yet he was held up as a corporate god in our culture. It greatly bothered me." Other chief executives, many of whom considered him an extremist, agreed that Dunlap's demise was a welcome relief.

During his time at Sunbeam, Dunlap's organisation design work reduced the number of factories from 26 to 8, cut $225m of costs, reduced the workforce by 6,000 and cut charitable contributions.[11] As Figure 7.2 shows, the result of his approach, far from saving a failing company, caused the share price to drop below the price it was when he took the helm with a mission to save it.

Recognise and reduce the fear people may have
Even people who trust their leaders may be fearful, for all sorts of reasons, at the thought of an impending organisation design change. Fear has a stultifying and demoralising effect, as Edmund Burke, an 18th-century philosopher, remarked: "No passion so effectively robs the mind of all its powers of acting and reasoning as does fear." People's fear of uncertainty, disruption and unknown outcomes may inhibit them from asking questions, participating in the design work or expressing a view about it. As Michael Carroll says in *Awake at Work*:[12]

> When the assistant who is rudely dismissed by his boss in a meeting becomes sullen and withdrawn, we see the silence of fear. When the accountant keeps her eyes down as the sales manager presents highly questionable sales numbers to the CEO, we again see such silence.

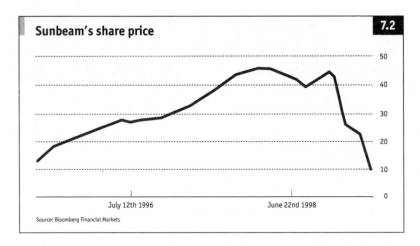

Sunbeam's share price 7.2

| | |
| July 12th 1996 | June 22nd 1998 |

Source: Bloomberg Financial Markets

It is rare for people to admit to being afraid, so looking for what is not being said and recognising that people are likely to be fearful is the first step towards creating the conditions in which they can face their fear and work with it positively. For a leader of an organisation design project, this means encouraging communication, involving people in the design work and decisions, and behaving in a respectful way to others. (See Chapter 6 for more on creating conditions for openness and dialogue.)

Use power wisely
Leaders who consistently use the same power source(s) usually fail, sometimes spectacularly, in achieving their mission. NASA is an example of an organisation that had leaders predominantly using their formal authority, control of decision processes and use of organisational structure, rules and regulations. This led, in part, to the tragic crashes of the space shuttles *Challenger* and *Columbia*. The Columbia Accident Investigation Board report notes that within the agency:[13]

> With Columbia, as with Challenger, the board found, decision-makers were overly influenced by pressures to launch on time. In blind adherence to safety rules, they ignored hunches and intuition about faulty equipment. They valued organizational charts over good communication. The report chastised the agency for habitually turning a deaf ear to outside critics, and for clinging to the belief that NASA alone knew best how to safely send people into space.

Signals were overlooked, people were silenced. Communication did not flow effectively up and down the formal chain of command.

Work skilfully with "followers"

Lao Tzu, author and founder of Taoism, described the ideal state in 6BC:

A leader is best when people barely know that he exists, not so good when people obey and acclaim him, worst when they despise him. "Fail to honour people and they fail to honour you." But of a good leader, who talks little, when his work is done, his aim fulfilled, they will all say, "We did this ourselves."

The way leaders do this depends on their style, and there is no best leadership style. What will work in one situation may not work in another. Knowing this, it pays to be alert to the nuances of different situations, and to behave consistently in similar ones. Random and unpredictable behaviour only confuses and alienates people; this is the opposite of what is required in an organisation design process.

A helpful framework for considering leadership style is Paul Blanchard and Kenneth Hersey's Situational Leadership Model.[14] It is based on the theory that leadership style is demonstrated by the amount of direction and support that a leader gives to "followers" and is represented in a grid (see Figure 7.3).

The premise is that leaders flex their style depending on the needs of the follower. This responsiveness creates a culture of openness where followers feel respected and valued.

Be conscious of the interests and motivations of other leaders in the programme or project

Gareth Morgan, in his discussion of organisations as political systems, suggests:[15]

People must collaborate in pursuit of a common task, yet are often pitted against each other in competition for limited resources, status, and career advancement.

Organisation design projects by definition shake things up – coalitions change as the project progresses. In most cases there are some leaders who feel that they will either win or lose from any proposed design and will then act to preserve their own interests at the expense of organisational

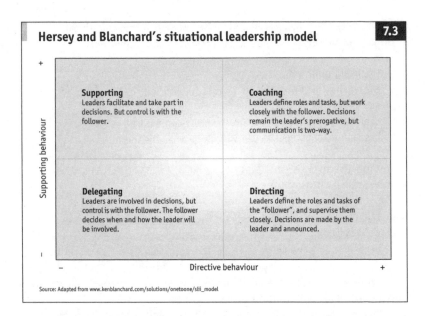

Hersey and Blanchard's situational leadership model 7.3

Supporting
Leaders facilitate and take part in decisions. But control is with the follower.

Coaching
Leaders define roles and tasks, but work closely with the follower. Decisions remain the leader's prerogative, but communication is two-way.

Delegating
Leaders are involved in decisions, but control is with the follower. The follower decides when and how the leader will be involved.

Directing
Leaders define the roles and tasks of the "follower", and supervise them closely. Decisions are made by the leader and announced.

Supporting behaviour

Directive behaviour

Source: Adapted from www.kenblanchard.com/solutions/onetoone/slii_model

interests. Being able to build what John Kotter calls a "guiding coalition" that balances both collaboration and competition becomes essential to project success on the basis that:[16]

> Efforts that don't have a powerful enough guiding coalition can make apparent progress for a while. But, sooner or later, the opposition gathers itself together and stops the change.

So formal leaders of organisation design projects face daunting challenges, but these can be met. Wayne Hale, the space-shuttle programmer at NASA in charge of the effort to get the shuttle flying again, talks about the *Columbia* space shuttle disaster in 2003:

> We dropped the torch through our complacency, our arrogance, self-assurance, sheer stupidity, and through continuing attempt[s] to please everyone. It is time to adjust our thinking.

Three years later, following significant organisational design work at NASA (it has estimated its *Columbia* investigation and return to flight efforts cost about $2.3 billion in 2006), *Discovery* was successfully launched on July 4th 2006. In the weeks leading up to the launch, two NASA officials, chief engineer Chris Scolese and chief safety officer Bryan O'Connor, gave a "no-go" for the launch:[17]

> [Michael] Griffin [NASA administrator] called the disagreements about
> the repairs a good sign that the culture at NASA has changed. The
> agency was faulted by the Columbia investigation board for having a
> conformity of opinion. "I personally want every engineer to express the
> best opinion that they can give us," Griffin said.

Following *Discovery*'s touchdown on July 17th, the commander of the shuttle, Steven Lindsay, noted:[18]

> I think we're back to space station assembly, to shuttle flights, but
> we're still going to watch and we're still going to pay attention. We're
> never ever going to let our guard down.

Achieving *Discovery*'s mission took a coalition of leaders in various leadership roles. Along the way any competing interests were managed and now NASA looks designed to achieve its goal announced in a speech by President Bush on January 14th 2004: to use the shuttle to finish the international space station by 2010, develop the crew exploration vehicle by 2014, return humans to the moon by 2020 and eventually move on to Mars – albeit at the expense of other NASA projects. As Griffin noted at a press briefing in Washington, DC: "NASA simply cannot afford to do everything that our many constituents would like us to do."

Informal leadership

Informal leaders emerge in organisations usually because they have a particular passion or belief and have characteristics which engage people in their cause. These informal leaders are found at any level in the hierarchy because what they spearhead is independent of hierarchy.

Lesson 9 of 18 lessons on leadership
Organization charts and fancy titles count for next to nothing
Organization charts are frozen, anachronistic photos in a workplace that ought to
be as dynamic as the external environment around you. If people really followed
organization charts, companies would collapse. In well-run organizations, titles are

also pretty meaningless. At best, they advertise some authority, an official status conferring the ability to give orders and induce obedience. But titles mean little in terms of real power, which is the capacity to influence and inspire. Have you ever noticed that people will personally commit to certain individuals who on paper(or on the organization chart) possess little authority, but instead possess pizzazz, drive, expertise, and genuine caring for team mates and products?

Source: Colin Powell, former US Secretary of State

Patricia Pearce and Derek Pereira are former British Airways cabin crew who in 1986 decided that they would find a way to fly sick children to Disneyworld on a dream flight and persuaded BA to support them in this venture. Today Dreamflight is an independent registered UK charity, still enjoying considerable support from BA, which sends one full flight of children on their Dreamflight each year. Sir Cliff Richard, patron of Dreamflight, says:[19]

> If anyone has any doubts about the value and impact of the Dreamflight charity on the lives of sick children, they should watch the faces of youngsters boarding a BA 747 for their trip of a lifetime to Disneyworld in Florida.
>
> I'm always humbled by their courage and inspired by the selflessness and compassion of so many of BA's staff and other escorts who give up their leave to accompany these children.
>
> I've often said that I find involvement with a charity often brings me far more than I could ever offer. Unarguably, that's true of Dreamflight.

This early venture into what is now called corporate responsibility paved the way for the current design of BA's department of corporate responsibility, which supports an extensive and wide-ranging programme. (In 2005 the company supported 130 projects with direct and indirect donations of £5.4m in 2005–06.)

In an engaging book, *Tempered Radicals*, Debra Meyerson describes people such as Pearce as wanting "to rock the boat and to stay in it".[20] She describes four approaches that they use to lead change:[21]

> Most subtle is "disruptive self-expression" in dress, office décor, or behavior, which can slowly change an unproductive atmosphere as people increasingly notice and emulate it. By using "verbal jujitsu" an

individual can redirect the force of an insensitive statement or action to improve the situation. "Variable long-term opportunists" spot, create, and capitalize on short- and long-term chances for change. And through "strategic alliance building" an individual can join with others to promote change with more force. By adjusting these approaches to time and circumstance, tempered radicals work subtly but effectively to alter the status quo.

Informal leaders muster support not only by their approach (in the Dreamflight example using strategic alliance building), but also by their use of referent power (which derives from the belief that people have in them after seeing them in action) and their personal characteristics. These include:[22]

- support of subordinates;
- intolerance of poor quality;
- lack of political orientation;
- high regard for competence;
- admission of error and failure;
- standing up for values and beliefs;
- outspokenness and candour;
- high ethics and integrity;
- calmness and effectiveness in crises;
- sharing of victories and a sense of fair play;
- ability to influence without authority.

Whistleblowers – those who expose misconduct in the workplace – share these characteristics and also have the power to change the design of the organisation. However, they usually find that they are not able to rock the boat and stay in it:[23]

Despite progress on the legal front, blowing the whistle remains a risky business. Whistleblower advocates say retaliation doesn't always occur, but the whistleblower should anticipate it. "The whistleblower will get hammered no matter what the protections," said Kris Kolesnik, executive director of the US National Whistleblower Center, which has lobbied successfully for better legal protections for whistleblowers. Kolesnik cautioned that even employers who appear grateful for the disclosures may be plotting to get rid of the whistleblower.

Exposing organisation malfeasance may well be better led by an outsider. Erin Brockovich, an administrator in a law firm, helped run a campaign that led to Pacific Gas and Electric paying $333m in compensation to the families of those who had suffered illness and death as a result of PG&E's pollution of land around its gas compressor station in Hinkley, California. PG&E also had to clean up the environment and stop using chromium 6, the cause of the pollution. By contrast, Karen Silkwood, who led a campaign against her employer Kerr-Mcgee, a plutonium fuels producer, ended up dying in a car crash in 1974. This was the subject of much speculation as she was in the middle of collecting evidence for the union to support her claim that Kerr-McGee was negligent in maintaining plant safety, and at the same time was involved in a number of unexplained exposures to plutonium. The plant closed the year after her death.

Informal leaders can initiate new organisation design work by their actions or they can intervene in an already initiated project. To achieve their goals they use predominantly referent power combined with an approach and a set of characteristics that enable them to muster support without jeopardising their position.

Being able to influence without authority is at the heart of informal leaders' ability to get what they want. This is often a tricky thing to do in difficult situations where, for example, there is no opportunity for a second chance, or there is a lot of resistance from another person or group. In these instances a systematic approach to influencing helps (see Figure 7.4).

Table 7.2 gives an example of the model in action. Ellen Thomas, a young African-American consultant, was given advice by her mentor, Joe, to unbraid her long cornrow braids before giving a high-profile public presentation. She interpreted this as meaning that she was to "look as white as possible".

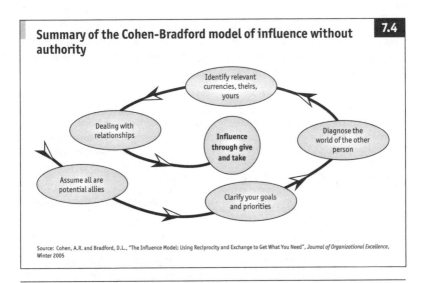

Summary of the Cohen-Bradford model of influence without authority `7.4`

Source: Cohen, A.R. and Bradford, D.L., "The Influence Model: Using Reciprocity and Exchange to Get What You Need", *Journal of Organizational Excellence*, Winter 2005

Table 7.2 **Influencing without authority**

Ellen knew it was a risk to ignore Joe's advice, but her hair was too tied to her sense of self to give in.	**1 Assume all are potential allies** It is easy to leap into an adversarial mode but imagine, instead, that things can be worked out in partnership or by forming an alliance. (Allies here are both Joe and the people she was presenting to.)
After some thought, Ellen was able to see this encounter as a test not just of her willingness to conform to fit this definition, but of the institution's willingness to adapt to the reality of its diverse workforce. She realised she had choices. This incident posed an opportunity to challenge Joe's biases and to help him appreciate the connection between this concrete incident and the organisation's espoused promise of valuing diversity.	**2 Clarify goals and priorities** There are usually several options, possibilities and choices in any situation. Think carefully about the trade-offs, cost benefits and outcomes of each of these. Depending on priorities it may, for example, be better to lose a battle and to win the war.
Ellen prepared for her presentation and delivered it with unimpeachable authority. She wore her hair in neat cornrow braids and dressed in a new conservative business suit. ... She knew she succeeded in conveying expertise; she also hoped that ... she signalled to others that professionals come in many different packages.	**3 Diagnose the ally's world** This means finding out what the other person cares about and seeing the world through their eyes. Someone who sees an organisation as a political system will have a very different perspective from a person who sees an organisation as a psychic prison.

She wanted to make sure her mentor learned something from this, but not in a way that jeopardised their relationship or put him on the defensive. Immediately following the presentation Ellen thanked Joe for caring enough to give her advice and gently asked him if he knew how it had affected her. As she suspected, he did not, and he asked her to explain. Ellen described why her hair was not just about "style", and why to her it was emblematic of her ethnicity. She let him know that she understood that he had not meant to offend her. She then explained that she chose this company because she thought it would accept her as a black woman.

4 Identify relevant currencies
People value and 'trade' in different things and these can become bargaining chips in an influencing exchange.

5 Deal with relationships
Cohen and Bradford describe this as having two aspects: the nature of the relationship – positive, neutral or negative – and the way each participant wants to be related to.

6 Influence through give and take
Once someone knows what they want, what the desired relationship is, and what currency is available to trade in then the exchange can take place.

She diverted the issue away from hairstyle and appearance to the much broader issues of the existing parameters of fitting in and the company's willingness to expand its implicit definitions of professionalism.

The result of this was that Ellen began to be known in the organisation as an informal leader of diversity issues.

Source of scenario in first column: Meyerson, D.E., *Tempered Radicals*, Harvard Business School Press, 2001, p. 66

Working together

Collaborative working, where people feel good about their interactions and the results they produce, is hard to achieve. Whatever the mix of formal and informal leaders in an organisation design project, the barriers to good outcomes are the same: territorial game playing, poor decision-making, the tendency to make assumptions, seeing things from only one perspective and failing to learn. Removing these is an imperative.

Territorial game playing

Who does not recognise that survival games are played in organisations? Joseph Heller exposes these brilliantly in *Something Happened*.[24] Here is an extract from the chapter "The office in which I work":

People in the company, for example, do their best to minimise friction. ... It is considered much better form to wage our battles sneakily behind each other's back than to confront each other directly with any semblance of complaint. ... We are all on a congenial, first name basis, especially with people we loathe. ... The right to this pose of comfortable intimacy does not extend downward.

Territorial games interfere with getting work done effectively. They cause bad feeling, poor-quality decisions and defensive behaviour. Yet there is great reluctance to expose and discuss game playing openly.

Overcoming this reluctance is the first step to understanding territorial instincts and choosing to work in more productive ways. The more people learn about the games they play the less effective destructive gamesmanship is (see Table 7.4 on page 212).

Poor management of agreement

Commitment is assumed when people publicly say they agree to a decision or course of action. (Sometimes they remain silent when asked if they agree and this is taken as tacit agreement.) If they have reservations about the decision but for various reasons are not willing to raise them, all sorts of problems can arise. The Abilene Paradox[25] (see Glossary) is a good illustration: a group makes a decision to drive for several hours to have dinner in the town of Abilene, but when they return it transpires that no one wanted to go but no individual was willing to say so. This paradox is commonly seen in organisations and results in loss of motivation and productivity.

The DESC process (see Table 7.3 overleaf) is a structured way of helping people to own up to and discuss misgivings they have about decisions that have been made or are about to be made. But someone has to take the first step.

The tendency to make assumptions

Making an assumption is presuming or believing something is true without first asking questions to determine if it really is. This has the effect of blocking thinking and/or shutting down possibilities. Often people do not know that they are making an assumption until they are questioned on it, but once the assumption is challenged new options emerge that allow people to move forward in more positive ways.

"These young people are smart, but in ways that can be dangerous. They're so sure they're right."[26] Imagine the effect this assumption might have if the "owner" of it were working with younger people on the team. A good, well-received challenge will open up the doors to new ways of collaboration.

Table 7.3 **The DESC process**

Describe how you feel	I want to talk to you about the project. I know we all, including myself, have been going along with it so far, but I don't think it's going to work, and I am anxious about it. I am concerned that I may end up misleading you and we may end up misleading one another.
Explain what you think are the causes	I think I've felt pressured to pursue a course of action because I'm fearful of reporting what our sponsor may not want to hear. I'm conscious that the reputation of the organisation is riding on this new design and we're in the public eye to deliver on it.
Suggest various options on ways forward	We can continue to go along a path which I think is likely to end in disaster. We can discuss options and see if there are ways we can make it work. We can recommend pulling the plug on it now if that makes the best sense.
Come to an agreement on how to proceed	I'd like to know where the rest of you stand and I would appreciate any thoughts about the project.

Seeing things from only one perspective

On its "your point of view" website (www.yourpointofview.com/ hsbcads_airport.aspx), HSBC, a global bank, has a series of airport advertisements. These consist of two photos repeated once to form a four-photo set illustrating opposing perspectives of the same thing. For example, one set, "Work Play", has a laptop labelled as "work" and a baby labelled as "play". The photos are repeated but the labels are switched, with the laptop labelled "play" and the baby labelled "work". A statement on the website points out:

> As the world gets more and more the same, we can each value other's opinions, however different they may be.

Leaders should heed this statement: "walking in another's shoes" establishes empathy which, in turn, leads to the possibilities of productive dialogue, mutual trust and co-operation.

Failing to learn is learning to fail

Well-structured organisation design projects have review points built into their management process. Even so, mistakes are repeated and lessons are not learned. During the 1990s many companies spent time and effort in trying to become learning organisations, but there is little evidence that any achieved this (or consensus on what it would look like if they did).

Nevertheless, making small efforts to learn during the course of a project means that there is less likelihood of having a major failure at the end of it. There are all sorts of small and informal ways to encourage learning, not just from mistakes and failures but during the normal course of working life. Look out for them. Ask "What have I learned from this experience? What could I do differently next time?" NASA's Wayne Hale periodically sends e-mails to staff about what he is learning as he goes through his working day. Here is one example.

From: HALE, N.W., JR (WAYNE) (JSC-MA) (NASA)
Sent: Friday, April 01, 2005 8:01 AM
To: Lots of people@nasa.gov
Cc:
Subject: What I learned at ISOS

I spent a couple of days at the Integrated Space Operations Systems review at Nashville, TN. ...

However, the biggest lesson I learned at ISOS occurred before any of the meetings at the convention center.

Source: www.spaceref.com/news/viewsr.html?pid=16028

In this e-mail Hale describes the big risks his great grandparents' generation took as pioneers and urges his staff to learn from them and consider the questions:

Have we lost the capability to weigh risk and reward, hardship and hope, difficulty and opportunity as they did? ... do we have those qualities that made our ancestors successful? Do we have the judgment to weigh it all in the balance? Do we have the character to dare great deeds?

History is watching.

CASE STUDY: CTC – design of the critical infrastructure protection practice

CTC International, a publicly quoted company, was founded by Miles Huberman to offer information technology consulting services. After two decades of steady growth, the company adopted a much more aggressive, primarily acquisition-based growth strategy. Six firms were acquired over the next five years, taking employee numbers from around 1,000 to 4,500 and annual revenue from $312m to $882m.

Each of the acquired companies had some expertise and leadership in infrastructure protection (one of the IT consulting services), but no overall leader of a specific infrastructure practice emerged within CTC. Therefore the organisation as a whole did not benefit from the critical infrastructure protection (CIP) knowledge and skills of the individual firms. Customers were confused as the acquired organisations were reluctant to shed their pre-acquisition identities, continuing to refer to themselves by their original company name, using their methodologies and operating according to their own philosophies and principles. As a result of this lack of coherence, CTC under-leveraged its CIP.

CTC was spurred into acting only when it unintentionally and unknowingly submitted two different proposals to a request from a potential client. The conflict was highly embarrassing and damaging to CTC's reputation, so experts representing the parent company and each of the six acquisitions met to figure out how to work together in a more efficient and co-ordinated way. The immediate concern was to avoid such overlaps in the future, but the overall goals of the discussion were to provide clients with higher-quality work, win new business, develop business opportunities, increase revenues and strengthen the group's reputation.

An initial stumbling block was determining who to invite to the meeting. There was no common definition for CIP – people used a number of terms to describe work that fell broadly in the area. There was no way of searching employees' CVs for key words that would pinpoint people with the relevant skills and experience. And few people knew others outside their own immediate network (which tended to be limited to their original company) whom they could recommend.

However, informal networks, referrals and getting the word out enabled a list of people to be drawn up. They were sent a one-page outline of the current CIP situation, preliminary thoughts on what the future could look like and some reasons for working towards this. This caused a flurry of queries and comments that were coloured with a mixture of hostility, curiosity and appreciation for the effort to bring people together. It also flushed out a handful of people not on the list who felt they ought to have been.

The 36 people eventually invited from the parent company and the six acquired companies included a senior vice-president of CTC and 13 vice-presidents. Some invitees led programmes, projects, or business divisions/units and others were leaders by virtue of their specialist expertise. The organisers suggested that the outcome of this meeting would be agreement on the value that a critical infrastructure protection practice would bring to CTC and a sketch of the design of such a practice (if it was agreed that a CIP practice would bring organisational benefits).

17 people attended and the meeting facilitator knew they had:

- as well as formal leadership roles, a variety of informal leadership roles, related to factors such as their length of service in the company, their social networks, their positions on external committees and boards;
- access to different sources of power;
- competing loyalties – to CTC, to their original company (which had been acquired by CTC) and to their clients;
- conflicts of individual interests (personal, career and what each wanted as meeting outcomes);
- assorted ways of playing territorial games.

Talking about the meeting after the event, one of the vice-presidents remarked:

For me, one of the positives of the meeting was simply to extend my network. Even though I've been with CTC 20 years and thought I knew everyone relevant to CIP, the introductions exposed some gaps. I don't think I've kept up with who we got in the acquisitions. We've got far more expertise at our disposal than I was aware of. It's certainly helped me think more carefully about ways of using our strengths more effectively.

I see the strengths as being the blend of policy, functional and technical expertise, which is also geographically dispersed and covers a broad customer base. The challenge is knitting this into a recognised CIP Practice if that's an appropriate thing to do. It's something I would like to see happen, and to be blunt I'd like to head it.

Another participant involved in business development noted:

CIP is a wide open field of expanding opportunities and if we don't get organised and co-ordinated as a company someone else will market themselves and establish their brand of "CIP expert" with our customer base.

We're suffering because we're not cohesive in our offering. To be frank, my job would be a lot easier if we could agree on a definition of CIP. We could then design a practice along the definition. This would mitigate the current risk of missing business opportunities because we are fractured in our organisation and don't have any shared or repeatable CIP processes across CTC. The current lack of integration means that we approach CIP with "small hat thinking" based on the clients we had before we were acquired by CTC rather than with "big hat thinking" – aiming for the clients we should be targeting if we took a whole CTC view.

A third person, involved in bids for work, had another perspective:

In an ideal state we'd know who all our clients are and what we're doing for them. We'd be up in front of the Request for Proposal process to make sure we are helping the client create it. We'd have access to viable performance qualifications and past experience and know the leads on similar projects. We'd share best practices through a knowledge management system and have a robust governance structure in place.

Currently my job is a nightmare. We don't know what proposals have a CIP component because there isn't a single point of entry, and beyond that it's very difficult to find the right people to contribute to the proposal-writing effort because there's no CIP rallying point, regular routine connection, or usable information to draw from. I'm all in favour of having some form of CIP organisation initially. It could be a loose confederation (there are lots of egos to contend with, so I don't want to suggest anything that will provoke turf battles) with centralised co-ordination. I'd like to see a design that's not too heavy on process but enough for me to be able to get the information I need to be able to write and deliver high-quality proposals to our clients.

The independent meeting facilitator reflected on some of the obstacles to achieving the goal of designing a CIP practice:

It seemed to me that people clearly articulated the value of having a better way of doing CIP client work and this led to a number of actions being suggested, all based in the notion of some form of CIP practice. The acid test will be if people are willing and able to put resources into making something happen. All too often this sort of talk results in either "strategic non-compliance" – that is, people agree to take action when they actually have no intention of taking it or are trying to buy time in order to find a way to avoid taking it – or "the invisible wall game" when people start to prevent progress that to their minds invades their territory whether that is business area, expertise, or something else.

Here, we had in the room a number of leaders. My guess is that several of them are jockeying for the position of CIP "point person" although only one has come right out and declared his hand. This means that individually they'll be using their various power sources to form a coalition to support their interest in being the CIP practice leader. This could be fine if they were all more transparent about declaring their ambition – it would help avoid some of the mud-slinging that goes on in these types of undercover power play situations. Outside of this meeting, for example, I've heard some of them openly cast doubts on the abilities of some of their peers to take on the leadership role.

Even without individual interests being brought to bear, they'll find it difficult to collaborate on forming a CIP practice while they're also expected to compete in other arenas. The performance management system (both individually and organisationally) does not reinforce or reward the collaborative work which is required for designing a CIP practice. For example, the focus on billable time means that non-billable work – which this is – will take a much lower priority on their task lists than billable work.

Could a viable CIP practice be designed? Of course, and I'm optimistic that it will be. They've identified their ideal state and they've found a common enemy in the potential for a competitor company beating them into the CIP expert space. Remember Aesop's fable:

"On a hot, thirsty summer's day a lion and a boar came to drink at a small spring. They started quarrelling over which should drink first and provoked each other to near mortal combat. But stopping for a moment to take breath, they looked round and saw vultures waiting to devour whichever of them was killed. The sight made them stop their quarrel. 'It is better for us to be friends,' they said, 'than to be eaten by vultures.'"

My feeling is that within 12 months you'll see a well designed and highly performing CIP practice.

Reflections on this case

This case illustrates leaders in an organisation starting to work on designing a new sphere of operation for the company. As is common in organisations, the design is being considered against a backdrop of many factors: there are several formal leaders with a vested interest in the game and each has at his disposal a variety of sources of power. These formal leaders want different things from a CIP practice: some want to lead it, some want to guard their existing client relationships, and some want to develop its reputation and expertise in specific aspects of CIP. None of these is mutually exclusive in a final design. But the leaders are faced with the usual challenges of balancing the work of designing a new area with the demands of their consulting day jobs, which require them to maintain high levels of billable client work. Inevitably, the design process sparks various turf-protection behaviours which could slow down or halt the intention to form a new CIP practice. Behind the scenes are the internal informal leaders and the other internal and external stakeholders who are likely to emerge as the design work proceeds. At this stage, to keep the formal leadership of the design process flowing, the facilitator recommended several actions:

- Putting together a smaller leadership team to drive the design work (bearing certain considerations in mind). In most cases it is difficult to get agreed actions initiated and followed through if the team is bigger than six people. However, the six people have to form a balance of capability to work successfully. A group of six "shapers" and no "evaluators",[27] for example, will struggle to carry through the design.
- Determining team operational processes, such as decision-making or conflict handling. Too frequently leaders foul up by having knee-jerk reactions, making intuitive decisions, getting heated, and so on. Having some simple processes or ground rules allows more considered discussions when the going gets hard.
- Engaging the formal leaders in open discussions about aspects generally relegated to the "too difficult" box. Even with established operational processes or ground rules it is worth setting aside time to reflect on the team process – sharing leadership, territorial games, power sources and the capabilities team members need to collectively exhibit. Leaders have very different motivations, interests and expectations and it helps oil the wheels if people discuss their ways of approaching the job. Steve Jobs and Peter Schneider differed in their approach to a deal, as the extract below shows. Knowing and discussing the differences helps the parties involved work through them.

Different approaches to a deal

Following Pixar's hit with *Toy Story* in 1995, Jobs and then chief financial officer Lawrence B. Levy gave themselves a crash course in movie business economics. That helped Jobs persuade Disney to agree to a far more lucrative distribution deal than Pixar had had in the past. Former Disney executive Schneider, who negotiated that deal with Jobs, says he applies equal parts industry knowledge, intensity, and sheer charisma. Jobs prefers to negotiate one-on-one, and let lawyers tie up the details after the handshake is done. "He says 'Fine, we have a deal,' and you're saying, 'Wait, wait, I need to check with Michael [Eisner],' and he's saying, 'No, it's done.'"

Source: Burrows, P. and Grover, R., "Steve Jobs' Magic Kingdom", *BusinessWeek Online*, February 6th 2006

Tools for this case
Understanding your territorial drive
Acknowledging the games people play to protect their territory helps stop the unco-operative and partisan behaviour that often accompanies organisation design work. One way of doing this is to use Table 7.4 as a framework for discussion within the leadership groups.

BATNA[28]
BATNA stands for best alternative to a negotiated agreement. BATNAS are critical to negotiation because a good decision about whether to accept a negotiated agreement can only be made when the alternatives are known. If the proposed agreement is better than the BATNA, accept it. If the agreement is not better than the BATNA, reopen negotiations. If the agreement cannot be improved, think about withdrawing from the negotiations and pursuing the alternative – though also consider the costs of doing that.

BATNAS are not always readily apparent but may be determined for any negotiation situation. Roger Fisher and William Ury outline a simple process for determining your BATNA:[29]

- develop a list of actions you might conceivably take if no agreement is reached;
- improve some of the more promising ideas and convert them into practical options; and
- select, tentatively, the one option that seems best.

Complex situations require the consideration of a broader range of factors and possibilities. For example, a community in the United States discovers that its water is being polluted by the discharges of a nearby factory. Community leaders first attempt to negotiate a clean-up plan with the company, but the business refuses to agree on a plan of action that satisfies the community. In such a case, what are the community's options for trying to resolve this situation? They could:

Table 7.4 **Understanding your territorial drive**

Territorial game	Used by you	Used by your peers	Used by your boss	Used by you
Occupation: Marking territory; maintaining an imposing physical presence; acting as a gatekeeper for vital information; monopolising relationships, resources or information				
Information manipulation: Withholding information, putting a spin on information, covering up, or giving false information				
Intimidation: Growling, yelling, staring someone down, scaring off, or making threats (veiled or overt)				
Powerful alliances: Using relationships with powerful people to intimidate, impress, or threaten others; using name dropping; making strategic displays of influence over important decision-makers				
Invisible wall: Actively instigating circumstances or creating counterproductive perceptions so that an agreed-upon concept is, if not impossible to implement, very, very difficult to implement				
Strategic non-compliance: Agreeing upfront to take action and having no intention of taking that action, or agreeing just to buy time to find a way to avoid taking that action				
Discredit: Using personal attacks or unrelated criticisms as a way of creating doubt about another person's competence or credibility				
Shunning: Subtly (or not so subtly) excluding an individual in a way that punishes him or her; orchestrating a group's behaviour so that another is treated like an outsider				
Camouflage: Creating a distraction, emphasising the inconsequential, or deliberately triggering someone's anxiety buttons just to distract him or her				
Filibuster: Using excessive verbiage to prevent action, out-talking any objectors at a meeting, talking until the time for discussion is exhausted or simply wearing others down by out-talking them				

Source: Simmons, A., *Territorial Games: Understanding and Ending Turf Wars at Work*, Amacom, 1998

- sue the business based on stipulations of the Clean Water Act;
- contact the Environmental Protection Agency and see what sort of authority that agency has in such a situation;
- lobby the state legislature to develop and implement more stringent regulations on polluting factories;
- wage a public education campaign and inform citizens of the problem. Such education could lead voters to support more environmentally minded candidates in the future who would support new laws to correct problems like this one.

In weighing these various alternatives to see which is best, the community members must consider a variety of factors:

- Which is most affordable and feasible?
- Which will have the most impact in the shortest amount of time?
- If they succeed in closing down the plant, how many people will lose their jobs?

These types of questions must be answered for each alternative before a BATNA can be determined in a complex environmental dispute such as this. Consider too the alternatives available to the other side.

Third parties can help disputants accurately assess their BATNAS through reality testing and costing. In reality testing, the third party helps clarify and ground each disputing party's alternatives to agreement.

Summary
Specific knowledge of sources of power, territorial games, the way informal and formal leaders interact and the barriers to collaborative working all help leaders get to successful design implementation. But technical knowledge about leading organisation design projects is not enough. Leading design projects also takes guts and a great deal of awareness – of self and of others – to carry things through, keep on learning, admit fallibilities and deal with consequences. NASA's Wayne Hale in an e-mail to staff describes his world of leading space projects – any organisation design leader will echo his thoughts:[30]

> I have given the Go 28 times. Every time was the toughest thing I have ever done. And I have never ever been 100 percent certain, it has always been gray, never a sure thing. But the team needs to have confidence that the decision was good. It is almost a requirement to speak the words much bolder than you feel, like it is an easy call. Then you pray that you were right.

8 Culture and group processes

Organization doesn't really accomplish anything. Plans don't accomplish anything, either. Theories of management don't much matter. Endeavors succeed or fail because of the people involved. Only by attracting the best people will you accomplish great deeds.

Colin Powell, former US Secretary of State

IN MOST CASES a "visioning" process kicks off an organisation design project. In these sessions executives and others gather to "blue-sky" the new organisation design, describe the ideal future state, and lay plans for becoming the "best we can be".

In these and subsequent sessions the cultural and group processes – typically the hidden dangers that block the route – are not discussed. Because they are caught up in the mindset of the "infinite possibility", participants choose not to acknowledge that the path between the current state and their desired future state is perilous and that they are often ill-equipped to take it. Unless design leaders ask and answer the sorts of questions listed below, they will be exposed like those Scott Fitzgerald describes in *The Great Gatsby* as careless, smashing up things and then retreating to "let other people clean up the mess they had made":

- How much is organisational design success dependent on factors such as local culture (both national and organisational) and human factors such as personalities?
- What specific aspects of an organisation's culture get in the way of a change process? How are these tackled?
- Are group processes – decision-taking, making sound judgments and managing consequences – effective?

Getting the cultural and process aspects of an organisation design journey right is challenging. Ernest Shackleton's apocryphal advertisement for men to accompany him to the South Pole in 1914 on the *Endurance* was rather different from the vision statement of most organisation design projects:[1]

Men Wanted for Hazardous Journey, Small Wages, Bitter Cold, Long

> Months of Complete Darkness, Constant Danger, Safe Return Doubtful.
> Honour and Recognition in Case of Success.

In mid-trip the *Endurance* was crushed by ice. Circumstances necessitated a complete new organisation design, including a change of purpose. (Some would say at this point that their project had failed because it did not achieve the intended mission. However, it illustrates the point that failure is relative and must adapt to circumstances.) In the event and after months of enduring staggeringly harsh conditions, the 28-man team under Shackleton's direct command returned safely.

To achieve this took strong group processes and a robust, well-functioning organisation culture. Indeed, Shackleton's report of the trip tends to mention only the positive aspects of these – friendly football games on the ice, and so on.[2] However, a recent perspective by Kelly Tyler-Lewis, writing about the expedition's base-camp party (members of whom did not accompany Shackleton's team), suggests a less rosy picture:[3]

> Shackleton's lack of clarity about the chain of command pitted
> Mackintosh against his subordinate, Ernest Joyce. "I have never in my
> experience come across such an idiot in charge of men!" Joyce wrote,
> while refraining from outright mutiny.

Both perspectives are probably right. However, imagine the likelihood of expedition success if group members had started with less of an idea of what they were letting themselves in for and then:

- blamed someone else for the situation they were in (a blame culture);
- wanted to hear only good news (a good-news culture);
- refused to discuss aspects of the expedition (the shadow side of the organisation);
- were unable to make quick decisions;
- failed to solve the problems they faced;
- escalated rather than managed conflicts.

One or more of these six factors commonly blocks an organisation design implementation. (Note that the first three relate to the culture of the organisation and the second three to group processes.) Clearly, there are other blockers and some are discussed in previous chapters – for example, leadership issues or stakeholder concerns – but realistic appraisal of aspects of culture and group process followed by effective management of them goes some way towards achieving either the desired outcome of an organisation design or being successful in its failure.

Shackleton acknowledges as much in the closing section of *South*:[4]

> That we failed in accomplishing the objective we set out for was due, I venture to assert, not to any neglect or lack of organization, but to the overwhelming natural obstacles ... To the credit side of the Expedition one can safely say that the comradeship and resource of the members of the Expedition was worthy of the highest traditions of Polar service; and it was a privilege to me to have had under my command men who, through dark days and the stress and strain of continuous danger, kept up their spirits and carried out their work regardless of themselves and heedless of the limelight.

This chapter looks at three aspects of organisation culture – blame culture, good-news culture and the shadow-side culture – and then at three group processes – making decisions, solving problems and dealing with conflict.

Organisational culture

It is surprising how few of the organisation design models shown in Chapter 2 specifically mention culture. They focus on aspects of organisation design that are explicit, whereas much about culture is implicit and difficult to describe because it is socially construed and manifested in norms, behaviours, expectations and "the way we do things round here". Nevertheless, as Edgar Schein says in *The Corporate Culture Survival Guide*:[5]

> Culture matters. It matters because decisions made without awareness of the operative cultural forces may have unanticipated and undesirable consequences.

Thinking about organisational culture at three distinct levels as shown in Table 8.1 makes it easier to gain awareness of the operative cultural forces that affect new organisation design implementation.

Organisation design work has a good chance of success when cultures are aligned, collaborative and open at all three levels. Take the example of MicroStrategy, a builder of business intelligence software, which was forced into design change following an investigation by the US Securities and Exchange Commission.

Table 8.1 **Three levels of culture**

Artefacts and behaviours	This is the observable level of culture, which consists of behaviour patterns and outward manifestations of culture: perks provided to executives; dress codes; who gets the latest technology device; and the physical layout of work spaces. All may be visible indicators of culture but difficult to interpret.
Espoused values	Values underlie and to a large extent determine behaviour, but they are not as directly observable as behaviours are. There may be a difference between value statements that organisations make and the values people use from day to day. People attribute their behaviour to underpinning values.
Assumptions	Assumptions derive from values, which are difficult to identify as they are taken for granted and drop out of awareness. People may be unaware of or unable to articulate the beliefs and assumptions forming their deepest level of culture.

Source: Schein, E.H., *Organizational Culture and Leadership*, 3rd edn, Jossey-Bass, 2004

MicroStrategy: a forced design change

Nearly every element of MicroStrategy's business model has been subjected to scrutiny and forced to change. But amidst these deep-seated strategic reforms, one element of the organization has remained intact so far: its equally deep-seated culture and values.

The fact that most employees were able to keep their heads, even as some heads were rolling, confirmed for Saylor [founder and CEO] that for all of his mistakes, he and his senior colleagues had done one important thing right. Their obsession with building a sense of shared purpose, their commitment to schooling all of their people in the big-picture vision behind the company's business, and their willingness to spend millions of dollars and hundreds of hours of CEO time to create a sense of shared responsibility, had become the glue that held things together.

"The past 12 months have really shown that culture is by far the most important thing in a company," Saylor says. "If we had constructed a culture that was based solely on stock price or on prestige, there wouldn't be a reason to be here now. At the end of the day, the thing that drives people through all of this pain and turmoil is the belief that the world is a better place because of what they do."

Source: Salter, C., "Updating the Agenda: MicroStrategy Inc.", *Fast Company*, May 2001

Cultures that are misaligned – for example, where there is a statement of values but these are not seen in practice, or are not open, for example where there is finger-pointing and back-biting – must be changed as part of the organisation design process if there is to be any chance of success.

Culture change is easy to effect at one level, for example changing the dress-code, or giving everyone the same size of office or workspace. Changing behaviour is harder and takes time, patience and resilience – as anyone with children (or dogs) knows. A TV series, *Super Nanny*, provides a model for behaviour change that organisation designers could well learn from:[6]

> Her simple methods stress consistency, communication and reasonable consequences for poor behaviour, all delivered with loving firmness. She emphasizes the importance of spelling out the new rules of the household to children in advance, as well as explaining the consequences for infractions. She also candidly points out to parents where they need to be more decisive, more flexible or even how they may need to adjust their expectations of a child's readiness for certain behaviours.

However, as with individuals so with organisations: it gets progressively more difficult to change espoused values and assumptions and it is at these levels that culture change is either not addressed in organisation design projects and/or fails to take root. Three types of culture which are particularly hostile to new organisation design and thus are essential to change are the blame culture, the good-news culture and the shadow-side culture.

The blame culture

Briefly, a blame culture is one where there is a search for someone or something to attribute lapses, mistakes or misdeeds to. In other words, people in a blame culture seek to pin responsibility, usually for a wrong action, on someone or something other than themselves.

The example of the response to an internet virus, discussed in relation to a generalised "software culture" similar to that found in many organisation's IT departments, illustrates the fact that blame cultures cost money, cut productivity, hinder innovation and learning, build dysfunctional relationships and stem the flow of good information.

Blame culture: response to an internet virus

This winter [2003], a worm known as Slammer rattled the internet violently enough to become what you might call a "CNN-level virus" – that is, it burrowed its way into the national consciousness.

The old game was to blame Microsoft. "Microsoft did not protect its customers", read a letter to the *New York Times* after the Melissa virus hit in 1999. A year later, after the I Love You virus infected Microsoft Outlook, a *Washington Post* editorial stated: "This is a software development problem."

Slammer, though, hasn't followed the old pattern. A developing consensual wisdom suggests that as woeful as Microsoft's products may be, CIOs have been equally sloppy. A February poll of more than 200 IT professionals, by antivirus company Sophos, showed that 64% of respondents blamed their peers' lax security practices for Slammer. Only 24% blamed Microsoft.

What frustrates ... security experts is the fact that this seemingly intractable problem is actually quite tractable. The tools and strategies to prevent another Slammer are just waiting to be used. In fact, the number of tools and strategies available – and available at a reasonable cost – makes it inexcusable for any CIO to fiddle while the software burns.

There is, after all, $60 billion on the table. A 2002 study by the National Institute of Standards and Technology (NIST) developed that number to describe buggy software's cost to the national economy. Improved software testing alone, NIST suggests, could shave $22 billion off that.

Why can't the software community motivate itself to grab all that cash? The answer lies in software culture.

Source: Berinato, S., "The Bug Stops Here", *CIO Magazine*, May 2003

The three levels of a blame culture typically appear as listed in Table 8.2.

Organisation design projects do not succeed in blame cultures because, inevitably, the project implementation process hits snags, bottlenecks and unforeseen circumstances. Although Shackleton's expedition hit all of these the prevailing culture was not one of blame, illustrating the point that in difficult conditions success relies on a culture of being accountable and taking responsibility. People know that "the buck stops here" and are able and confident to admit to errors, work with the situation as it is and learn from it, not waste time and energy casting around to find someone to scapegoat.

An example of successful culture change is Motorola, where CEO

Table 8.2 **Three levels of blame culture**

Artefacts and behaviours	CYA (cover your arse) behaviour "If at first you don't succeed, remove all evidence you ever tried"
Espoused values	"Eagles may soar high, but weasels don't get sucked into jet engines" The secret of success is knowing whom to blame for your failures No single raindrop believes it is to blame for the flood
Assumptions	People are out to get you Someone will stab you in the back if you're not careful The harder you try the dumber you look

Ed Zander turned around a blame culture. The organisation has seen a number of changes since he joined in 2004, one of which is the way that teams have learned to co-operate to develop new handsets:[7]

> Co-operation improved ... because each group became willing to try something difficult that might help the others – without worrying too much about who would get blamed if they failed.

This sort of atmosphere is hard to achieve unless the boss takes it seriously, and unless everyone in the company knows that the rules really have changed. By encouraging Motorola's people to push themselves in this way, Mr Zander has changed the company's frame of mind.

The good-news culture

Similar to a blame culture is the good-news culture. Here people refuse to listen to the operational realities of a situation that is not going as planned. The three levels of a good-news culture are illustrated in Table 8.3.

Good-news cultures often reflect the need of leaders to have their image of themselves as successful leaders bolstered. Consequently, people in these cultures are not valued for their success in their jobs but for their ability to provide evidence that things are going well, do deals and make their superiors look good. Typically, senior executives are unwilling to hear anything which suggests that there are problems.

Bob Woodward in his book *State of Denial* illustrates the good-news culture in action in his description of Jay Garner, head of the Iraq Postwar Planning Office, meeting President Bush:[8]

> Of course with all the stories, jocularity, buddy-buddy talk, bluster and confidence in the Oval Office, Garner had left out the headline. He had

Table 8.3 **Three levels of good-news culture**

Artefacts and behaviours	Present data selectively to show only the good news Push bad news under the carpet Dismiss negative findings or make them more palatable
Espoused values	You aren't being paid to do what you believe is right Avoid candour Remain cocooned
Assumptions	You'll be punished for being the bearer of bad news It is a career limiter to discuss difficulties openly There's no support for admitting errors or mistakes

not mentioned the problems he saw, or even hinted at them. He did not tell Bush about the three tragic mistakes. Once again the aura of the presidency had shut out the most important news – the bad news.

It was only one example of a visitor to the Oval Office not telling the president the whole story or the truth. Likewise, in these moments where Bush had someone from the field there in the chair beside him, he did not press, did not try to open the door himself and ask what the visitor had seen and thought. The whole atmosphere too often resembled a royal court, with Cheney and Rice in attendance, some upbeat stories, exaggerated good news, and a good time had by all.

In another example, the good-news culture prevailing at the National Australia Bank led to massive foreign-currency losses:[9]

A key finding of both the Australian Prudential Regulation Authority report and a controversial PricewaterhouseCoopers investigation into the currency losses was the need for sweeping changes to the bank's culture.

It was described as being too bureaucratic and focused on process and documentation, rather than understanding the substance of issues, "taking responsibility and resolving matters".

All levels of management were criticised for encouraging a "good news culture" that cocooned top decision makers from information that might have enabled the bank to avoid a string of corporate mishaps, ranging from the $3.5 billion HomeSide losses to the currency scandal.

The issue for people introducing new organisation designs into a good news culture is that they feel pressured to cover up aspects of the project implementation that would be better exposed and dealt with before it gets too late or spins out of control. Helen Fraser, formerly managing director of Penguin Books, makes the point:[10]

> You have to make it easy for someone to be able to tell you the bad news. We all like hearing good news, but they have to be able to tell you that they have made the most terrible mistake and know that you won't completely lose it. The mistakes may not always be redeemable, but you hope you have learned for next time.

The shadow-side culture

In his book *Working the Shadow Side*, Gerard Egan defines the shadow-side culture as:[11]

> All the important activities and arrangements that do not get identified, discussed, and managed in decision-making forums that can made a difference. The shadow side deals with the covert, the undiscussed, the undiscussable, and the unmentionable. It includes arrangements not found in organisational manuals and company documents or on organisational charts.

Although it appears from this definition that there is something wrong about the shadow side, this is not necessarily the case. And characterising the shadow side in terms of three levels of culture is not helpful as it does not exhibit in that way. A better way is to think of the organisation's culture as being a brain with a left and right hemisphere: the left being the rational, logical side and the right being the intuitive, and creative. Using this analogy the two sides manifest as shown in Table 8.4.

Taking this brain analogy, it is clear that having a shadow side is normal and that organisations are likely to survive best by working with both parts of the "brain", in exactly the same way that human potential is realised through the whole brain and not through only one hemisphere. Unfortunately, organisation design projects are often initiated and planned using predominantly the rational (left side) of the cultural brain which means that the mess, unpredictability and chaos of day-to-day implementation creates anxiety and lack of confidence in project leaders. Those that have the skills to engage openly in the right side of the cultural brain as well as the left are more likely to adapt, innovate and find creative solutions as they work on their design.

Table 8.4 **Rational and shadow sides of an organisation**

Rational elements (left hemisphere)	Non-rational shadow-side elements (right hemisphere)
Directives	Trust
Strategic plans	Friendships
Organisation charts	Jealousy
Job titles	Fear and insecurity
Policies	Power struggles
Training courses	Ambition
Budgets	Grapevine

Source: "An Introduction to the Shadow Side", www.organisational-leadership.com/intro_shadowside.cfm

Group processes

Organisation design work depends on groups of people being able to work effectively together to meet the project's goals. This is easier said than done. Although group members may know what they have to achieve – the outcomes or objectives – they may lack skills to do it. Consequently, groups commonly stall on things like making decisions, problem-solving, handling conflicts, communication and boundary management (which includes obtaining resources, sharing information, admitting people into the group, and relationships between the group and the wider organisation/environment). A meeting at Marks & Spencer when Sir Richard Greenbury was running the company illustrates difficulties on almost all these counts:[12]

> One of Greenbury's former aides said: "The thing about Rick is he never understood the impact he had on people – people were just too scared to say what they thought. I remember one meeting we had to discuss a new policy and two or three directors got me on one side beforehand and said they were really unhappy about it. Then Rick made his presentation and asked for views. There was total silence until one said, 'Chairman we are all 100% behind you on this one.' And that was the end of the meeting."

Group process knowledge and skill in handling interpersonal dynamics are critical competences for organisation designers because they work with a range of groups including project teams, advisory committees, task-forces, steering boards and stakeholder constituencies. Without the process skills to build confidence, bring people along, generate commitment and help people listen to each other, designers will struggle to make their projects successful.

Reporting annually on what makes IT projects work – and large scale IT implementations are a common driver of a new organisation design – the Standish Group has noted that lack of user group involvement traditionally has been the principal reason for failure. Recognising this, the group developed a one-day workshop called The Six Senses (sight, hearing, touch, smell, taste, instinct), all of which are related to developing group process skills in IT project managers. This is an interesting, touchy-feely foray into a world traditionally associated with geeks and techies (see Glossary) not known for their people skills.

First Workshop: Sense of Sight

What is the necessary expertise a project manager needs in development to be able to fully use the sense of sight to improve project management success? Can a project manager see the future and move people and the process in ways without criticizing, condemning or complaining to keep the project moving in the right direction? In this workshop we will work together on this sense to improve the sense of sight and eliminate blind spots.

Source: "The Six Senses of Project Leadership", www.standishgroup.com/events/chaos.php

As well as being skilled in group processes, designers and managers who develop and use the mindset of a critical practitioner as they work will fare better than those who do not. This means: [13]

- being constructively not negatively critical;
- coping with uncertainty and change;
- using knowledge with awareness of personal biases;
- adopting no moral direction, apart from the fundamental professional commitment to social justice for others and empowering, anti-oppressive work.

Developing these skills in critical practice involves five interlocking and overlapping domains. The International Masters Programme in Practising Management (IMPM), a radically different alternative to a traditional MBA, co-founded by Henry Mintzberg, Cleghorn Professor of Management

Studies at McGill University and author of *Managers Not MBAs*, aims to develop managers able to manage:[14]

- themselves (the reflective mindset);
- organisations (the analytical mindset);
- context (the worldly mindset);
- relationships (the collaborative mindset);
- change (the action mindset).

The critical practitioner mindset that this type of study develops should be a mandatory mindset for managers in group situations where people have a tendency to do extraordinary things for good or bad. In most cases the good things go largely unrecognised – no news is good news – while the bad things surface, wreaking all kinds of damage. This is cleverly documented in "The Human Behaviour Experiments", produced by Alex Gibney, in which past social psychology experiments are re-enacted and discussed in order to answer questions about why human beings commit unethical acts under particular social conditions:[15]

> Why would four young men watch their friend die, when they could have intervened to save him? Why would a woman obey phone commands from a stranger to strip-search an innocent employee? What makes ordinary people perpetrate extraordinary abuses, like the events at Abu Ghraib? ... [There is] a fierce debate about just how much the situation – or the system – determines our actions, and how much individual personalities are to blame.

Three situations particularly relevant to management practice in organisation design work are the group processes involved in decision-making, problem-solving and managing conflict, where an experienced critical practitioner can help head off disaster and navigate towards success.

Decision-making

> Decisions are the essence of management. They're what managers do – sit around all day making (or avoiding) decisions. Managers are judged on the outcomes, and most of them – most of us – have only the foggiest idea how we do what we do ... decision making is a kind of fortune-telling, a bet on the future.
>
> Thomas Stewart[16]

Making this kind of bet on the future is risky. Take the case of Hewlett Packard, a large computer and printer company, whose CEO Mark V. Hurd made the decision to approve an elaborate "sting" operation on a reporter in February 2005 in an attempt to plug leaks of competitive and sensitive information to the media. According to the *Washington Post*:[17]

> Internal e-mails show senior HP employees who were given the task of identifying anonymous news sources concocted a fictitious, high-level HP tipster who sent bogus information to a San Francisco reporter in an attempt to trick her into revealing her sources.

In this instance what started off as an apparently good decision to find out how the leaks occurred resulted in an internal investigation into the sting operation that then led to criminal probes and became the subject of a congressional hearing. Hurd explains in his Congressional Written Testimony on September 26th 2006:[18]

> What began as a proper and serious inquiry of leaks to the press of sensitive company information from within the HP board became a rogue investigation that violated HP's own principles and values. There is no excuse for this. ...
>
> How did such an abuse of privacy occur in a company renowned for its commitment to privacy? The end came to justify the means. The investigation team became so focused on finding the source of the leaks that they lost sight of the privacy of reporters and others. They lost sight of values that HP has always represented.

The result of this kind of reputational disaster, which has wide-ranging repercussions in respect of share price, employee trust in management, and so on, inevitably leads to organisation design work as roles and processes are realigned to keep the business stable. Hurd, continuing his testimony, explains the measures taken:

> We have appointed Bart Schwartz, the former head of the criminal division of the US Attorney's Office under Rudy Giuliani, to do an assessment of current practices and develop future best practices so that our processes will always be legal, ethical, appropriate and without peer.
>
> We are putting into place new measures to maintain the highest levels of information privacy. Let me elaborate on those internal policies.

In an attempt to minimise the risks inherent in group decision-making in organisations, various tools and techniques are brought into play. Simplifying considerably, these come from two schools of thought: first, teaching that good decisions come from a structured, analytical and rational approach; second, teaching that decisions are made in a naturalistic way involving experience, intuition, sense-making, and so on. Generally, managers are taught to make organisational decisions using the first – a structured way of getting to a situational decision. A common method is the Vroom-Yetton-Jago model of decision-making, which has two steps:[19]

Step 1: Answer seven questions in order. Each question has only a yes or no answer. Follow the tree diagram shown (Figure 8.1) from left to right. The questions are indicated on the top row by a letter of the alphabet and the boxes in the column under each letter indicate the point to ask each question.

A. Is the quality of the decision important?
B. Is there sufficient information to make a high-quality decision right now?
C. Is the problem structured?
D. Is acceptance of the decision by subordinates important for effective implementation?
E. If the leader was to make the decision by him or herself, is it reasonably certain that is would be accepted by subordinates?
F. Are subordinates motivated to attain organizational goals?
G. Are subordinates likely to disagree with proposed solutions?

Step 2: Apply one of the decision processes that is shown at the end of the path through the tree. There are five possible processes.

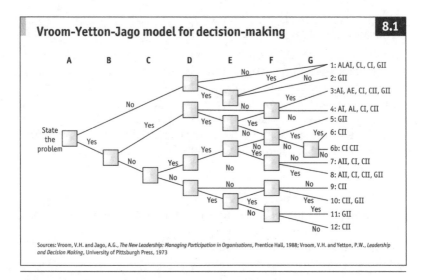

8.1

Vroom-Yetton-Jago model for decision-making

Sources: Vroom, V.H. and Jago, A.G., *The New Leadership: Managing Participation in Organisations*, Prentice Hall, 1988; Vroom, V.H. and Yetton, P.W., *Leadership and Decision Making*, University of Pittsburgh Press, 1973

Table 8.5 **Decision processes**

Autocratic decision-making	AI: Leader makes decision with current information. AII: Leader obtains needed information from subordinates, then makes the decision him or herself.
Consulting decision-making	CI: Leader shares the problem with subordinates individually and gathers their input. Leader makes the decision that may or may not reflect their input. CII: The same as CI but the leader gathers input from subordinates in a group.
Group decision-making	GII: The leader shares the problem with subordinates as a group. Collectively, group members generate and evaluate alternatives. They choose a solution that has group consensus.

For example, in the case where the quality requirement is low (for example, the nature of the solution is not critical), choose the "no" branch at point A. If in reference to question D acceptance of this decision by subordinates is also not critical, choose method AI. Alternatively at point D, if acceptance is critical, ask question E regarding certainty of acceptance if the decision is made without reference to others. If people are likely to accept the decision, again choose method AI. If, however, acceptance of the decision is not reasonably certain, opt for a consensual group method (GII) to help overcome this.

The naturalistic method suggests that decisions are made in a much

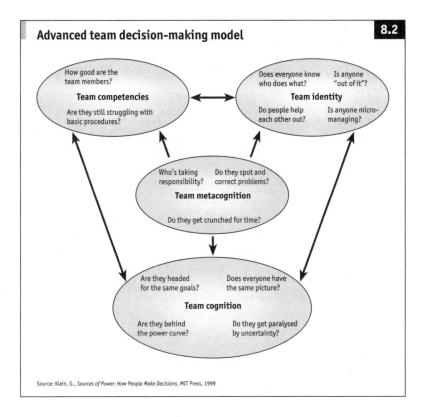

Advanced team decision-making model 8.2

How good are the team members?
Team competencies
Are they still struggling with basic procedures?

Does everyone know who does what? Is anyone "out of it"?
Team identity
Do people help each other out? Is anyone micro-managing?

Who's taking responsibility? Do they spot and correct problems?
Team metacognition
Do they get crunched for time?

Are they headed for the same goals? Does everyone have the same picture?
Team cognition
Are they behind the power curve? Do they get paralysed by uncertainty?

Source: Klein, G., *Sources of Power: How People Make Decisions*, MIT Press, 1999

less analytical way drawing on a range of sources. Gary Klein presents a model (Figure 8.2) for assessing whether a team is likely to have good decision-making processes.[20] The answers to the questions in each of the four areas give an indication of the soundness of a team's decision-making process.

In this naturalistic model a team with a sound process usually has:

■ high skill levels, and shared practices and routines (team competencies);
■ a good sense of what they collectively, rather than individually, own and control (team identity);
■ a shared understanding of the situation they are in with methods of communicating changes and preparing for them (team cognition);
■ an ability "to create new and unexpected solutions, options, and interpretations, drawing on the experience of all team members

to generate products that are beyond the capabilities of any of the individuals"[21] (team metacognition).

Researching the characteristics of team decision-making, Klein describes a team of newly organised wildland firefighters with good processes:[22]

> Marvin Thordsen was on location during a forest fire in Idaho, a large one that covered six mountains. He watched the command staff assemble a team of 4,000 firefighters, drawing them from all over the country. They put together a working organisation in only a few days and sent them out to fight the fire. It is hard to manage an intact organisation of 4,000 people, to give directions and make policies, even in stable and safe bureaucratic settings. Here, in less than a week, they were building that organisation and trusting it enough to risk lives. Why are they so good? ...
> The command staff met twice a day to make difficult decisions. After years of working together, the team members knew how to plan together. They did not waste time on politeness, and their egos were strong enough to take criticism without bristling. They were also sensitive to issues of morale. Someone who disagreed with the commander's action would confront the commander in the meeting only if it was necessary. Otherwise, the disagreement would be expressed in private. They did not want to waste staff time on lower-priority fights or create a feeling of divisiveness.

In reality teams use a blend of the two approaches, sometimes helped by technology tools like Decision Lens or CogNexus, both allowing groups to participate in a range of decision-making situations by identifying decision options and enabling electronic voting.

Because organisation design work is complex and involves decisions being made across a range of objectives, processes, policies, systems, technologies, skills, incentives, and so on (see Figure 1.2 on page 5), making design decisions usually requires trade-offs whatever the method used. John Mackey, CEO of Whole Foods, a US natural and organic food retailer, is designing an expansion to his organisation. His answer to the question "Are there sustainable measures that you wish you could implement, but can't because of practical bottom-line concerns?" illustrates this:[23]

> If you speak to the totally pure, you will cease to exist as a business. I made these decisions 25 years ago. My first store was a little tiny store

called Safer Way. I opened it in 1978. It was a vegetarian store. We did $300,000 in sales the first year. And when we made the decision to open a bigger store, we made a decision to sell products that I didn't think were healthy for people – meat, seafood, beer, wine, coffee. We didn't think they were particularly healthy products, but we were a whole food store, not a "holy food" store. We're in business not to fulfil some type of ideology, but to service our customers.

Going through a process gives a group the opportunity to look at a decision from various angles and consider the consequences of different courses of action. But even a good process is no guarantee of a good outcome. The value of the process lies in "checking the results of a decision against its expectations, showing executives what their strengths are, where they need to improve, and where they lack knowledge or information".[24]

Problem-solving

Some problems are so complex that you have to be highly intelligent and well informed just to be undecided about them.

Laurence J. Peter, The Peter Principle[25]

From the moment the design work is conceived, organisation design teams are faced with problems that may be latent, showing signs of becoming problems, or already evident (see Figure 8.3 overleaf).

At whatever stage they are, the problems may have existed before the project was conceived or they may arise at any stage during the progress of the project. This means that organisation design teams need the skill to:

- anticipate problems before they emerge – this is linked to risk assessment;
- identify the symptoms of a problem early enough so it can be managed before it gets bigger – an analogy here is containing a grievance before it develops into a strike;
- take action on an evident problem – often design work focuses on one aspect while ignoring others.

The BP example illustrates an organisation that had problems at each of the stages shown above.

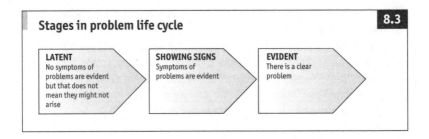

BP: problems at every stage

An interim report into a fatal oil refinery explosion accuses BP of ignoring "catastrophic safety risks" and of knowing about "significant safety problems" at another 34 facilities around the world.

The US Chemical Safety Board (CSB), which publishes the damning findings today, believes that BP may have been aware for years of major problems at its Texas City refinery, which exploded in March last year killing 15 workers and injuring 180.

Carolyn Merritt, the CSB chairman, said: "The CSB's investigation shows that BP's global management was aware of problems with maintenance, spending and infrastructure well before March 2005. BP did respond with a variety of measures aimed at improving safety. However, the focus of many of these initiatives was on improving procedural compliance and reducing occupational injury rates, while catastrophic safety risks remained."

Source: Hotten, R., "BP 'ignored safety risks over refinery disaster'",
Daily Telegraph, October 31st 2006

In this case the recognised problem was ignored and people focused instead on improving compliance and reducing injury rates. They failed to identify the symptoms of disaster at that particular plant with the result that there was a catastrophic explosion, and they did not anticipate the problem (reputational and otherwise) that an explosion would cause. In other words, they did not manage the risks of this. The result of the explosion is an investment of an estimated $1 billion of organisation design work aimed at improving and maintaining the site.

BP: repairing the damage

"The report clearly describes the underlying causes and management system failures which contributed to the worst tragedy in BP's recent history," said Ross Pillari, president of BP Products North America Inc. "We accept the findings, and we are working to make Texas City a complex that attains the highest levels of safety, reliability and environmental performance."

Some of the actions recommended by the investigation team have been completed. Many are underway. Texas City site manager Colin Maclean has established a special project team to plan and drive execution of the improvement program.

The company will install modern process control systems on major units, transition to a more powerful maintenance management system, improve worker training, remove blow down stacks and implement the other recommendations contained in the final report. The project team will also develop plans for reconfiguring and simplifying the operation of the Texas City refinery.

Source: BP press release, December 9th 2005, www.bp.com/genericarticle.do?categoryId=201
2968&contentId=7012963

Problem-solving, like decision-making, is best approached in a disciplined way, selecting tools and approaches appropriate for each stage in the life cycle (see Table 8.6).

Note that Table 8.6 shows both rational and naturalistic tools. Blend these as the situation demands and also realise that although the tools are associated with a particular stage, this does not preclude using them in other stages. Remember, too, that no method can predict all possible problems as Michael Saylor, founder and CEO of MicroStrategy, ruefully acknowledges:[26]

What a difference a year makes. Saylor is still young, but it seems as though he's aged 10 years in 12 months. His dark hair has started to turn gray. He says that he's much more cautious as a result of MicroStrategy's meteoric rise and fall – and more humble. While he still answers questions in long, eloquent passages, they sound less like a lecture and more like a confession. "If I was a better manager, if I had had more experience, if I was more careful, if I was more competent, maybe this wouldn't have happened," he concedes. "It's like being a parent whose children were playing in the front yard, and one of

Table 8.6 **Examples of tools for each stage of a problem life cycle**

Problem life cycle *Group process tools for each stage*

Problem life cycle	Group process tools for each stage
Anticipate problems before they emerge	Use tools and approaches associated with risk assessment: ◪ Brainstorming ◪ Questionnaires ◪ Business studies which look at each business process and describe both the internal processes and external factors which can influence those processes ◪ Industry benchmarking ◪ Scenario analysis ◪ Simulation exercises ◪ Risk assessment workshops ◪ Incident investigation ◪ Auditing and inspection ◪ HAZOP (Hazard and Operability Studies)[a]
Identify the symptoms of a problem early	◪ Spotting anomalies ◪ Pattern recognition ◪ "Connecting the dots" ◪ Using intuition – "something doesn't smell right here" ◪ Tracking trends ◪ Seeking confirmatory or disconfirmatory information ◪ Comparison of past and current experience ◪ Seeing the invisible ◪ Filtering out noise
Take action on a recognised problem	Use tools and approaches associated with Six Sigma DMAIC (define, measure, analyse, improve, control) methodology, eg: Kaizen SIPOC Work-Out Pareto Chart Regression Analysis Cause and Effect/Fishbone Diagram 5 Whys

a The Institute of Risk Managers, *The Risk Management Standard*, 2002, available to download from www.theirm.org

the kids got struck by lightning, and now he's dead. You didn't have a lightning rod on your roof, because you were planning to take care of doing that next year. Now people walk by your house, point, and say, 'Look, that's where the kid got struck by lightning.' It's an awful feeling."

Managing conflict

Those involved in organisation design projects frequently find themselves in conflict with others. Recognising that conflict is inevitable and learning to manage it constructively rather than trying to avoid it is critical. Richard Duran, senior director of human resources at Ben & Jerry's Homemade (bought by Unilever in April 2000), makes the point:

> I have come to expect it [conflict] as a part of my everyday routine in dealing with business issues. If we walk away from conflict and don't understand it, we are doomed to repeat and recreate the conflict. Not working through problems just slows down the process of understanding. Avoiding conflict creates tension and frustration. On the other hand, if I work through the conflict, I can both understand the other person's point of view and express my perspective. The process then begins to build trust and understanding. I would not be successful, or a survivor, if I did not deal with conflict openly. It would eat me up inside or cause me political problems within the organization.

People's attitudes to conflict depend on a range of variables – what will inflame one person may not even be noticed by another. Conflicts are most likely to occur when a person or a group feels that their social, psychological, emotional, physical or other space is threatened, and only some form of dialogue will resolve the conflict. There are six steps in a conflict cycle (see Figure 8.4).

Conflict is often thought to be a negative group dynamic, but if managed effectively at steps four and five (interpretation of situation and response to situation), it can be positive (see Table 8.7).

Individual conflict style and the process a group uses for managing conflict have the greatest impact on the outcome of a potential conflict situation. It is therefore helpful to know what individual and team role styles are and how conflict styles can be assessed. There are several tools and models available for individual conflict style assessment, most based on a five-mode response model with two dimensions (see Figure 8.5). A popular one is the Thomas-Kilmann Conflict Mode Instrument.[27]

In this model the "concern for self" axis is the degree to which a person aims to satisfy his or her personal concerns or needs, and the "concern for others" axis reflects how much someone is concerned with meeting others' needs or concerns:

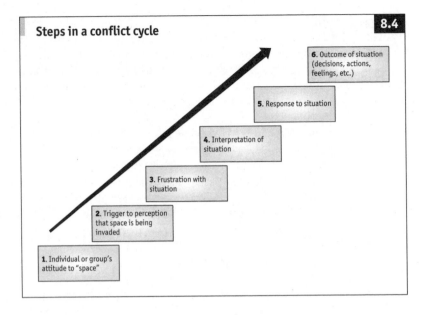

Steps in a conflict cycle   8.4

6. Outcome of situation (decisions, actions, feelings, etc.)

5. Response to situation

4. Interpretation of situation

3. Frustration with situation

2. Trigger to perception that space is being invaded

1. Individual or group's attitude to "space"

- ◪ The competing or dominating style emphasises winning at the expense of other people – it is highly assertive and unco-operative.
- ◪ The collaborating or integrating style involves high concern for self and high concern for others – it is both assertive and co-operative.
- ◪ The avoiding or neglecting style shows low concern for self

---

Table 8.7 **Positive and negative outcomes of group conflict**

Positive effects of conflict	*Negative effects of conflict*
Causes problems to surface and be dealt with	Frustrates individuals
Clarifies points of view	Reduces cooperation
Stimulates and energises individuals	Destroys trust
Motivates the search for creative alternatives	Diminishes performance and motivation
Provides vivid feedback	Causes lasting damage
Creates increased understanding of individual conflict styles	Communication breakdown
Tests and extends capacities of group members	Builds stress
Provides a mechanism for adjusting relationships	Breaks up relationships

Source: Mitchell, R.C., "Constructive Management of Conflict in Groups", 2002, www.csun.edu/~hfmgt001/cm_gp.htm

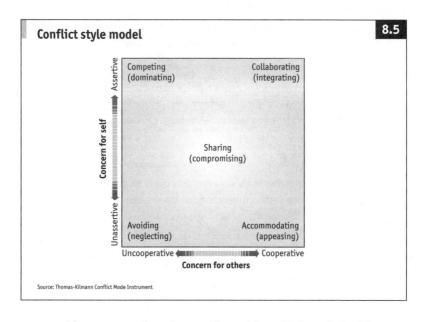

Conflict style model 8.5

Source: Thomas-Kilmann Conflict Mode Instrument

and low concern for others evidenced by withdrawal, denial or sidestepping confrontations.

- The accommodating or appeasing style reflects low concern for self and high concern for others, akin to self-sacrificing and acquiescing.
- The sharing or compromising style shows moderate concern for self and for others. It takes a middle ground that involves trading concessions, splitting the difference, and so on.

A tool such as Belbin's team-roles, which is an inventory designed around nine clusters (team-roles) of behaviour, each having a combination of strengths and areas for development, can be used to assess the part individuals play in groups.[28] Using this form of assessment in combination with an assessment of team-member conflict style is a powerful way of thinking about managing conflicts that may arise. Some interesting research by Aitor Aritzeta, Sabino Ayestaran and Stephen Swailes, who used the Belbin team-role tool, suggests that:[29]

> Creating a high performing work team is not just about putting well-trained individuals together and giving them the autonomy to take decisions. Such teams also need to be built in a complementary way where different team role preferences are present and individuals have

the abilities to manage conflict. Knowing how team role preferences are related to conflict management styles will help practitioners to build balanced teams.

Other ways of managing conflict focus on the processes and strategies used by participants either at the point of conflict or as the conflict escalates up the management ladder.[30] Strategies for managing at the point of conflict include:

- devising and implementing a common method for resolving conflict (for example, collaboration, mediation, team counselling);
- providing people with criteria for making trade-offs (for example, between speed in getting a new process up and running and ensuring its seamless integration with existing ones);
- halting the escalation of conflict, rather than accepting it, and coaching people to manage it at their level. IBM, for example, runs training programmes with back-up resources for staff. One of these lists the types of conversations that might occur and suggests some methods of managing these.

Strategies for managing conflict as they start to escalate include:

- establishing and enforcing a requirement of joint escalation (that is, people present a disagreement jointly to their manager or managers);
- requiring managers to resolve escalated conflicts directly with their peers;
- making the process for escalated conflict resolution transparent.

Jamie Dimon, CEO of JPMorgan Chase, notes his way of stopping the escalation of conflicts as he designs the company to be less bureaucratic:[31]

You have all these meetings, and people come and see you privately afterward and say, "Well, I know what we said there, but here's what I really think about it." And my reaction is, "Hey, am I your messenger? You couldn't say it in the meeting?" The response is, "Well, I thought so-and-so would get upset." And I say, "I don't care whether he or she gets upset. Say it next time." I have no problem with someone coming in and saying, "Hey, we met. We don't agree. Here are the facts on which we agree; here are the things we disagree on. Can we talk about this now?" That's what mature management does.

CASE STUDY: management of roles and conflicts

Enterpriseaccess.org is the official business link to a major western country's government, and is managed by the Department of Enterprise in a partnership with more than 20 other government departments. This partnership, known as Enterprise Access, is an initiative that provides a single access point to government services and information to help the country's businesses with their operations.

Enterprise Access initially focused on starting, growing and financing small businesses. More recently users said they needed help in complying with government regulations, a need that was not being met by any other government programme. To meet that need Enterprise Access was relaunched to provide a one-stop compliance assistance shop for businesses. It held over 20,000 compliance-related documents from 94 government websites and for the first time businesses were able to go to a single website for all their compliance assistance resources. One business owner reported:

It's a real breakthrough. I've browsed the site and already I can see it's going to save me hours of time and a lot of money. The maze of stuff I have to submit to comply is a nightmare and I was never sure if I got it right. The burden has almost put me out of business, but with this resource and the way it's organised I don't have to know which of the 90 or more departments to contact, or navigate millions of documents returned from general web directories and search engines.

The team behind the portal's new look comprised Enterprise Agency staff and external consultants and the project had not gone smoothly. Malcolm Silcock, the programme manager, said:

Quite honestly this has been a difficult project. On the client side, we've had five changes in the client we reported to, the government stakeholders have been inconsistent and unreliable, we've had to handle a lot of budget unknowns because the funding comes from the 20 partnering departments which all have the option to withdraw funding. On our side, our company was acquired which has led to team turnover with all that entails, and we weren't sure for almost a year precisely what the project aimed to achieve which caused a lot of tension and in-fighting.

I clearly remember the day when we had everyone together and finally nailed the direction. It was a real turning point. People stopped blaming each other for hold-ups and there was a reduction in gossip and emotional responses. Other issues remained unresolved but once we had a common goal we became motivated. We started to say "let's do this together", instead of "this is never going to work". I'm really proud that we've achieved the first goal of getting the site renewed and relaunched. Now our task is to drive traffic to the site and give the users good reasons for returning. In a year from now I'd like to be seeing an extended user base and hearing success stories that they put down to the site's content and ease of use.

To recalibrate the project (starting again but from where the company was then) and set the tone for the next phase, Silcock decided to run a one-day workshop:

What I'd like to come out of it is that we have a common view of what the current situation is, and what we would like to achieve in the coming year. To do this we need to agree why we should bother working towards this – what's in it for all the players? Of course it can't be just a talking shop, we also need to draft a high-level plan of what work has to be done together with a timeline and critical milestones so we're in a better position to respond as the situation changes.

Silcock and the facilitator he brought in to orchestrate the day carefully designed it in the spirit of appreciative inquiry (see Chapter 2). The opening session included questions like: What do you most enjoy about your work? What works well in the team you currently work with? What surprised participants was their realisation that they had successfully met their target because, for the most part, once they had an agreed direction they had managed to achieve an open team culture where they shared information, sought creative solutions to issues and valued the diversity in the team. The morning progressed in a similar vein, and the client manager reported:

My eyes were really opened when we did that transferable skills exercise [see Tools for this case below] where we all identified the three or four things we were most competent at and I saw how much capability we had available to us. It made me see more clearly that people are wired differently and that we could use this diversity more effectively. In the discussion we had about some of the conflicts we'd had I could see that a lot of it was probably due to people trying to place their standards on others. Also we'd been under very tight time pressures to get the software right and didn't take time to have face-to-face discussions. Had we done that we probably would have identified the root problems and solved these rather than arguing about the symptoms we had to deal with.

The exercise on capturing achievements to date led to other insights. The software architect said:

> What I enjoyed hearing was not just the range and level of achievements we'd had but the discussion around what made these possible. It pulled out the reasons why we were successful in some aspects and suggested that if we applied similar approaches in those cases where we'd had difficulties things might have worked out differently. For example, I remember a tremendous blow-up in the early stages when the technical solution failed on all counts – I don't think we realised that some of what happened was due to our not defining our terms properly. There was frustration because some of our partners felt their territory was being encroached on, and we worried too much about trying to hide our problems from the client rather than sharing openly and honestly what was going. The client, who was our point of contact at that stage, was very difficult too. To protect ourselves we felt obliged to hide all the issues from him as he couldn't cope with anything but good news. This led to all kinds of complications which, with the current client manager, we simply don't have. Her view is that an unhealthy culture develops if people can't express openly what's going on.

The afternoon session focused on the practicalities of drafting a high-level plan, and again to the surprise of some of the participants the session ran smoothly. It began with the facilitator reminding people of some of the attributes for group success that participants had identified in the morning: listening carefully before responding, sticking to the issues in hand, keeping the behaviour and vocabulary level, not overreacting, and calling truces for rethinking, cooling off, or recovering.

Six months after the event the programme manager commented:

> I had in mind what the streams of work should be but as the discussion progressed I started to change my mind, and in fact, stopped even thinking about my solution and went with the flow of the group. It made a lot of sense because I was new to the project and they'd all been working on it for various lengths of time. What we came up with was radically different from what I planned to propose but I could see how it made sense to start from a clean slate. What was more important was that we arrived at a jointly agreed solution that everyone subscribed to. I must admit that I'm rather impatient and over the course of the three hours or so that it took I wondered if we were ever going to get to closure but I'm glad that I stuck with it. The thing that catalysed it for me was that graphic that the facilitator showed (Figure 8.6).

My approach was going to be that of the common design scenario building

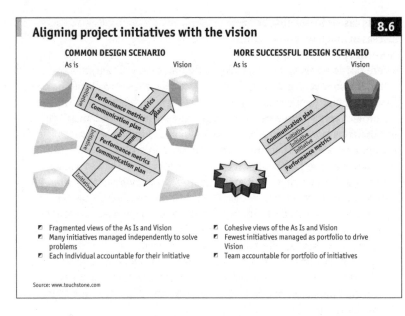

Aligning project initiatives with the vision

8.6

COMMON DESIGN SCENARIO | MORE SUCCESSFUL DESIGN SCENARIO

- Fragmented views of the As Is and Vision
- Many initiatives managed independently to solve problems
- Each individual accountable for their initiative

- Cohesive views of the As Is and Vision
- Fewest initiatives managed as portfolio to drive Vision
- Team accountable for portfolio of initiatives

Source: www.touchstone.com

on what already existed, and what we've got now is the more successful design scenario reflecting a whole view of the project in the system and not a piecemeal view. By celebrating their success and acknowledging the different strengths people bring to the table, the team has been able to find a creative solution to recalibrating the project. What's striking is that we're getting a lot of kudos for the way things are going. For example, we've now got trade associations' support and other government departments are using us as a model of success for one-stop information and are seeking our input on how to apply our learning to their projects. Of course it hasn't all been easy. We've had to put a lot of effort into defining our own operating processes – decision-making, problem-solving and managing the inevitable conflicts. But it seems that this investment is paying off and we are almost able to say that the Enterprise Access project is running like a well-oiled machine.

Reflections on this case

Having to redesign project organisations when they have reached specific milestones (in this case the website launch) or when some other event occurs (such as a significant change in stakeholder support) is extremely common.

This case is interesting because on the face of it the project had achieved success in that it was on schedule, within budget and well received. Probing more deeply using appreciative inquiry revealed a number of aspects where participants agreed that they could do things differently and much better. It also revealed how they had been able to be successful in the first phase. Crucial to their success was agreeing the vision and mission of the project and thus having a common direction for their work. With this and the constraints of time and budget they had tight boundaries to work within, and were able to move from a culture of blame towards a more participative "one for all and all for one" approach. With the appointment of the new client contact they were able to move away from a good-news culture. Both these events meant a shift in the shadow side of the project organisation towards a healthier, more trusting working environment. The shifting context had clear impacts on the project.

Team members handled decision-making less well than they felt they should. For example, they knew they had to make a decision on data harmonisation as they were getting information in different formats from the various departments, but they had procrastinated on this which led to upstream difficulties.

They all felt pretty good about problem-solving. But looking again at how they did it, they understood that they were not using the diversity of the team to come up with innovative solutions. They had a tendency to limit discussion to people in their work streams which they felt could lead to missed opportunities.

Managing conflict was an aspect that they felt they could improve on. Team members recognised that negative conflicts arose over things like administrative procedures, resource issues, deadlines, overruns and not prioritising carefully enough. However, team members also saw that there were some positive conflicts that they found energising and capacity building provided that they followed the "rules": listening effectively, acknowledging people's positions, responding without defensiveness and looking for the causes of issues rather than trying to deal with the symptoms.

Tools for this case

Transferable skills cards

These cards, available from Lifeskills Publishing,[32] are used to help individuals and groups identify and apply their skills and values to work choices. Users identify their transferable skills and then classify their level of ability in applying them, choosing one of four levels (very competent, competent, adequate for task, undeveloped) for each skill. Skills cards are classified under data, ideas, people and things. Work values are identified by levels of importance and considered with respect to paid and unpaid work. Guidelines and support materials are available in *Build Your Own Rainbow*.[33]

The prisoner's dilemma

The prisoner's dilemma shows that, in certain circumstances, if the members of a group trust each other, they can choose a course of action that will lead to the best possible outcome for the group as a whole. Without trust, each individual will aim for his or her best personal outcome, which can lead to the worst possible outcome for all.

In the prisoner's dilemma, two players act as prisoners who have been jointly charged with a crime (which they did commit) but they are questioned separately. The police have enough evidence to secure a conviction for a minor offence but not enough for the more serious crime.

The prisoners made a pact that if they were caught, they would not confess or give evidence against each other. If both prisoners keep their word, they will only be convicted of the lesser offence. The dilemma occurs when the police offer each prisoner a reduced prison term if they confess to the serious offence and give evidence against the other prisoner.

This is a good exercise in group dynamics when played with a pack of playing cards (instructions are available at www.indiana.edu/~econed/issues/v31_3/3.htm). Individuals can also play the Open University's interactive prisoner's dilemma (www.open2.net/trust/dilemma/dilemma_game.htm).

Summary

This chapter discusses aspects of group culture and dynamics, putting the view that successful organisation design work is characterised by a no-blame culture, telling it like it is and reducing the negative power of the shadow side. Team members working on organisation design projects must be able to work effectively with group processes and dynamics, specifically methods of decision-making, problem-solving and conflict management.

Even so, success is not guaranteed. Returning to Shackleton's expedition:

> Whether there is one book or 20, the fate of the Ross Sea Party
> deserves to be told and retold. "There are," wrote the Edinburgh
> Evening Dispatch, "some failures as glorious as successes. Sir Ernest
> Shackleton's is one of them". No less important, no less memorable, is
> the story of The Lost Men.[35]

9 Morphing not future proofing

Things fall apart; the centre cannot hold.

W.B. Yeats, *The Second Coming*

Prediction is difficult, especially about the future.

Yogi Berra, baseball catcher (1925–)

ORGANISATION DESIGNERS look for assurances that their design is right and that it will endure. They aspire to "future proof" its success, but this is impossible because they are not designing a static building or a monument. An organisation is a dynamic system with its own life cycle. Consider designing the right shape, size and operating processes for a shoal of fish. Organisation design is done in an analogous context – environmental conditions and constituent parts are constantly changing. Thus:[1]

> there is no common (design) solution that fits all organisations; there
> is no common approach to even finding a solution; and there is no
> agreement on what constitutes an adequate solution.

No organisation design will last forever (or even very long), but this does not mean that the organisation itself is necessarily under threat. Like a shoal of fish, an organisation continuously changes shape, size and membership, yet lasts over time. Threats generally come from externalities, such as environmental change or predators, which can be subtle or cataclysmic. So it is with organisation designs. Go into a design process knowing that it will not endure. This is not defeatist, just realistic.

Begin with the view that the design is dynamic, has a life cycle and will change as the context demands, and there will be fewer charges of design failure and more support from stakeholders (who usually want quick results from a new design yet cold-shoulder the notion of a redesign if the results are not delivered). Good designs are not a one-shot effort; they allow for meeting continuous change while simultaneously keeping the business operations running successfully. The best designs consciously develop the organisational capacity to morph[2] from one form to another in the same way that Morph, a plasticine being who could change shape at will, demonstrated in a UK television show, *The Amazing Adventures of Morph*.

This chapter discusses why morphing capacity is required and then presents several ways in which organisation designs can work to invigorate and revitalise an organisation while building renewal and regeneration capability.

Why morphing capacity is required

> Everybody has accepted by now that change is unavoidable. But that still implies that change is like death and taxes – it should be postponed as long as possible and no change would be vastly preferable. But in a period of upheaval, such as the one we are living in, change is the norm.
>
> Peter Drucker[3]

The list in Table 9.1, forwarded by e-mail in March 2006, reveals why change is the norm because even a month or two after it was circulated it seemed dated.

Table 9.1 **YOU KNOW YOU ARE LIVING IN 2006 when...**

1	You accidentally enter your password on the microwave.
2	You haven't played solitaire with real cards in years.
3	You have a list of 15 phone numbers to reach your family of 3.
4	You e-mail the person who works at the desk next to you.
5	Your reason for not staying in touch with friends and family is that they don't have e-mail addresses.
6	You pull up in your own driveway and use your cell phone to see if anyone is home to help you carry in the groceries.
7	Every commercial on television has a website at the bottom of the screen.
8	Leaving the house without your cell phone, which you didn't have the first 20 or 30 (or 60) years of your life, is now a cause for panic and you turn around to go and get it.
10	You get up in the morning and go online before getting your coffee.
11	You start tilting your head sideways to smile. :)
12	You're reading this and nodding and laughing.
13	Even worse, you know exactly to whom you are going to forward this message.
14	You are too busy to notice there was no 9 on this list.
15	You actually scrolled back up to check that there wasn't a 9 on this list.

Take, for example, number 3 (you have a list of 15 phone numbers to reach your family of 3). By mid-2006 companies started to offer a one-number service, eliminating the multiple phone number issue:[4]

> Grand Central, a new service [set up in 2006] based in California, provides you with one number that you can essentially "forward" anywhere, keeping you in touch forever and ever with your friends, family, and associates. It also centralizes your voice-mail and e-mail functions. The interactive website provides some unique features, such as letting you record customized greetings for each caller, switch phones in mid-call, listen in on voicemail while a caller leaves a message, and block unwanted callers; it also offers lifetime voicemail storage, access to voicemail via web, phone, or e-mail, and call announcement and handling.

Or take number 4 (you e-mail the person who works at the desk next to you). During the year IM (instant messaging) became a common rival to e-mail among co-workers:[5]

> If we pay close attention to the online habits of people using the Web, we can't help but see that this is a huge sea change. The tide is now moving out on email. Moving away from standalone email as the primary messaging tool is a huge deal, for platform makers, software makers, and the people who use them.
> Google also did an interesting thing along these lines. They combined email and messaging in Gmail. It started off as a "hey, that would be cool" type of idea. But it morphed into something that really speaks to the convergence of messaging. So when you go to your email account you have a choice, do you want to send someone email or simply start a chat? If they're online and you have a couple minutes, you'll probably chat. If they're offline or you don't want to have a full conversation, you'll probably email. It's kind of like calling your neighbour ... you call them instead of going over when you don't want to talk long.

These examples illustrate that organisations exist in a context of continuous flux, where small and big things happen in the environment and people respond (or not) to them. Interestingly, people appear more responsive to contextual changes in their personal lives than they do at work. One explanation for this is that organisations often encourage employees to be narrowly focused and therefore blinkered. Organisation control devices such as reporting lines, performance appraisals, scorecards and measures suggest that employees have to achieve certain targets to a specific schedule, so the wider perspective is not considered.

Because the systems and processes that control organisations militate against those organisations developing morphing capability, organisation designers find it difficult to design in adaptability. However, a design that takes a narrow, short-term focus and ignores the wider context is liable to fail to achieve its objectives. To lay the foundations for design flexibility it is necessary to keep abreast of three particular aspects in the organisation's external context and three in the internal context:

- ◪ External context
  - new businesses and models
  - our responsibility for the future
  - new markets
- ◪ Internal context
  - corporate governance
  - psychological contracts
  - workforce demographics

Of course there are other external and internal context factors to bear in mind, but these six are the ones currently having the most impact upon organisations.

External context: new businesses and business models

An astonishing array of new businesses and business models have emerged since 2000. The rise of blogs and all the businesses associated with them is one example, and the timeline shown in Table 9.2 illustrates just how fast this method of interpersonal networking grew in its first ten years.

This example illustrates the swift rise of a new type of business model that directly competes with a more traditional one. Blogs are now a rich source of material that was traditionally the territory of print publications: newspapers, newsletters, journals and magazines.

With the rise of blogs came a shift in the print newspaper industry. According to the World Association of Newspapers, in 2005 circulation sales increased by 1.7% in Asia, 3.7% in South America and 0.2% in Africa, and decreased by 0.24% in Europe, 2.5% in North America and 2% in Australia and Oceania, compared with the previous year. These

Table 9.2 **A brief history of blogs**

1997, December	Jorn Barger invents the term "weblog" to describe his own website
1998, December	An inventory of all known weblogs is taken; it tallies all of 23 sites
1999, April	Peter Merholz coins the shorter term "blog"
1999, August	Pyra Labs launches Blogger, a free blog-hosting service
2001, October	Six Apart releases Movable Type for making blogs
2002, December	Political bloggers drive Trent Lott from US Senate majority leader post over allegedly racist comments
2003, February	Google buys Pyra Labs and its Blogger.com; becomes the world's top blog host
2003, March	The Oxford English Dictionary lists blog as a noun and a verb
2003, September	Worldwide blog count soars to 1m
2004, August	Bloggers are cleared to cover US political conventions
2005, May	Blogosphere explodes to 10m blogs
2005, September	Google introduces blog search features
2005, November	Blogosphere doubles in size again; now at 20m outposts
2006, December	Technorati is tracking 60m blogs and according to Technorati data, there are over 175,000 new blogs (that is just blogs) every day. Bloggers update their blogs regularly to the tune of over 1.6m posts per day, or over 18 updates a second

Sources: Up to 2005, *Forbes*, November 14th 2005; 2006, www.technorati.com/about

figures represent a trend evident over the previous five years of decreasing circulation in the more developed countries. In response to the growth of alternative online sources of news, many traditional newspapers opened new distribution channels, ranging from daily free newspapers to online editions. As the Newspaper Association of America in its publication *The Source* reported (with generous use of boldface):

> The key to the future of newspapers is the effort to **build a broad portfolio** of products around the core product, the traditional newspaper, and to **connect** with both general and targeted audiences. Newspapers across the country have established their **presence on the Web** and are aggressively developing additional online products. They are launching niche publications and reaching out to new audiences,

particularly minorities. It's all part of a critical **transformation**: from newspaper companies to information companies.

Blogs were only one example of new types of businesses and business models appearing in the early 2000s. Table 9.3 lists many others that threatened more traditionally offered products and services.

Table 9.3 **Traditional and new business models**

Traditional model	New model
Press release	RSS feed
Marketing collateral	Blog
Media tour	Webcast
Event	Social network
Customer reference	Community advocate
Data sheets	e-newsletters
Newspapers	Blogs
E-mail newsletters	Syndication (RSS)
Encyclopaedia	Wikipedia
Phone	Skype, IM
Classifieds	Craig's list
Music stores	iTunes
Blockbusters	Netflix
Traditional music industry	MySpace, Podcasting
TV	Rich web media, Video blogging
Radio	Podcasting, XM radio
Travel agencies	Online travel websites
Magazines	Blogs, RSS
Talent agents (music, film, modelling)	MySpace, Blogs, other social networking
Middleperson	Internet
Banks/financial services	Online banking

The impact that networking and other technologies have had and are continuing to have on businesses cannot be underestimated. With what seems like hyperbole, *Fast Company* noted:[6]

> It's hard to overstate the coming impact of these new network technologies on business: They hatch trends and build immense waves of interest in specific products. They serve giant, targeted audiences to advertisers. They edge out old media with the loving labor of amateurs. They effortlessly provide hyperdetailed data to marketers. If your customers are satisfied, networks can help build fanatical loyalty; if not, they'll amplify every complaint until you do something about it. They are fund-raising platforms. They unify activists of every stripe, transforming an atomized mass of individuals with few resources into an international movement able to put multinational corporations and governments on the defensive. They provide an authentic, peer-to-peer channel of communication that is far more credible than any corporate flackery[7].

Nevertheless, the message is clear and rings true. The traditional newspaper industry is only one of many that are under possible terminal threat; others include retailing, telecommunications, software, pharmaceuticals and advertising.

Organisations must take account of changing businesses and business models. This is easier said than done, although there are some examples of established organisations being successful. A good example is Nokia, which began in 1865 as a wood-pulping company, between the two world wars turned to paper, rubber and cables, and in 1966 merged with Finnish Rubber Works and Finnish Cable Works. In 1991 the company transformed from a conglomerate into one that focused on telecommunications. There are some organisations, however, which may not be able to achieve the radical redesigns necessary to survive and prosper; the challenge for them is to ensure that their demise is as well planned and painless as possible.

External context: responsibility for our future

> We are made wise not by the recollections of our past, but by the responsibility for our future.
>
> George Bernard Shaw

Global issues loom larger by the day. Table 9.4 lists 20 that have an impact on organisation design and highlight the increasing responsibility organisations feel they have to help shape a sustainable future for the world at large as well as their own business.

Table 9.4 **Global issues affecting organisation design**

Environmental issues	Global warming
	Biodiversity and ecosystem losses
	Fisheries depletion
	Deforestation
	Water deficits
	Maritime safety and pollution
Humanitarian issues	The fight against poverty
	Peacekeeping, conflict prevention, combating terrorism
	Education for all
	Global infectious diseases
	Digital divide
	Natural disaster prevention and mitigation
Regulatory issues	Taxation
	Biotechnology rules
	Financial systems
	Illegal drugs
	Trade, investment and competition rules
	Intellectual property rights
	E-commerce rules
	International labour and migration rules

Source: Rischard, J.F., *High Noon: 20 Global Problems. 20 Years to Solve Them*, Basic Books, 2002

Organisations designing in aspects of global responsibility include GE, which launched ecomagination in May 2005.

GE: ecoimagination

A broad portfolio of new technologies that will provide solutions to our energy needs and revolutionize how we power the world. It's all part of the company's exciting new growth initiative called ecomagination.

Ecomagination is GE's commitment to help our customers and society at large solve its most pressing energy and environmental challenges. Under ecomagination, GE has committed to:

◪ Doubling its research investment in environmentally friendly technologies from $700m to more than $1.5 billion over the next five years.

◪ Introducing new products and services that offer significant and measurable

environmental performance advantages to its customers.
- ☑ Reducing its greenhouse gas emissions (GHG) and improving its energy efficiency.
- ☑ Keeping the public informed. GE has pledged to publicly report its progress in meeting its goals.

GE's philosophy in this rapidly changing energy market is that "Green is Green" – good environmental policy makes good economic sense. The billions of dollars we are investing in new, eco-technologies today will mean billions more in sales and revenues for the company in the future.

Source: www.ge.com/research/grc_2_1_1.html

Almost every day other household name companies, not previously associated with greenness or sustainability, join the ranks of those announcing their intention and commitment to address one or more of these aspects of common concern. In doing so they are effecting a new design of their organisation.

Take the example of the Mojo Bar produced by Clif Bars. Michael, category insights manager, when asked "Which Clif product best describes you?", said:[8]

> I think I'd have to go with the Mojo Bar because in its prior life, it was a lot less organic than it is now. Since coming here, I've learned a lot about ingredients, what goes into food, organic foods versus conventionally-farmed foods and also about using less energy, riding your bike to work, about bio-diesel and all of these other things that are much more sustainable for the environment. Mojo, in its old version, wasn't really all that organic but now it's up to 70%.

Think of the organisation design work that followed the decision to make this one bar 70% organic. It included rethinking sourcing processes, making cultural changes, adjusting production systems, and so on.

Responses to global issues such as those made by GE and Clif Bars require the morphing capacity to transform the organisation design from old product or service to new product or service without missing an operational beat.

External context: emerging economies
Besides the business challenges of technology and global responsibilities

there are the twin challenges of entering new markets in the emerging
– and faster growing – economies and competing with rapidly growing
businesses being established within the emerging economies. (Definitions
of what is an emerging economy differ but generally speaking they are
economies where income per head is low to middle.) *The Economist* tracks
more than 30 countries within the six groups shown in Figure 9.1, which
indicates the annual average GDP growth of emerging economies.

Organisations used to doing business in the developed world are
entering these new markets with greater or lesser success. Wal-Mart, for
example, pulled out of South Korea because of "sluggish" business:[9]

> US giant Wal-Mart Stores, the world's largest discount store chain, will
> sell its South Korean business to local retail group Shinsegae for 825
> billion won (US$874 million), officials said yesterday.
>
> Shinsegae, which operates discount chain E-Mart as well as
> department stores, said it would buy all 16 outlets run by Wal-Mart in
> South Korea in a bid to expand its discount store business.
>
> Under the deal, the stores will be absorbed by E-Mart and operate
> under the E-Mart brand name. The US chain has invested 812 billion
> won since it opened its first store in South Korea in 1998.

But many companies are expanding successfully in emerging markets.
Intel, for example, is investing $1bn (£522m) in building two produc-
tion plants in a science park outside Ho Chi Minh City in Vietnam, and
Motorola is one of many companies investing in China:[10]

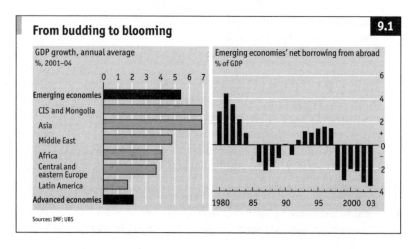

From budding to blooming 9.1

GDP growth, annual average %, 2001–04

Emerging economies
CIS and Mongolia
Asia
Middle East
Africa
Central and eastern Europe
Latin America
Advanced economies

Emerging economies' net borrowing from abroad % of GDP

1980 85 90 95 2000 03

Sources: IMF; UBS

BEIJING, China – 14 November 2006 – Motorola, Inc. (NYSE: MOT) today announced the opening of its Broadband Wireless China Research Center in Beijing. The center will focus on researching key technologies for future broadband wireless systems and helping develop global standards. "The opening of the center is a further testament of Motorola's China strategy: to develop China as a production and R&D base. Today Motorola has nearly 3,000 engineers working in 18 R&D centers in China, the largest R&D presence any global company has established here," said Greg Brown, president of Motorola Networks and Enterprise.

Conversely, some emerging-market companies are expanding into the developed world. Lenovo (originally named Legend), for example, which was established in 1984 by 11 computer scientists in Beijing, by 2004 had a 25% market share in China and went on to acquire IBM's personal computing division in May 2005, giving the company global reach. Today Lenovo is a leader in the global PC market, with approximately $13 billion in annual revenue.

Competing in this emerging-economy space requires careful thinking about an organisation's design. Wal-Mart, for example, tried to export a successful US-based design and failed to adapt the design to meet local requirements. Starbucks in China faced an uphill battle in 2003:[11]

> Walking the tightrope between hip and Western is difficult in China. After Starbucks opened a store in Beijing's hallowed Forbidden City in December 2000, outraged local media reported that 70% of people they surveyed would rather not see the chain there. Chinese customers have different priorities than their American yuppie counterparts. ... Tweaks to the furniture, store layout, artwork and food options make Starbucks more friendly to Chinese eyes, but coffee remains the core offering.

However, three years later Starbucks chairman Howard Schultz was able to report:[12]

> Starbucks has grown from a single Beijing shop in 1999 to a network of 238 now [2006]. The secret was "respecting the consumer and the culture," Schultz said. "Especially in a country like China," he said, "you have humbly to earn their respect and gain their trust." One of Starbucks' first acts in China was to create a $5 million scholarship fund for disadvantaged children. The company did it "not just to issue a

press release" but to show that it was committed to balancing profit and social conscience.

In October 2006, the company confidently announced its international growth strategy for 2007, including opening in Brazil, Russia, India and Egypt (all emerging economies):[13]

> "Our international growth strategy balances accelerated development in line with the long-term retail potential of existing countries, while entering several promising new markets," said Coles. "The company's entrance into the three large markets of Brazil, Russia and India as well as establishing our first African location will propel Starbucks' International expansion towards meeting its long-term store potential of 20,000 locations, which is up from 15,000 previously targeted."

Internal context: corporate governance

Definitions of corporate governance vary widely. They tend to fall into two categories. The first set of definitions concerns itself with a set of behavioural patterns: that is, the actual behaviour of corporations, in terms of such measures as performance, efficiency, growth, financial structure, and treatment of shareholders and other stakeholders. The second set concerns itself with the normative framework: that is, the rules under which firms are operating – with the rules coming from such sources as the legal system, the judicial system, financial markets, and factor [labour] markets.

Stijn Claessens[14]

Regardless of definition, an organisation's board influences its design, and this is true whether board members are active, aiming to contribute value to the organisation, or passive, doing little more than ensuring regulatory compliance.

Corporate governance continues to be a fast-changing aspect of organisational life. It has been moving up organisational agendas for various reasons since the early 1990s, following a number of corporate scandals or crises that led to board members taking action, often to replace a chief executive or other directors.

Beyond the scandals and crises (themselves a symptom of weak organisation design), other factors have led to governance issues coming to the fore:[15]

- The private, market-based investment process – underpinned by good corporate governance – is now much more important for most economies than it used to be.
- Because of technological progress, liberalisation and opening up of financial markets, trade liberalisation and other structural reforms, the allocation within and across countries of capital among competing purposes has become more complex, as has monitoring of the use of capital.
- The mobilisation of capital is increasingly one step removed from the principal owner, given the increasing size of firms and the growing role of financial intermediaries. The role of institutional investors is growing in many countries, with many economies moving away from pay-as-you-go retirement systems.
- Programmes of deregulation and reform have reshaped the local and global financial landscape.
- International financial integration has increased, and trade and investment flows are increasing.

All this has led to board members paying closer attention to their role in providing their organisations with strong and appropriate direction and oversight. This in itself has given rise to organisation design work that reflects the measures of corporate governance that are becoming parts of organisational reporting. Governance Metrics International, for example, has developed ratings for six aspects of corporate governance (see Table 9.5) based on securities regulations, stock-exchange listing requirements and various corporate governance codes and principles. It monitors companies by geographic region and red flags aspects of governance concern.[16]

In carrying out their role, board members have to engage in some or all of the following activities:[17]

- Approving a corporate philosophy and mission.
- Selecting, monitoring, evaluating, compensating and – if necessary – replacing the CEO and other senior executives, and ensuring management succession.
- Reviewing and approving management's strategic and business plans, including developing a depth of knowledge of the business being served, understanding and questioning the assumptions upon which such plans are based, and reaching an independent judgment as to the probability that the plans can be realised (referred to as "constructive engagement" in strategy).

Table 9.5 **Governance Metrics International sample rating**

	Global rating	Home market
Overall rating	2.5	1.5
Board accountability	3.0	1.5
Financial disclosure and internal controls[a]	1.0	1.0
Shareholder rights	4.0	2.0
Remuneration	3.5	1.5
Market for control	2.0	1.0
Corporate behaviour[a]	1.0	1.5

a GMI alert
Source: www.gmiratings.com/(c3q0ul55hz2qyeuw12joi355)/products.aspx

- ◪ Reviewing and approving the corporation's financial objectives, plans and actions, including significant capital allocations and expenditures.
- ◪ Reviewing and approving transactions not in the ordinary course of business (if the transaction would cause the disappearance of the corporation or the sale of all its assets, then only the board can make this decision; it may not be delegated to a committee or to management).
- ◪ Monitoring corporate performance against the strategic and business plans, including overseeing the operating results on a regular basis to evaluate whether the business is being properly managed.
- ◪ Ensuring that the corporation has in place systems to encourage and enable ethical behaviour and compliance with laws and regulations, auditing and accounting principles, and the corporation's own governing documents.
- ◪ Assessing its own effectiveness in fulfilling these and other board responsibilities (subject to minimum statutory requirements such as quorum requirements for meetings under state corporation law).
- ◪ Performing such other functions as are prescribed by law, or assigned to the board in the corporation's governing documents.

This list shows how integral board members' involvement is to much organisation design work, not least because they are guardians of their organisations and their future. In the words of Steve Odland, CEO of Office Depot:[18]

> Strong corporate governance and high ethical standards are not simply matters of personal and public morality. They are also essential for long-term corporate success and world economic leadership by this nation. ... A corporation and a society based on strong governance principles and high ethical standards are in the best position to face unexpected challenges, overcome them, and flourish.
>
> And as long as we can keep that idea central, we can continue to look forward to greater prosperity and human progress.

Organisations have to have the capability to keep pace with fast-evolving governance principles and to predict and respond to board-member activity. Stakeholder analysis (see Chapter 6) identifies the level and extent of board involvement required for any particular design project. It is worth bearing in mind that although this section is concerned with corporate governance, the principles and frameworks are, of course, applicable to programme governance (see Chapter 7).

Internal context: employee relationships

> Future firms must become both creators of competence and providers of personality. Once it was money for mastery. Now, it must also be meaning for membership. Talent wants value and values. To thrive, organisations must learn how to combine skill and soul.
>
> Jonas Ridderstrale and Kjell Nordstrom[19]

Responsiveness to changes in the employer/employee relationship is another area requiring morphing capability. Changes in the labour market in the developed world mean that employees want to gain value from a better work–life balance and employers want to gain value in workforce flexibility. These twin wants are resulting in changes to both the implicit psychological contract (that is, "the perceptions of the two parties, employee and employer, of what their mutual obligations are towards each other"[20]) and the explicit employment contract between employers and employees.

The psychological contract is something that is read between the lines of the employment contract and is then interpreted by the employee as something that the employer promises. What individuals read varies from person to person, is highly subjective and, again unlike an employment contract, is not legally binding. In spite of this, the implied psychological contract can have a strong influence on employee behaviour, well-being, attitudes and performance:[21]

> For example, an employee can feel let down about some issue at work and take a day off. Not being inclined to go to work can be due to a number of factors, such as wanting to get back at the organization for something it has done or not done for you, so that you don't feel so committed to the organization, or you feel demoralized about your job. When an employee believes that the organization has failed to deliver its promises on a regular basis, he or she will question whether it makes sense to continue contributing to that organization or whether it might be better for them to move on to another.

Employers are offering explicit and binding job contracts in many different forms: short-term contracts, flexible working, home-working, teleworking, casual jobs, job shares, compressed working (working 80 hours – two 40-hour weeks – over nine days instead of ten days) and annualised hours, and so on. Bank of America is one company offering flexible working.

Flexible work arrangements

You may be able to take advantage of a work arrangement that gives you flexibility in balancing your life and work schedules. Flexible work arrangements are mutually agreed upon by a manager and an associate.

Work arrangement options
- ☑ FlexTime. The opportunity to alter starting and/or departure times.
- ☑ Compressed workweeks. Condenses a full-time workweek into fewer days.
- ☑ Telecommuting. The ability to perform all or part of your work from a location other than your normal work site.
- ☑ Select time. Reduces your work schedule and job responsibilities for a specific need.
- ☑ Phase-in. The option to gradually return to a regular work schedule after a medical leave.

Source: Bank of America

Although the relationship between employment and psychological contracts is complex, designing as much flexibility into the legal contracts as possible and carefully managing the implicit promises of the psychological contract contribute to an organisation's morphing capability. Trader Joe's, a US food retailer, recognises the value of carefully managing the psychological contract, as the employee testimony below implies.

TRADER JOE'S

Crew Member

Meet Charlotte!
With a Bachelors degree in Fitness and a desire to become a Physical Therapist, it might seem odd to find Charlotte working checkout at her local Trader Joe's. But according to Charlotte, it all makes sense. "Trader Joe's will help me reach my goals by allowing me the flexibility of working different shifts that accommodate my school schedule."

Internal context: workforce demographics
The age structure of the world's population is changing. According to UN estimates, the number of people aged 60 or over will grow from 688m in 2006 to almost 2 billion by 2050, when older people will outnumber children for the first time in history. By 2050 one person in five will be aged 60 or over. The percentage of older people is currently much higher in the more developed than in the less developed countries, but the pace of ageing in developing countries is more rapid, and their transition from a young to an old age structure will occur over a shorter period. Average life expectancy at birth has increased by about 20 years since 1950, to its current level of 66 years, though there are startling differences between countries – 30 years in Swaziland, for example, compared with 83 years in Japan. On average, of those surviving to age 60, men can expect to live another 17 years and women an additional 21 years.[22]

These demographic shifts have significant implications for the design of organisations, in terms of leadership succession, knowledge transfer and workforce productivity, and they will continue to do so in the future as emerging talent shortages among younger employees exacerbate these problems.[23] A report commissioned by IBM and the American Society for Training and Development (ASTD) comments that human resources managers have identified that:[24]

Knowledge transfer, removing barriers to learning for mature workers, and meeting the needs of the next generation of employees [are] their greatest challenges related to changing workforce demographics. Yet, less than half think their organisations are doing enough to tackle these challenges, and only about 40% believe their companies are addressing their overall skill and capacity needs over the next three to five years. These findings suggest that many organisations remain unprepared for workforce shifts of potentially "tectonic" magnitude.

Similarly, a 2005 study by the AARP, a US organisation aimed at improving the quality of life for people as they age, and human-resources consultants Towers Perrin says that employees aged 50 and over will account for 20% of the US workforce by 2012, compared with 13% in 2007. As a result firms are adapting their employment policies and practices to meet the desires of older workers. To acknowledge the companies that do this well, the AARP's Annual Best Employers Program for Workers Over 50 highlights 50 companies and organisations "whose best practices and policies for addressing aging workforce issues are roadmaps for the workplaces of tomorrow".[25] Two companies exemplify the qualities that AARP is looking for:

- John Deere, a manufacturer of industrial equipment and commercial machinery, offers comprehensive health benefits to any employee working at least one hour per week. These include individual and family medical coverage, prescription drug coverage, vision and dental insurance as well as long-term care coverage. The company also offers a phased retirement programme and offers retirees the following work arrangements: temporary work assignments, consulting/contract work, telecommuting as well as part-time and full-time work.
- Centegra Health System has made significant changes to its benefits plan and services to promote work–life balance over the past three years. For example, it offers associates their own complimentary personalised concierge service which takes care of dry cleaning, oil changes, car washes, restaurant reservations, gift wrapping and purchase, floral delivery, as well as shoe and watch repair. The hospital also allows employees to phase into retirement through flexible scheduling options such as part-time work, summers off and weekend programmes.

Building the capability to morph

Leaders need to accept that their current organisation design will inevitably give way to a future design, and would do even better if they understood and acted on the necessity to be continuously and consciously thinking about the whole organisation design. They should also grasp the fact that designs must be constructed to respond to dynamic environments and that building adaptive capability into any design is a necessary part of the process. Unfortunately, they rarely do. For a number of reasons many leaders:[26]

- do not know enough about the processes and theories for designing effective organisations and fail to appreciate the range of options open to them;
- choose designs that are more political and more complex than they need be, less than optimal because they exclude important knowledge crucial to the success of a new organisational design, and resisted when implemented;
- work on a design that solves a specific symptom rather than the underlying cause giving rise to it (identifying the root cause of issues and responding to these is crucial to the success of an organisational design project);
- separate a new design from their organisation's strategy and external environment, when they should realise that a good organisation design is a means for implementing strategy and can also open up new strategic options;
- fail to recognise how much of their time and active involvement is required in organisational design work and cannot delegate their role to consultants;
- overlook the fact that organisational design is a multi-stage process during which the organisation must continue to operate and change, so the design process must synchronise with the dynamic of the organisation.

The capacity to overcome some of these leadership obstacles, execute in the present and adapt to the future requires leaders and designers to work on the shelf-life principle; invest in formal and informal research and development; and most importantly do everything in their power to develop and enable adaptive capabilities in the workforce.

Working on the shelf-life principle

This means acknowledging that an enterprise has a shelf life in a particular form and can last only so long before it becomes obsolete. In *A History of American Business*, C. Joseph Pusateri lists the 25 largest US corporations in 1917, 1957 and 1986.[27] Of the 25 corporations in the 1917 list, 13 made it into the 1957 list. Only seven – if US Steel and USX are treated as the same firm – made it into the 1986 list. Only 12 firms on the 1957 list made it to the 1986 list:[28]

> At the top of the 1917 list is U.S. Steel. When formed through the merger of eight large steel firms in 1901, U.S. Steel became the world's largest private business: it had a total capitalisation of $1.4 billion and accounted for 65.7% of all steel sales in the United States. By 1917, U.S. Steel had assets valued at over $2.4 billion, more than four times the assets of Standard Oil of New Jersey [Exxon], the next largest corporation. But U.S. Steel's market share was down to 45%. Forty years later, U.S. Steel was only the third largest company and its market share was less than 30%. Today U.S. Steel is no longer U.S. Steel but USX, and has a market share in steel of less than 10%, receives more revenue from petroleum than steel, and is number 121 in the list of the largest U.S. corporations, ranked by assets. The moral of the U.S. Steel story applies to all corporations: no firm is impervious to market competition.

Of the original 100 companies in 1917, only 13 still survive independently today, and of these most have not achieved high performance in their sectors or relative to the market overall.[29]

One way of thinking about shelf life is in terms of an organisational life cycle. Typically, it takes the form of an S curve (see Figure 9.2), sometimes called the sigmoid curve.

There is a theory that the organisational maturing and decline cycle can be interrupted by jumping into another sigmoid curve at an appropriate point, thus avoiding the inevitability of decline. The jump is usually made at the midpoint of the maturity phase before the upwards curve reaches its peak and starts to head down (see Figure 9.3).

However, this is hard to do for two reasons: it is difficult to judge when an organisation is at the midpoint; and when things appear to be going well, as they typically do in the first half of the maturity phase, there is usually little incentive to change.

It therefore requires long-term planning – for example, the type of

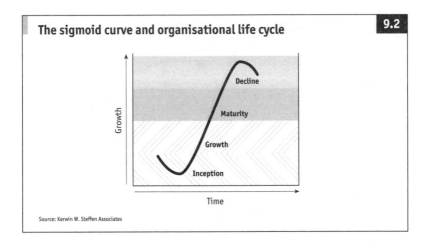

The sigmoid curve and organisational life cycle `9.2`

Source: Kerwin W. Steffen Associates

scenario planning that was developed by companies such as Shell in the 1970s. Glen Meakem, founder and CEO of FreeMarkets (acquired by Ariba in 2004), which created business-to-business online auctions, was asked what he felt when he realised that his business model had become out of date:[30]

> It was painful, but whether you're running a start-up or an established company, there are turning points where you need to assess critically how you're positioned and ask, "Is the market coming toward us or running away from us?" And thank God we did what we did. And it's hard, because you need to move. Your board and your investors and everybody in the company need to face up to it. We made a big bet and we just ran with it. As CEO, you can't be scared of making bold decisions. It's tough, but you have to be able to do it.

Making a decision to review an organisation's core values is equally tough. One organisation which regularly reviews its core values is IAP2 (International Association for Public Participation), a non-profit organisation that working "through its members, helps organisations and communities around the world improve their decisions by involving those people who are affected by those decisions". It has a set of core values that define the organisation's public participation practice.[31]

The IAP2's board of directors has adopted a policy of formally reviewing the association's core values every five years with the objective of maintaining their relevance in changing contexts. To do this it has established

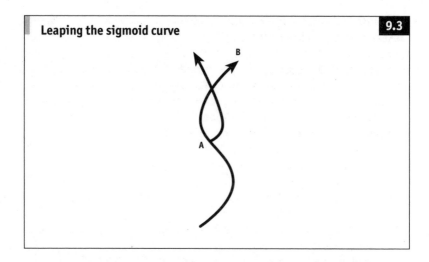

Leaping the sigmoid curve 9.3

a core value working group and invites contributions to the discussion on core values from its members around the world. During 2006, after significant participation and input from members, the decision was made to reword Core Value 1 from:

> The public should have a say in decisions about actions that could affect their lives.

to:

> Public participation is based on the belief that those who are affected by a decision have a right to be involved in the decision-making process.

This may not appear to be a significant shift, but the impact of the change affects many aspects of IAP2's organisation as it focuses on defending the "right" of the public to be involved in the decision-making process rather than supporting their "say" in it.

Difficult as it is to leap to a new sigmoid curve and assess core operating values for continuing relevance, these two activities contribute to thinking of an organisation design as having a shelf life. With this thought it becomes easier to morph towards new and improved organisation designs.

Investing in formal and informal research and development

Research and development (R&D) activity is also important if organisations are to be capable of adapting. Most large enterprises have their own R&D groups keeping an eye on the future, usually in a combination of three ways: by using a variety of techniques to look ahead, by assessing consumer behaviour, and by analysing economic, financial, and other data. Ian Pearson, a member of the foresight and futurology group at telecommunications company BT, explains his role:[32]

> I work as a futurologist. I study the future. My day-to-day work, currently with BT, involves tracking developments across the whole field of technology and society, figuring out where it is all going next, and how that will affect our everyday lives. I take account of as many technology and social factors as possible. My main tools are a strong background in science and engineering, trends analysis, common sense, reasonable business acumen, knowing when to listen to other people, and a lot of thinking. I usually get it right, but since the future is never totally predictable, I sometimes get it wrong too, about 15% of the time. But I specialise in doing long term stuff. ...
>
> Although I use the slightly wacky sounding title of futurologist, I'm just an engineer making logical deductions about tomorrow based on things we can already see happening. For example, if someone is investing heavily in a particular development, and there aren't any obvious barriers to success, there is a good chance that they will succeed in due course. Keeping up with externals such as political, economic and social factors helps improve judgement as to whether products are likely to succeed, and how they might be used. Anyone with reasonable intelligence can do it, but it takes a lot of time to internalise the very many factors involved before you start getting it right. I learned from experience that computers are of limited use, because although there are many computer tools on the market, it usually takes longer to explain all the interconnections to a program than it does to analyse them yourself. I make no claim to be able to predict the future with absolute accuracy, but I think of it as like driving a car through fog. You can't see a very clear picture of what is ahead, and sometimes you will misinterpret an apparent shape in the distance, but few of us would drive through fog without bothering to look out the window. Blurred vision is a lot better than none at all! The same is true for business, which is why BT employs me.

As well as in-company R&D activity, a number of profit and non-profit organisations have been established for those seeking insights into what might be ahead. In the UK, for example, Demos, the Global Ideas Bank and the Centre for Future Studies are three mentioned in an article in the *Independent*, a UK newspaper, listing 20 of the UK's top think-tanks, only one of which (at BT) was a company in-house unit.[33]

R&D also occurs through open-source (see Glossary) and similar techniques, whereby consumers or others play an active role in process redesign, product development strategies, new channel development and solving complex problems. Linux software development is one example (see www.linux-foundation.org). Research by the Forrester Group indicates that there will be increasing expansion in the role that consumers play in the development and execution of new products, services and processes (see Figure 9.4).

If they are to continuously adapt, organisations must be future aware, and then use not just their own expertise but the input of others (amateurs, consumers) to help them work through ways of meeting the future in good shape.

Enabling adaptive capabilities in the workforce

It is not only at an organisational level that adaptive capability needs to be generated and regenerated. Individual employees must also be able to meet the future with equanimity and imagination. One way of encouraging this is to minimise the number of behavioural rules necessary to keep the enterprise operational yet adaptive.

In 1986 Craig Reynolds was looking for a way to model the flocking behaviour of birds. He was looking for a small set of behavioural rules to achieve the desired result and managed to come up with just three:[34]

1 Separation: steer to avoid crowding local flock mates.
2 Alignment: steer towards the average heading of local flock mates.
3 Cohesion: steer to move toward the average position of local flock mates.

These three rules are sufficient to generate flocking behaviour (see Figure 9.5 on page 270). Note that:

- there is no leader who says "follow me" – at any time any flock member could be the leader;
- each member follows the same rules – there is no hierarchy of rules;

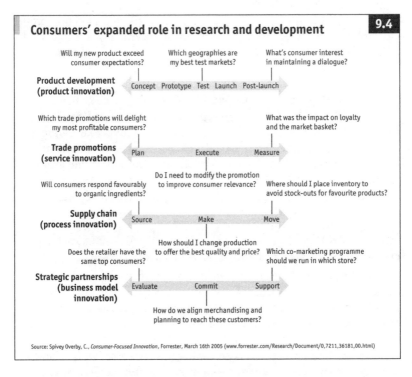

Consumers' expanded role in research and development `9.4`

Will my new product exceed consumer expectations?
Which geographies are my best test markets?
What's consumer interest in maintaining a dialogue?

Product development (product innovation)
Concept Prototype Test Launch Post-launch

Which trade promotions will delight my most profitable consumers?
What was the impact on loyalty and the market basket?

Trade promotions (service innovation)
Plan   Execute   Measure

Do I need to modify the promotion to improve consumer relevance?

Will consumers respond favourably to organic ingredients?
Where should I place inventory to avoid stock-outs for favourite products?

Supply chain (process innovation)
Source   Make   Move

How should I change production to offer the best quality and price?

Does the retailer have the same top consumers?
Which co-marketing programme should we run in which store?

Strategic partnerships (business model innovation)
Evaluate   Commit   Support

How do we align merchandising and planning to reach these customers?

Source: Spivey Overby, C., *Consumer-Focused Innovation*, Forrester, March 16th 2005 (www.forrester.com/Research/Document/0,7211,36181,00.html)

- each member is concerned only with what its neighbours are doing – there is no attempt to try to comprehend the behaviour of the whole;
- the rules are not directly concerned with global-level behaviour. The appearance of flocking is an "emergent" property resulting from all of the mutual interactions between members.

Such simple rules when applied to an organisation make for flexibility, autonomy and adaptability without losing overall control. They make organisational behaviour visible, and once articulated it becomes possible to discuss whether the behaviours they generate are the ones the organisation wants or needs in order to keep adapting or whether design work should aim to change them.

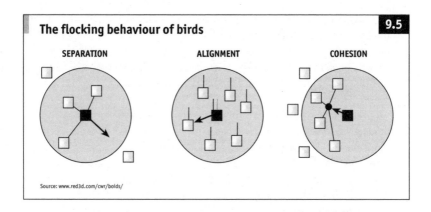

The flocking behaviour of birds 9.5

SEPARATION   ALIGNMENT   COHESION

Source: www.red3d.com/cwr/boids/

CASE STUDY: how to keep an organisation continuously morphing

Margaret Johns, vice president of a forecasting firm, faced the conference. Her audience of business administration students had invited her to present her views on how organisations could meet the future. Her strongly held view was that businesses have to have the capacity to be continuously transformable. This is what she said.

We're not living in a fairy story where the frog gets turned into a prince and that's it. We're living in a world where what we are today is not what we're going to be tomorrow and that's different again from what we're going to be the following day. This requires a different way of thinking but unless we take that path our company will be in trouble.

I learned this early in my career when I worked for Cummins Engine Company. Theirs is an interesting story that is still continuing. In the early 1980s, when I joined Cummins, it was faced with declining sales, new foreign competition and the need for its diesel engines to meet higher environmental standards. It was mature in its market, sales were declining and a number of other things were going wrong. It seemed to be entering its death throes and analysts were beginning to say so.

In the late 1980s three options were presented to the board of directors:

1 To sell the company.
2 A "harvest strategy", that is, consciously running current production out to maximise cash flow.
3 To redesign the company with the goal of improving its product mix and manufacturing processes.

Option three was the one recommended because it was felt that this was the only option that balanced the needs of the long-term shareholders with other stakeholders. Also, it focused the discussion on ways of developing new markets, products and organisational processes. But it was a risky strategy involving heavy investment and a long time lag before it would be possible to see any results.

To cut a long story short, the firm was redesigned to achieve high productivity in new markets, including China and India, with new products in those markets. This was done by deploying techniques and processes around three areas: customer-led improvement; internally led improvement; and internal cultural change, benchmarking the firm against its main competitors. Although I left a year or two into the new design, I stayed in touch with people there and kept up to date with progress, so it did not come as much of a surprise to me when I read in the press:[35]

> Investing in local manufacturing. Grooming managers for the long term. Exporting when it makes sense, and tapping local engineering brainpower. Many multinationals are now emulating these strategies in China and India. Cummins figured it out well before the competition.

During my time at Cummins I learned six things that have informed my style of operating over the years:

1 A strong and involved board of directors and governance process is crucial to success. At Cummins we were able to work with the directors and get their support to take a risky decision which they stuck behind in the long term. It is clear to me that there is real value in developing governance standards and approaches.

2 Business models must adapt to changing circumstances – you have to keep reviewing the design. Taking the principle that form follows function, as the function of the organisation changes so must its form. In the Cummins case the function adapted to being successful in new markets with new products; thus the form had to follow suit. Too often companies get stuck in one design and think that's it for all time.

3 Every single day you have to keep things going and change things. Thinking in terms of projects and initiatives implies a beginning and an end point and will not breed a successful organisation. We had to simultaneously keep Cummins going and manage a new design implementation. We could not do that by thinking too much in terms of projects and initiatives; we had to think of it as a culture and mindset

change that imbued everything we did every day all of the time. I have transferred this thinking into my daily life: each day I try to change either one aspect of a process or the environment it exists in. For example, today I reordered the way I hang clothes in my wardrobe to make the dressing process quicker. Tomorrow, I'm going to change the light bulb in my wardrobe so I can see the colours better.

Successful organisations learn how to interrupt their rituals and habits and look for day-to-day improvement possibilities. Trying out new ways develops adaptability and minimises the fear of change.

4 Enabling people to be part of the next generation of the company requires involving them in what is going on, listening to their ideas, and helping them live their whole lives and not just their work lives. This develops strong employee/employer bonds – the psychological contract holds firm. Helping staff "run hard and dream big" (in Cummins's vocabulary) because they are contributing to their future, the organisation's future and the planet's future is a philosophy I've tried to practise in all the subsequent enterprises that I've worked in.

5 People who can run hard and dream big are generally curious and innovative and these capabilities need managerial nurturing. This is hard to do in many organisations that formalise innovation in things like R&D units. To my mind this doesn't work. Humans are naturally curious and inventive – look at the way a child constantly asks "Why?". Too often organisations squash these capacities even though they are human enterprises. It is hard to genetically code them into forward thinking without having a regenerative culture that comes from empowered people finding expression every day.

6 I discovered that people and organisations benefit from a diverse workforce where differences spark positive energy. In my current organisation, demographic changes are bringing some surprises. For example, younger people are now managing people much older than themselves. Simultaneously, we are consciously recruiting people with a great deal of experience and they are able to mentor and coach the younger ones. No one can claim technology expertise as we are all getting to grips with wave upon wave of new technologies.

So what am I telling people who come to me for career advice? Steve Jobs said it well: "You've got to do what you love." The highest-performing and best-run organisations help people do that. Look for companies that intentionally morph and transform, honour their implicit agreements with people and work responsibly for the future good.

Reflections on this case

Johns's story illustrates how her early work experiences in transforming an organisation helped shape her thinking about how best to guide the morphing process in organisations she worked in subsequently. She chose to work in a forecasting firm as it provided a match to her interests and skills. In her position she can model the way she advises the leaders in her client companies to work. She knows that she must scan her external context for new businesses and models that might catch her unawares if she is not careful. With this her business strategy is focused on opening new markets even as she operates in existing markets. She is aware of her company's responsibility for the future and through various means is assiduous in helping her staff live whole lives, thus keeping the psychological contract strong. She is an advocate of strong and involved governance used wisely. The changes in the demographic profile lead to recruitment and retention challenges, but she is astute enough to see the value in having a diverse workforce where individuals are encouraged to use their strengths to help solve their client's problems. For the most part she is doing a job she loves in an organisation that she is hopeful will show its ability to leap the S curve and morph to meet a successful future.

Tools for this case

Keeping an organisation leaning into the future requires a tolerance (and even seeking out) of chaos combined with a certain discipline in intentionally changing the organisation's design on a continuing basis. Two tools help with this.

Good to Great Diagnostic Tool

The Good to Great diagnostic tool was developed by Jim Collins and is available online (www.jimcollins.com). It is a four-stage tool that assesses the organisation's capability meet the future successfully.

Good to Great Diagnostic Tool

Our research shows that building a great organisation proceeds in four basic stages; each stage consists of two fundamental principles:

STAGE 1: DISCIPLINED PEOPLE
Level 5 Leadership. Level 5 leaders are ambitious first and foremost for the cause,

the organisation, the work – not themselves – and they have the fierce resolve to do whatever it takes to make good on that ambition. A Level 5 leader displays a paradoxical blend of personal humility and professional will.

First Who ... Then What. Those who build great organisations make sure they have the right people on the bus, the wrong people off the bus, and the right people in the key seats before they figure out where to drive the bus. They always think first about "who" and then about what.

STAGE 2: DISCIPLINED THOUGHT

Confront the Brutal Facts – the Stockdale Paradox. Retain unwavering faith that you can and will prevail in the end, regardless of the difficulties, AND AT THE SAME TIME have the discipline to confront the most brutal facts of your current reality, whatever they might be.

The Hedgehog Concept. Greatness comes about by a series of good decisions consistent with a simple, coherent concept – a "Hedgehog Concept". The Hedgehog Concept is an operating model that reflects understanding of three intersecting circles: what you can be the best in the world at, what you are deeply passionate about, and what best drives your economic or resource engine.

STAGE 3: DISCIPLINED ACTION

Culture of Discipline. Disciplined people who engage in disciplined thought and who take disciplined action – operating with freedom within a framework of responsibilities – this is the cornerstone of a culture that creates greatness. In a culture of discipline, people do not have "jobs"; they have responsibilities.

The Flywheel. In building greatness, there is no single defining action, no grand programme, no one killer innovation, no solitary lucky break, no miracle moment. Rather, the process resembles relentlessly pushing a giant heavy flywheel in one direction, turn upon turn, building momentum until a point of breakthrough, and beyond.

STAGE 4: BUILDING GREATNESS TO LAST

Clock Building, Not Time Telling. Build an organisation that can adapt through multiple generations of leaders; the exact opposite of being built around a single great leader, great idea or specific programme. Build catalytic mechanisms to stimulate progress, rather than acting as a charismatic force of personality to drive progress.

Preserve the Core and Stimulate Progress. Adherence to core values combined with a willingness to challenge and change everything except those core values – keeping clear the distinction between "what we stand for" (which should never change) and "how we do things" (which should never stop changing). Great companies have a

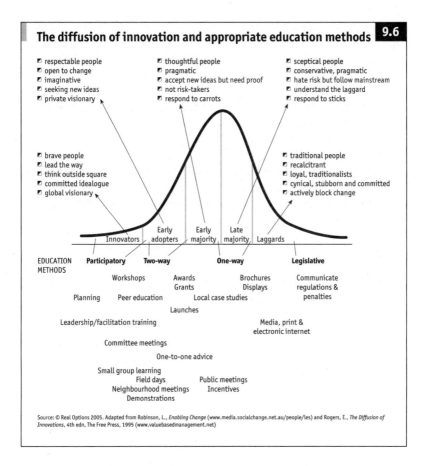

The diffusion of innovation and appropriate education methods `9.6`

- respectable people
- open to change
- imaginative
- seeking new ideas
- private visionary

- thoughtful people
- pragmatic
- accept new ideas but need proof
- not risk-takers
- respond to carrots

- sceptical people
- conservative, pragmatic
- hate risk but follow mainstream
- understand the laggard
- respond to sticks

- brave people
- lead the way
- think outside square
- committed idealogue
- global visionary

- traditional people
- recalcitrant
- loyal, traditionalists
- cynical, stubborn and committed
- actively block change

Innovators / Early adopters / Early majority / Late majority / Laggards

EDUCATION METHODS: **Participatory**   **Two-way**   **One-way**   **Legislative**

Workshops   Awards   Brochures   Communicate
Grants   Displays   regulations &
penalties
Planning   Peer education   Local case studies
Launches

Leadership/facilitation training   Media, print &
electronic internet

Committee meetings

One-to-one advice

Small group learning
Field days   Public meetings
Neighbourhood meetings   Incentives
Demonstrations

Source: © Real Options 2005. Adapted from Robinson, L., *Enabling Change* (www.media.socialchange.net.au/people/les) and Rogers, E., *The Diffusion of Innovations*, 4th edn, The Free Press, 1995 (www.valuebasedmanagement.net)

purpose – a reason for being – that goes far beyond just making money, and they translate this purpose into BHAGs (Big Hairy Audacious Goals) to stimulate progress.

Source: www.jimcollins.com

The diffusion of innovation and appropriate education methods

This tool (Figure 9.6) provides a snapshot of the type of activity needed to keep an organisation's constituents moving along the adoption and adaptation curve.

Summary

This chapter begins with the premise that no organisation design could or should last forever. Indeed, it is better to think that any design is transitory and must have the built-in capability to morph to a different design without causing disruption to the operation of the enterprise.

Getting this right in an environment that has multiple challenges both internally and externally is hard. But certain approaches and techniques employed in the development and implementation of the design can help move things in the right direction.

Since it seems that the forecast for most companies is continued chaos with a chance of disaster, learning to handle this successfully or accept the outcomes is a prerequisite for boards, leaders and the workforce.

Notes

General

The URLs for the websites referred to in this book were correct and active at the time of going to press. However, the author and the publisher cannot guarantee that they will remain active or that the content they relate to will not change.

The Economist house style is to use British spelling. In this book, American spelling has been retained in quotations from American sources.

All unattributed charts are by the author.

1 Introducing organisation design

1 www.bdo.co.uk/BDOSH/Website/bdouk/websiteContent. nsf/vAll/023F13FFCD2B07E380257243005538F2?OpenDocument
2 Rheingold, J., "Still Angry After All These Years", *Fast Company*, October 2003.
3 Senge, P.M., *The Fifth Discipline: the Art and Practice of the Learning Organization*, Currency, 2006.
4 Lawrence, E., *Strategic Thinking: A Discussion Paper*, Personnel Development and Resourcing Group, Research and Communications Branch, Public Service Commission of Canada, 1999 (archived at epe.lac-bac. gc.ca/100/200/301/psc-cfp/strategic_thinking-e/pdf/strathink_e.pdf).
5 www.gore.com
6 www.creatingthe21stcentury.org/Larry-IIB-about-work.html
7 Kotter, J., "Leading Change: Why Transformation Efforts Fail", *Harvard Business Review*, March–April 1995.
8 Deutchsman, A., "The Fabric of Creativity", *Fast Company*, December 2004.
9 Covey, S., *Seven Habits of Highly Effective People*, Simon & Schuster, 1999.
10 Gupta, R. and Wendler, J., "Leading change: An interview with the CEO of P&G", *McKinsey Quarterly*, August 2005.
11 Ibid.
12 Ibid.

13 Weisbord, M. and Janoff, S., "Faster, Shorter, Cheaper May Be Simple; It's Never Easy", *The Journal of Applied Behavioral Science*, Vol. XX, No. X, 2004 (www.futuresearch.net/news/articles/JABS273248.pdf).
14 Ibid.

2 Models, approaches and designs

1 Box, G.E.P., "Robustness in the strategy of scientific model building", in Launer, R.L. and Wilkinson, G.N. (eds), *Robustness in statistics*, Academic Press, New York, 1979, pp. 201-36.
2 www.ichnet.org/glossary.htm
3 Magretta, J., "Why Business Models Matter", *Harvard Business Review*, May 2002.
4 Friedman, T., *The World is Flat*, Farrar, Straus and Giroux, 2005, p. 180.
5 Goold, M. and Campbell, A., "Do You Have a Well-Designed Organization?", *Harvard Business Review*, March 2002.
6 Nadler, D. and Tushman, M., "The Organisation of the Future: Strategic Imperatives and Core Competencies for the 21st Century", *Organisational Dynamics*, Vol. 28, Issue 1, Summer 1999, pp. 45-60.
7 Adams, M.G., *Change Your Questions, Change Your Life: 7 Powerful Tools for Life & Work*, Berrett-Koehler Publishers, 2004.

3 Organisational structures

1 moneycentral.msn.com/content/P136436.asp, posted January 12th 2005.
2 For a challenge to Mayo's work see Stewart, M., "The Management Myth", *Atlantic Monthly*, June 2006.
3 Senge, P., Scharmer, C.O., Jaworksi, J. and Flowers, B.S., *Presence: Exploring Profound Change in People, Organisations and Society*, Nicholas Brealey Publishing, 2005.
4 Morgan, G., *Imaginization: New Mindsets for Seeing, Organizing, and Managing*, Berret-Koehler Publications and Sage Publications, 1997.
5 De Geus, A., *The Living Company*, Harvard Business School Press, 1997.
6 Senge, P. *et al.*, op. cit.
7 Senge, P., Scharmer, C.O., Jaworski, J., Flowers, B.S., "Awakening Faith in an Alternative Future", *Reflections*, Vol. 5, No. 7, 2004.
8 Ibid.
9 www.chevron.com/news/archive/chevron_speech/1998/98-1-28.asp

10 Galbraith, J.R., *Designing a Reconfigurable Organisation*, undated. Available from www.jaygalbraith.com/resources/reconfigurable_org. pdf

11 Drucker, P., *Management: Tasks, Responsibilities, Practices*, HarperBusiness, 1993.

12 "Take a deep breath", *The Economist*, January 19th 2006.

13 Goold, M. and Campbell, A., op. cit.

14 Copyright 1998 Richard M. DiGeorgio & Associates. All Rights Reserved (www.change-management.net/articlespan.htm)

15 Simons, R., *Levers of Organization Design*, Harvard Business School Press, 2005.

16 Simons, R., "Designing High Performance Jobs", *Harvard Business Review*, July–August 2005.

4 Planning and sequencing the organisation design

1 Weisbord, M. and Janoff, S., op. cit.

2 Office of Government Commerce, Successful Delivery Toolkit (www. ogc.gov.uk/sdtoolkit). This website is a source of excellent practical information on running successful projects.

3 Hanessian, B. and Sierra, C., "Leading a Turnaround: An Interview with the Chairman of D&B", *McKinsey Quarterly*, No. 2, 2005.

4 Van Exel, A. and Fisher, S., *Winning Internal Support for United's New Airline*, Melcrum Publishing, 2005.

5 Hanessian and Sierra, op. cit.

6 Ghislanzoni, G. and Shearn, J., "Leading Change: An Interview with the CEO of Banca Intesa", *McKinsey Quarterly*, No. 3, 2005.

7 London, S., "Why the bunker mentality has become a corporate liability", *Financial Times*, September 14th 2005.

8 Davenport, T.H., "Competing on Analytics", *Harvard Business Review*, January 2006.

9 Ibid.

5 Measurement

1 For a fascinating discussion on this, see Taleb, N.N., *Fooled by Randomness*, Random House, 2005.

2 Wieck, K., *Sensemaking in Organizations*, Sage Publications, 1995.

3 Reichheld, F.F., "The One Number You Need to Grow", *Harvard Business Review*, December 2003.

4 It was similar to the Satmetrix Customer Acid Test (www. loyaltyrules.com/loyaltyrules/acid_test_customer.html).

5 Diski, J., *Rainforest*, Penguin Books, 1987.
6 Institute of Chartered Accountants in England and Wales, *Guide to professional ethics*, Retrieved on June 2nd 2006 from www.icaew. co.uk/viewer/index.cfm?AUB=TB2I_31547, Chapter 2.0 Section A
7 AA1000 Stakeholder Engagement Standard.
8 *The Stakeholder Engagement Manual, Volume 2: The Practitioner's Handbook on Stakeholder Engagement*, available from www. accountability.org.uk
9 UK National Audit Office, *Choosing the right FABRIC: A framework for performance information*, March 2001 (www.nao.gov.uk).
10 www.spo.noaa.gov/pdfs/PerfGuidelinesOnly_030805.pdf

6 Stakeholder engagement

1 www.j-sainsbury.co.uk/cr/index.asp?pageid=112
2 Wylie, I., "Talk to Our Customers? Are You Crazy?", *Fast Company*, July 2006.
3 www.triodos.co.uk/uk/about_triodos/organisation/people_at_triodos/ ?lang=
4 Mayer, R.C., Davis, J.H. and Schoorman, F.D., "An integrative model of organizational trust", *Academy of Management Review*, 20, 1995, pp. 709–34.
5 www.vodafone.com (page on "Earning the Trust of Customers" within the Corporate Responsibility section)
6 "For whom the Dell tolls", *The Economist*, May 11th 2006.
7 *American-Statesman*, May 15th 2006.
8 www.businessweek.com/print/technology/content/may2006/ tc20060519_475997.htm
9 www.edelman.com/news/ShowOne.asp?ID=102
10 One of these is Line, R. *et al.*, "The Production of Trust During Organisational Change", *Journal of Change Management*, Vol. 5, No. 2, June 2005, pp. 221–45.
11 Ibid.
12 Adapted from Bellman, G., *The Consultants Calling*, Jossey-Bass, 2002.
13 www.ibm.com/ibm/values/us/
14 Reichheld, F.F., "The Loyalty Effect: The Forces of Loyalty vs. Chaos", *Bain Strategy Brief*, Essay No. 4, April 1998 (www.bain.com/bainweb/ publications/publications_detail.asp?id=21&menu_url=publications_ results.asp).

15 Marsden, P., Samson, A. and Upton, N., *Advocacy Drives Growth: customer advocacy drives UK business growth*, LSE Institute of Social Psychology, 2005.
16 www.reliefresources.com
17 Ibid.
18 Cohen, B. and Warwick, M., *Values-Driven Business*, Berrett-Koehler, 2006.
19 "Life beyond Pay", *The Economist*, June 15th 2006.
20 Urban, G.L., "The Emerging Era of Customer Advocacy", *MIT Sloan Management Review*, Winter 2004.
21 www.pampers.com
22 mopat405, April 4th 2005, www.epinions.com
23 "Buzz Marketing", *BusinessWeek Online*, July 30th 2001.
24 "How to Communicate Business Strategy to Employees", www.melcrum.com/store/products/product.shtml?id=2900, January 2006.
25 Power, S., "Top Volkswagen Executive Tries US-Style Turnaround Tactics", *Wall Street Journal*, July 18th 2006.
26 Labovitz, G. and Rosansky, V., *The Power of Alignment: How Great Companies Stay Centered and Accomplish Extraordinary Things*, Wiley, 1997.

7 Leadership and organisation design

1 Evans, P. and Wolf, B., "Collaboration Rules", *Harvard Business Review*, July–August 2005.
2 Adapted from Morgan, G., *Images of Organization*, Sage Publications, 1997.
3 French, J.P.R. Jr and Raven, B., "The bases of social power", in Cartwright D. and Zander A. (eds), *Group Dynamics*, Harper and Row, 1960, pp. 607–23.
4 Kahn, M., "Unions Take Wal-Mart to Court of Public Opinion", Reuters, August 30th 2005.
5 September 20th 2001, Profile: British Airways, news.bbc.co.uk/2/hi/business/1554140.stm
6 Roach, J., "NASA Budget Diverts Funds From Science to Spaceships", *National Geographic News*, February 8th 2006.
7 Borrus, A. and Arndt, M., "Executive pay: Labor strikes back", *BusinessWeek Online*, May 26th 2003 (www.businessweek.com/magazine/content/03_21/b3834075.htm).
8 Stanford, N., *Fitting in and Getting On: the performance of senior executives joining new companies*, unpublished PhD thesis, 2002.

9 Schein, E.H., "Organizational culture and leadership", in Shafritz, J. and Ott, J.S. (eds), *Classics of Organization Theory*, Harcourt College Publishers, 2001.

10 "How Al Dunlap Self Destructed", *Business Week*, June 25th 1998.

11 www.hedricksmith.com/site_bottomline/html/dunlap.html

12 Carroll, M., *Awake at Work*, Shambhala, 2006.

13 Dickey, B., "NASA'S Next Step", *Government Executive*, April 15th 2004.

14 Blanchard, K. and Zigami, P., *Leadership and the One Minute Manager: Increasing Effectiveness Through Situational Leadership*, William Morrow, 1999.

15 Morgan, G., *Images of Organization*, op. cit.

16 Kotter, J., op. cit.

17 CNN, "Independence Day Lift-off for Discovery", July 4th 2006 (www.cnn.com/2006/TECH/space/07/04/shuttle.launch/index.html).

18 Malik, T., "Landing Day: Space Shuttle Discovery Returns to Earth", July 17th 2006 (www.space.com/missionlaunches/060717_discovery_return.html).

19 www.dreamflight.org

20 Meyerson, D.E., *Tempered Radicals*, Harvard Business School Press, 2001.

21 Meyerson, D.E., "Radical Change the Quiet Way", *Harvard Business Review*, October 2001.

22 Weiss, A., *"Good enough" isn't enough: Nine Challenges for Companies that Choose to be Great*, Amacom, 1999.

23 Taylor, S.T., "Whistleblowers End Up Lonesome", *Orlando Sentinel Online*, August 18th 2002.

24 Heller, J., *Something Happened*, Vintage, 1995.

25 Harvey, J.B., *The Abilene Paradox*, Jossey-Bass, 1996.

26 Kruger, P. and Mieszkowski, K., "Stop the Fight", *Fast Company*, August 1998.

27 See www.belbin.com/ for an explanation of Belbin's Team Roles (one of several methods of assessing the profile of a team).

28 Adapted from Spangler, B., "Best Alternative to a Negotiated Agreement (BATNA)", in Burgess, G. and Burgess, H. (eds), *Beyond Intractability*, Conflict Research Consortium, University of Colorado, posted June 2003 (www.beyondintractability.org/essay/batna).

29 Fisher, R. and Ury, W.L., *Getting to Yes: Negotiating Agreement Without Giving In*, 2nd edn, Penguin Books, 1991.

30 Boyce, N., *Wayne Hale's Insider Guide to NASA*, June 30th
   2006. Retrieved from www.npr.org/templates/story/story.
   php?storyId=5522536

8 Culture and group processes

1 This is a widely quoted advertisement that makes good reading but
  to date no one has found its original publication. The closest to it
  appears to be a letter from Ernest Shackleton printed in *The Times* on
  December 29th 1913, p. 6.
2 Shackleton, E., *South*, The Lyons Press, 1998.
3 Watkins, P., "Lost in the Sea of Ice", *The Times*, August 26th 2006, in a
  review of Tyler-Lewis, K., *The Lost Men*, Bloomsbury, 2006.
4 Shackleton, op. cit.
5 Schein, E.H., *The Corporate Culture Survival Guide*, Jossey-Bass, 1999.
6 Retrieved from abc.go.com/primetime/supernanny/about.html
7 "Face Value: The Cutting Edge", *The Economist*, October 7th 2006.
8 Woodward, B., "State of Denial (excerpt)", *Newsweek*, October 9th
  2006.
9 Hughes, D., "NAB chief urges staff to share the vision", *Sydney
  Morning Herald*, May 22nd 2004.
10 Kean, D., "Profile: Helen Fraser", *The Bookseller*, Issue 5076, May 5th
   2003.
11 Egan, G., *Working the Shadow Side*, Jossey-Bass, 1994, p. 4.
12 Bevan, J., *The Rise and Fall of Marks & Spencer*, Profile Books, 2007.
13 Brechin, A., Brown, H. and Eby, M. (eds), *Critical Practice in Health and
   Social Care*, The Open University, 2000.
14 www.impm.org
15 Retrieved from www.cbc.ca/bigpicture/human.html
16 Stewart, T.A., "Did You Ever Have to Make Up Your Mind?", *Harvard
   Business Review*, January 2006.
17 Nakashima, E. and Noguchi, Y., "HP CEO Allowed 'Sting' of
   Reporter", *Washington Post*, September 21st 2006.
18 Retrieved from news.com.com/pdf/ne/2006/hurd_remarks.pdf
19 Vroom, V.H. and Jago, A.G., *The New Leadership: Managing
   Participation in Organisations*, Prentice Hall, 1988; Vroom, V.H. and
   Yetton, P.W., *Leadership and Decision Making*, University of Pittsburgh
   Press, 1973.
20 Klein, G., *Sources of Power: How People Make Decisions*, MIT Press,
   1999.
21 Ibid.

22 Ibid.
23 Griscom-Little, A., "The Whole Foods Shebang", *Grist*, December 17th 2004.
24 Drucker, P.F., *The Effective Executive: The Definitive Guide to Getting the Right Things Done*, HarperCollins, 2002.
25 Peter, L.J., *The Peter Principle*, first published in 1969.
26 Salter, C., "Updating the Agenda: MicroStrategy Inc.", *Fast Company*, May 2001.
27 www.kilmann.com/conflict.html
28 See www.belbin.com and the Glossary for more information on the team-role inventory.
29 Aritzeta, A., Ayestaran, S., Swailes, S., "Team Role Preference and Conflict Management Styles", *International Journal of Conflict Management*, Vol. 16, Issue 2, 2005.
30 Weiss, J. and Hughes, J., "Want Collaboration? Accept – and Actively Manage – Conflict", *Harvard Business Review*, March 2005.
31 Deutsch, C.G., "Building the global bank: An interview with Jamie Dimon", *McKinsey Quarterly*, Issue 4, 2006.
32 Lifeskills Publishing, Guidance House, York Road, Thirsk, North Yorkshire, YO7 3BT; tel: 01845 526699; e-mail: info@lifeskillspublishing.co.uk; website: www.lifeskillsintl.net
33 www.lifeskillspublishing.co.uk/businesspubpages/resources.asp
34 Watkins, op. cit.
35 Ibid.

9 Morphing not future proofing

1 www.emacassessments.com/majorapproach.htm (Mackenzie, K.D.).
2 Short for metamorphosing, morphing refers to a technique in which one thing is gradually turned into another.
3 Drucker, P., *Management Challenges for the 21st Century*, Collins, 1999.
4 www.grandcentral.com/
5 bokardo.com/archives/on-the-convergence-of-email-and-chat-google-and-apple-get-it/ November 9th 2006.
6 Kamenetz, A., "The Network Unbound", *Fast Company*, June 2006.
7 Flackery comes from "flack", an informal word for someone who allegedly invents news, or gives out news that people want to hear. In this instance flackery is a synonym for hype.
8 www.clifbar.com/ourstory/document.cfm?location=people

9 "Wal-Mart pulls out of South Korea on 'sluggish' business", *Taipei Times*, May 23rd 2006 (www.taipeitimes. com/News/worldbiz/archives/2006/05/23/2003309675).

10 www.motorola.com/mediacenter/news/detail. jsp?globalObjectId=8419_8350_23#

11 Corliss, B., "Not Lost in Translation", *Herald Net*, April 20th 2006 (www.heraldnet.com/stories/06/04/20/100bus_hubiz001.cfm).

12 www.globalpolicy.org/globaliz/cultural/2003/0710starbucks.htm

13 www.starbucks.com/aboutus/pressdesc.asp?id=705

14 Claessens, S., *Global Corporate Governance Forum Focus 1*, World Bank, 2003 (Foreword by Sir Adrian Cadbury).

15 Summarised from Claessens, op. cit., p. 7.

16 The National Association of Corporate Directors (www.nacdonline. org) provides a list of others.

17 www.nacdonline.org/FAQ/details.asp?faq=1#8

18 www.businessroundtable.org/newsroom/document.aspx?qs=5946BF 807822B0F1AD1458022FB51711FCF53CE Corporate Governance Task Force chairman Steve Odland, Speech to the FBI Corporate Fraud Training Conference on "Ethics, Corporations and Fraud", Boston, Massachusetts, August 25th 2005.

19 Nordstrom, K.A. and Ridderstrale, J., commenting on their book *Karaoke Capitalism: Managing for Mankind*, Pitman Publishing, 2004 (see www.funkybusiness.com/funky).

20 Guest, D.E. and Conway, N., *Pressure at work and the psychological contract*, CIPD, 2002.

21 Conway, N. and Briner, R.B., *Understanding Psychological Contracts at Work*, Oxford University Press, 2005.

22 www.mercerhr.com/referencecontent.jhtml?idContent=1231640

23 www.un.org/esa/population/publications/ageing/ageing2006chart. pdf

24 www-03.ibm.com/press/us/en/pressrelease/20387.wss

25 www.aarp.org/states/il/il-news/aarp_honors_best_employers_for_ worker_over_50.html

26 Adapted from *Major Approaches to Organizational Design*, www. emacassessments.com/majorapproach.htm (Mackenzie, K.D.).

27 C. Joseph Pusateri, *A History of American Business*, 2nd edn, Harlan Davidson, 1988.

28 www.fee.org/publications/the-freeman/article.asp?aid=2917; Matthews, D., "Does Big Mean Bad? The Economic Power of Corporations", *The Freeman*, Vol. 46, No. 2, 1996.

29 Beinhocker, E.D., "The Adaptable Corporation", *The McKinsey Quarterly*, No. 2, 2006.
30 "Market Makers Bid for Success", Harvard Business School: Working Knowledge for Business Leaders, May 30th 2000 (hbswk.hbs.edu/item/1540.html).
31 www.iap2.org/displaycommon.cfm?an=3
32 www.btinternet.com/~ian.pearson/
33 news.independent.co.uk/uk/this_britain/article9181.ece
34 www.red3d.com/cwr/boids/
35 www.businessweek.com/magazine/content/05_34/b3948463.htm; Engardio, P. and Arndt, M., "How Cummins Does It", *BusinessWeek Online*, August 22nd 2005.

Appendix 1
Organisation design models

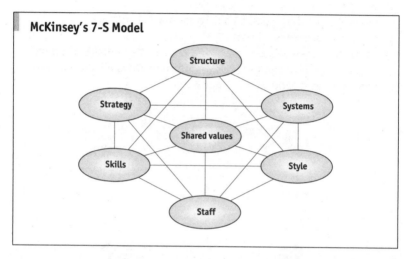

McKinsey's 7-S Model

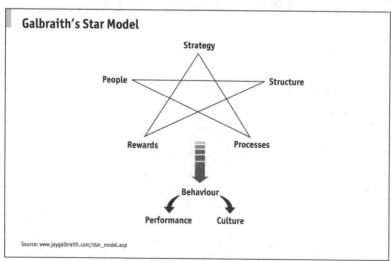

Galbraith's Star Model

Source: www.jaygalbraith.com/star_model.asp

Weisbord's Six Box Model

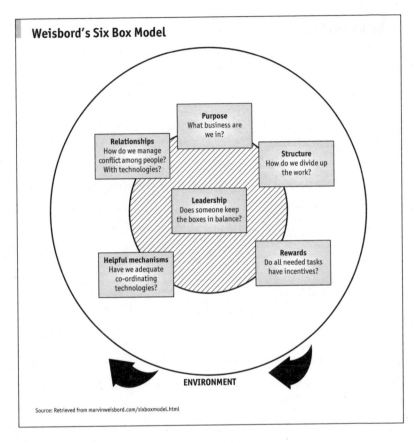

Source: Retrieved from marvinweisbord.com/sixboxmodel.html

Nadler and Tushman's Congruence Model

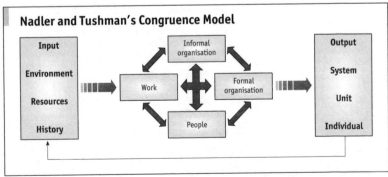

Burke-Litwin Causal Model

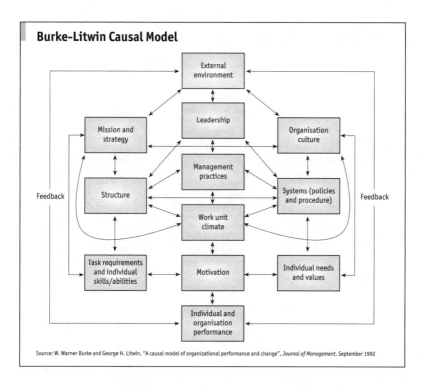

Source: W. Warner Burke and George H. Litwin, "A causal model of organizational performance and change", *Journal of Management*, September 1992

Fractal web

Ethos and values artery

Competitors

Innovations

Project space

Customers

Resources

Chill out

Futures

Externals

Global perspectives

Opportunities

a b c

Heart

e d

Legals

Safeties

Risks

Experiences

Learning

Shareholders

Project space

Local/national perspectives

Intelligence artery

Purpose artery

External landscapes

Source: McMillan, E., "Considering Organisation Structure and Design from a Complexity Paradigm Perspective", in Frizzelle, G. and Richards, H. (eds), *Tackling Industrial Complexity: The Ideas That Make a Difference*, Institute of Manufacturing, University of Cambridge, 2002

Ralph Kilmann's Five Track Model

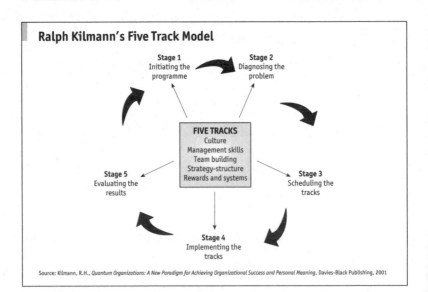

Stage 1
Initiating the programme

Stage 2
Diagnosing the problem

FIVE TRACKS
Culture
Management skills
Team building
Strategy-structure
Rewards and systems

Stage 5
Evaluating the results

Stage 3
Scheduling the tracks

Stage 4
Implementing the tracks

Source: Kilmann, R.H., *Quantum Organizations: A New Paradigm for Achieving Organizational Success and Personal Meaning*, Davies-Black Publishing, 2001

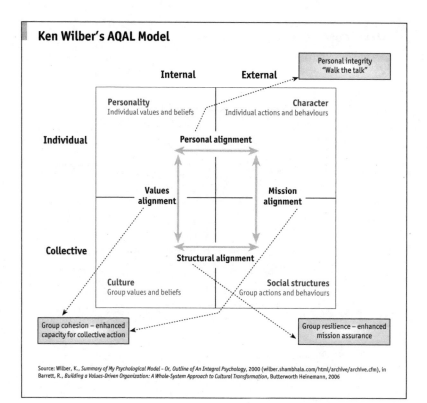

Ken Wilber's AQAL Model

Internal   External

Personal integrity
"Walk the talk"

Personality
Individual values and beliefs

Character
Individual actions and behaviours

Individual

Personal alignment

Values alignment

Mission alignment

Collective

Structural alignment

Culture
Group values and beliefs

Social structures
Group actions and behaviours

Group cohesion – enhanced capacity for collective action

Group resilience – enhanced mission assurance

Source: Wilber, K., *Summary of My Psychological Model – Or, Outline of An Integral Psychology*, 2000 (wilber.shambhala.com/html/archive/archive.cfm), in Barrett, R., *Building a Values-Driven Organization: A Whole-System Approach to Cultural Transformation*, Butterworth Heinemann, 2006

Nadler's Updated Congruence Model

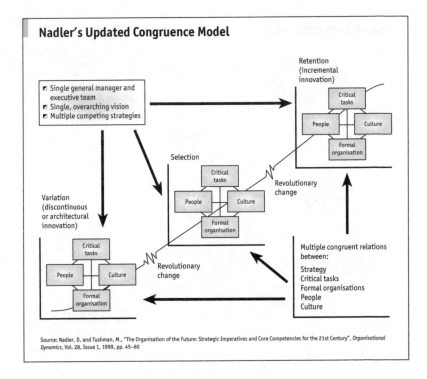

Source: Nadler, D. and Tushman, M., "The Organisation of the Future: Strategic Imperatives and Core Competencies for the 21st Century", *Organisational Dynamics*, Vol. 28, Issue 1, 1999, pp. 45–60

Holonic Enterprise Model

EC: execution control
CE: control execution
E: execution

Source: © World Scientific Publishing Company. Ulieru, M. and Unland, R., "Enabling Technologies for the Creation and Restructuring Process of Emergent Enterprise Alliances", *International Journal of Information Technology & Decision Making*, Vol. 3, No. 1, 2004, pp. 33–60

Appendix 2
Useful sources of information

This listing is a gallimaufry of resources that the author frequently returns to. Thus it represents some personal favourites. It should not be taken either as an exhaustive list or as an endorsement of any of the products, services, or content represented on the websites listed.

Books
Allen, D., *Getting Things Done: the Art of Stress Free Productivity*, Penguin, reprinted 2002.
A refreshing look at self-organisation with enough hints, ideas and common sense to help anyone who has struggled to get more done with less feel slightly less overwhelmed.

Block, P., *Flawless Consulting: A Guide to Getting Your Expertise Used*, 2nd edn, Jossey-Bass/Pfeiffer, 1999.
An introduction to becoming a consultant, taking the reader through the key principles in a lively, straightforward, practical way.

Cameron, J. and Bryan, M., *The Artist's Way at Work*, Quill, 1999.
A series of reflective exercises designed to encourage anyone working in an organisation to learn how to work effectively in it and develop skills in working with others.

Deal, T.E. and Kennedy, A.A., *Corporate Cultures*, Perseus Publishing, 2000.
An established book in the field of corporate culture first published in 1982.

Deal, T.E. and Kennedy, A.A., *The New Corporate Cultures*, Perseus Publishing, 2000.
Revisits corporate cultures in the light of mergers, downsizing and re-engineering.

Drucker, P.F., *The Effective Executive: The Definitive Guide to Getting the*

Right Things Done, HarperCollins, 2002 edition.
A book that is as vivid in its recommendations today as when it was first published in 1967. Some things stay the same, such as not enough time, difficulty in making decisions and making effective contributions.

Gerstner, L.V., *Who Says Elephants Can't Dance? Inside IBM's Historic Turnaround*, HarperBusiness, 2002.
A well told story of leadership, participation and involvement. Easy to read with lots of tips on what worked and what did not work with some lessons to learn from.

Morgan, G., *Images of Organization*, 2nd edn, Sage Publications, 1996.
A more academic book, this is a fascinating survey looking at organisations through different lenses: as psychic prisons, as political systems and as machines, among others.

Prochaska, J.O., Norcross, J.C. and Diclemente, C.C., *Changing for Good*, Quill, 2002.
A grounded and practical approach to helping individuals change their behaviour. Although aimed at personal change, it has assessments, discussions and suggestions that work in organisational settings.

Scott, W.R., *Organizations: Rational, Natural, and Open Systems*, 5th edn, Prentice Hall, 2003.
An overview of key aspects of organisational theory. This is more a textbook than a "how to" book, giving insights into how and why organisations have evolved in the way they have.

Senge, P.M. *et al.*, *The Dance of Change: The Challenges to Sustaining Momentum in Learning Organizations*, Doubleday/Currency, 1999.
A readable and sensible look at methods of helping organisations develop by providing the conditions for individuals to develop.

Stacey, R.D., Griffin, D. and Shaw, P., *Complexity and Management: fad or radical challenge to systems thinking?*, Routledge, 2002.
A discussion of complexity science and its application to organisation development. Provides an alternative to traditional thinking of organisations as systems.

Journals, magazines and newspapers

Business Week
A weekly US print publication covering news, technology, media and national (US) and global business.
Website: www.businessweek.com

E:CO
A quarterly journal published in print and online by the Complexity Society, the Institute for the Study of Coherence and Emergence, and Cognitive Edge, blending academic and practical insights and moderated with academic publishing standards and processes.
Website: www.emergence.org

The Economist
A weekly UK print publication billed as an "authoritative weekly newspaper focusing on international politics and business news and opinion".
Website: www.economist.com

Fast Company
A monthly print magazine aiming to chronicle how companies create and compete, to highlight new business practices, and to showcase the teams and individuals who are reinventing business.
Website: www.fastcompany.com

Financial Times
A daily international business newspaper printed on distinctive salmon-pink broadsheet paper covering UK and international business, finance, economic and political news, comment and analysis.
Website: www.ft.com

Forbes Magazine
A bi-weekly US print magazine featuring in-depth coverage of current business and financial events for "the world's business leaders".
Website: www.Forbes.com

Fortune Magazine
A weekly US print magazine, known especially for its annual features ranking companies by revenue.
Website: money.cnn.com/magazine/fortune

Harvard Business Review
A monthly general management journal with articles including research project findings and their practical application to management issues and opportunities.
Website: harvardbusinessonline.hbsp.harvard.edu/b01/en/hbr/hbr_home.jhtml

Inc. magazine
A monthly print publication covering information and advice on business and management tasks, including marketing, sales, finding capital and managing people.
Website: www.inc.com/

Industry Watch
A quarterly UK publication that investigates recent economic trends and predicts business failures across a range of industry sectors, published by BDO Stoy Hayward.
Website: www.bdo.co.uk/industrywatch

McKinsey Quarterly
A quarterly journal of business management strategy articles, surveys and interviews, covering global business strategy, management and economics.
Website: www.mckinseyquarterly.com/home.aspx

Slate
A daily internet magazine, founded in 1996, with analysis of and commentary on politics, news, culture, business and technology.
Website: www.slate.com

Wall Street Journal
A daily newspaper providing international and national news with a business and financial perspective.
Website: www.wsj.com

Wired
A monthly print journal focusing on the effects of computing and technology on business culture, the economy and politics.
Website: www.wired.com

Organisations and communities

The Business Innovation Factory
A community of innovators collaborating to explore and test better ways to deliver value. BIF members and partners explore business model innovation through a series of experiences designed to get ideas off of the whiteboard and onto the ground as quickly and cost-effectively as possible.
Website: www.businessinnovationfactory.com

The Center for Human Systems
A professional and personal development organisation focusing on improving organisation and human systems.
Website: chumans.com/index.html

collaboratioNation
Looks at how people work together across boundaries.
Website: collaborationation.com

Leader to Leader Institute
Provides innovative and relevant resources, products and experiences that enable social-sector leaders of the future to address emerging opportunities and challenges with the goal of leading social-sector organisations towards excellence in performance.
Website: www.leadertoleader.org

Organization Design Forum
An international professional association for those interested in organisation design, dedicated to advancing the theory and practice of the organisation design through expertise, education and resources.
Website: www.organizationdesignforum.org

Plexus Institute
A non-profit organisation providing an introduction to complexity science.
Website: www.plexusinstitute.org

Royal Society of Arts
Runs a programme of projects and lectures based on five manifesto challenges: encouraging enterprise, moving towards a zero-waste society,

developing a capable population, fostering resilient communities, advancing global citizenship.
Website: www.rsa.org.uk

Sante Fe Institute
An organisation devoted to creating a new kind of scientific research community, emphasising multidisciplinary collaboration in pursuit of understanding the common themes that arise in natural, artificial and social systems.
Website: www.santafe.edu

Spirit in Business
An organisation founded on the premise that creating businesses that respect life rather than destroy it requires a shift in the mind, a change in consciousness. Its mission is to explore and further the role of consciousness, ethics and values in business leadership.
Website: www.spiritinbusiness.org/new/content/home.php

Strategy as Practice
A community of scholars interested in the practice of strategy and strategic change in organisations, applying a variety of different theoretical approaches, such as practice perspectives on organisations, sense-making, discourse analysis and script theory.
Website: www.strategy-as-practice.org

Tavistock Institute of Human Relations
Offers research, consultancy, evaluation and professional development work to support change and learning, as well as publications in the fields of inter-organisational relations, the emergence of the knowledge society and problems of organisation, particularly in the delivery of public policy.
Website: www.tavinstitute.org/index.php

Virtual organisation
A website focusing on theoretical and empirical research related to virtual organisations, virtual teams, network organisation and e-commerce. It issues regular newsletters and event details.
Website: www.virtual-organization.net

Resources and tools

Beyond Intractability
A free knowledge base on more constructive approaches to destructive conflict.
Website: www.beyondintractability.org/

Buros Institute
Provides professional assistance, expertise and information to users of commercially published tests, tools, surveys and inventories, and promotes appropriate test selection, utilisation and practice. Offers reviews and information on nearly 4,000 tests, tools, surveys and inventories.
Website: www.unl.edu/buros

Businessballs
Provides free resources, tools and inspiration for the ethical development of people, business and organisations.
Website: www.businessballs.com

Center for Effective Organizations, Marshall School of Business
Offers a Certificate Programme in Organisation Design.
Website: www.marshall.usc.edu/web/CEO.cfm?doc_id=8297

Change Management Learning Center (sponsored by Prosci)
The Change Management Toolkit includes detailed planning templates, readiness assessments and guidelines for building executive sponsorship and managing resistance.
Website: www.change-management.com/change-management-toolkit.htm

Change Readiness Questionnaire
See Buros Institute.

Economist Intelligence Unit
Provides analysis and forecasts for more than 200 countries and eight key industries, delivered online, in print, in customised research as well as through conferences and peer interchange.
Website: www.eiu.com

Executive Briefing (Economist Intelligence Unit)
Provides industry forecasts, country analysis and management insights.
Website: www.viewswire.com/index.asp?layout=homePubTypeEB

Gallup Organisation
As well as conducting independent polls, the Gallup Organisation publishes books and inventories on employee and customer engagement and articles and white papers on a range of human performance topics.
Website: www.gallup.com

Organisational Culture Inventory (OCI)
See Buros Institute.

Reuters.com
A source for news including business, financial and investing news, and personal finance and stocks.
Website: www.reuters.com

The Strozzi Institute
Provides training, books and information on leadership development based on the principle of mind and body interaction. The theory is that developing leadership skills involves language, action and meaning (here called "somatics") and martial arts, principally Aikido, form the vehicle for this.
Website: www.strozziinstitute.com

Team Effectiveness Inventory
See Buros Institute.

Appendix 3
Glossary

Abilene Paradox A story of mismanaged agreement. A course of action was suggested by one member of a group and no one raised any objection to it. The group took this course. Subsequently, it transpired that several people had not agreed with the original proposal but went along with it for various reasons. (See Harvey, J.B., *The Abilene Paradox and other Meditations on Management*, Jossey-Bass, 1996.)

Action management A systematic method of managing actions planned to achieve business goals. Various action-management software programs are available to help track, monitor, control and respond to actions.

Action planning Decide business goals and then determine the actions to take to achieve these. From this build an action plan, a sequenced series of steps that include task assignments, milestones, timelines, resource allocations and performance measurement.

Analysis tools Analysis is the systematic approach to problem-solving. Complex organisational problems are made simpler when they are separated into smaller, more understandable elements. The selection of the right analysis tool depends on the nature of the problem. An example of an analysis tool is a SWOT (strengths, weaknesses, opportunities, threats) analysis.

Appreciative inquiry An analysis and assessment approach that seeks to find what works in an organisation and to build designs from that. The results of this positively oriented process are statements that describe the future state of the organisation based on the high points and good aspects of where it has been.

Blue-sky thinking Similar to brainstorming in that it asks people to create a range of options and possibilities in an ideal world where there are no constraints.

Business process An end-to-end series of activities starting with inputs to a product or service and ending with the output. There are three types of business process: management, operational, support.

Capability Organisational capability is the collective skills, abilities and expertise of an organisation vested in its employees. Capability is maintained and developed through various human resource practices including job design, training, rewards and recognition, and career development. Organisational capability is an intangible asset that, managed well, can be a valuable competitive differentiator.

Change readiness Before launching any type of project involving a change to working conditions, it is helpful to assess factors such as the perception of the need for change, how much (or little) support the change is likely to get from stakeholders, what the driving and blocking forces might be to achieving project success, and leadership ability to manage the change.

Competence An individual's ability to carry out tasks and activities to the standards required in employment using an appropriate mix of knowledge, skills and attitudes. Many organisations have competence frameworks that define levels of ability against which employees' performance is measured.

Complexity theory In the case of organisations and management, complexity theory is concerned with the conditions that affect predictability and self-organising behaviour. Oversimplifying, the theory suggests that a complex system is inherently unstable and therefore unpredictable (mathematics demonstrates that the unpredictability is not random), but that direction emerges and self-organisation happens around this. (See Stacey, R.D., *Complexity and Management: Fad or Organizational Challenge*, Routledge, 2000.)

Culture The values, traditions, customs, stories, habits and attitudes that a group of people share that define for them their general behaviour and way of working in an organisation. A common shorthand for the definition is "the way we do things round here".

Dashboard A method of presenting easy-to-read and easy-to-assimilate information on the metrics being used to track and measure project status. It is called a dashboard because the visual display of the information resembles that of a car dashboard.

Derailers The character traits that contribute to leadership failure by undermining their effective characteristics. Dysfunctional attributes that take leaders off track include arrogance, volatility, micromanagement and an abrasive interpersonal style. (See www.hoganassessments.com for tools to assess derailers.)

Emotional intelligence In 1995 Daniel Goleman wrote a book, *Emotional Intelligence: Why It Can Matter More Than IQ* (Bantam, reprinted 1997), describing five dimensions of emotional intelligence: self-monitoring, self-regulation, self-motivation, empathy and social skills. He suggested that people who are clearly more capable in demonstrating these attributes are more successful than those who have lower levels of emotional intelligence (EI). The book sparked a commercial and research industry in the concepts of EI. (See the Consortium for Research on Emotional Intelligence in Organizations at www.eiconsortium.org.)

Engagement approaches
The communication and other methods used to involve stakeholders in an organisational change. The aim is to develop and maintain support for the change from those who will be involved in it and affected by it.

Facilitated sessions
Events or workshops orchestrated by a facilitator. Facilitators do not need to have knowledge of the content of the workshop as their skill is using their knowledge of group processes to determine approaches and techniques that help a group achieve the objectives of the session. (See the International Association of Facilitators at www.iaf-world.org.)

Focus groups
Small groups of stakeholders who participate in facilitated discussions on questions related to organisation change. The purpose of the discussion is to collect views and opinions on the proposed or enacted changes in order to inform future planning.

FTE
Short for full-time equivalent. In reporting numbers of employees on a payroll, figures are expressed as a full-time equivalent statistic representing the number of full-time employees that could have been employed if the reported number of hours worked by part-time employees had been worked by full-time employees. This statistic is calculated by dividing the part-time hours paid by the standard number of hours for full-time employees.

Future Search
A conference-style approach involving large numbers of internal and external stakeholders

jointly working on a design with facilitator support. Briefly, some initial questions are posed and the "delegates" use a combination of structured activities to agree answers/solutions. This method has the benefit of generating feelings of ownership among stakeholders thus getting speedily to the implementation stage.

Gallup Q12

Gallup Consulting has identified 12 questions that measure employee engagement and link powerfully to relevant business outcomes, including retention, productivity, profitability, customer engagement and safety. These questions – the Q12 – measure dimensions that leaders, managers and employees can influence.

1 I know what is expected of me at work.
2 I have the materials and equipment I need to do my work right.
3 At work, I have the opportunity to do what I do best every day.
4 In the last seven days, I have received recognition or praise for doing good work.
5 My supervisor, or someone at work, seems to care about me as a person.
6 There is someone at work who encourages my development.
7 At work, my opinions seem to count.
8 The mission/purpose of my company makes me feel my job is important.
9 My associates (fellow employees) are committed to doing quality work.
10 I have a best friend at work.
11 In the last six months, someone at work has talked to me about my progress.
12 This last year, I have had opportunities at work to learn and grow.

(www.gallupconsulting.com/content/?ci=52)

Geeks and techies

People with a passionate interest in the detailed technical attributes of something. They focus on this to the exclusion of many other aspects of life. There is now a magazine, *Geek Monthly*, targeted at self-identified geeks (www.geekmonthly.com).

Global Reporting Initiative   The vision of the Global Reporting Initiative (GRI) is that reporting on economic, environmental and social performance by all organisations becomes as routine and comparable as financial reporting. The GRI accomplishes this vision by developing, continually improving and building capacity around the use of its Sustainability Reporting Framework. (See www.globalreporting.org/home)

Governance   The way an organisation design programme is directed, controlled, organised, managed and administered through various policies and procedures.

Hierarchy theory   A theory concerned with levels of organisation. It uses a small number of principles to monitor complex structures and behaviours of multiple level systems. The theory's foundation paper, "The Architecture of Complexity: Hierarchic Systems", was written by Herbert Simon (*Proceedings of the American Philosophical Society*, Vol. 106, December 1962).

Holonic systems   From the Greek *holos* meaning whole, a holonic system is composed of autonomous entities (called holons) that can deliberately reduce their autonomy, when the need arises, to collectively achieve a goal. It is a complex, co-operative system, able to evolve and self-organise over time to optimise survivability, adaptability, flexibility, efficiency and effectiveness. (See Koestler, A., *The Ghost in the Machine*, Penguin, reprinted 1990.)

Interventions   Planned activities designed to change the communication track of a process, for example a workshop aimed at determining ways to communicate differently with stakeholders.

Interview

A verbal exchange between two or more people either face to face or via a phone line with the interviewer taking the lead in asking questions. The primary purpose of interviews in organisation design work is to obtain information to feed into project planning.

Jumpstart event

An approach that quickly moves participants through the early phases of organisation design work. Jumpstart events provide a spark that gets people going in the same way that jump leads get a car with a flat battery going.

Mapping techniques

In organisation design work, mapping means assessing the attributes and relationships between organisational elements to get a sense of the organisational landscape. The aim is to find out what the focus of the various elements is, how they are ordered in relation to one another, what the areas of similarity and difference are, and how they are oriented with each other.

Measurement

A formalised activity (assessing, monitoring, gauging, ascertaining, surveying, and so on) aimed at producing structured data that are then interpreted and applied in the process of making judgments, decisions and choices.

Noise

In organisation design work, noise is the information generated by all the day-to-day organisational communication channels, formal and informal, including e-mail, gossip, websites and news briefs. Organisational designers have two challenges related to noise: sifting out what is relevant, such as useful feedback on progress, from background noise; and getting their messages heard clearly over other messages.

Open source Forums, usually web-based, for sharing problems and challenges and working together on solutions. Commonly associated with development of software, for example Linux, the term and concepts are now being applied to a range of other arenas where collaborative problem-solving or product development benefits from widespread outsider (often those with expertise tangential to the problem's field) thinking. See www.innocentive. com for examples of open source challenges in science.

Organisation A relatively durable, reliable and accountable social structure "created by individuals to support the collaborative pursuit of specified goals" (Scott, R.W., *Organizations: Rational, Natural, and Open Systems*, Prentice Hall, 2003). Any organisation comprises interacting components, each having an impact on one another.

Organisation design The sequence of work that results in an alignment of vision/mission, values/operating principles, strategies, objectives, systems, structure, people, processes, culture and performance measures. The outcome of intentional activities that align all the components of an organisation in a way that keeps it adaptable in its operating context.

Predictive modelling A process of creating a model and with this analysing past performance data to predict probable future performance.

Principal/agent problems The difficulties that arise when one person (the principal) delegates work to someone else (the agent) without having the means to ensure that the agent will act in the principal's interest and not in self-interest.

Processes The end-to-end work flow from input to output of a product or service. For example, a recruitment process typically includes the following steps: develop job specification, determine selection criteria, advertise vacancy, provide information to candidates, shortlist applicants, interview applicants, make offer, negotiate contract, sign contract.

Programme management
The co-ordinated management of a portfolio of projects to achieve a set of business objectives which will be realised more effectively with a consolidated approach. Managing a programme commonly involves using a set of tools and methodologies to take the programme in a systematic way from inception to closure (see Chapter 4).

Project management
The application of specific tools and techniques to initiate, plan, execute, control and close a time-related piece of work that has stated objectives.

Quantum theory
Formulated in a well-defined mathematical language, quantum theory makes predictions for the probabilities of various possible outcomes, but not for which outcome will occur in any given case. Interpretation of the calculations, in words and images, often leads to statements that seem to defy common sense. Because quantum events occur on an extremely small scale, many aspects of quantum behaviour seem strange and even paradoxical. (Adapted from www2.slac.stanford.edu/vvc/theory/quantum.html.)

Reorganise
Shuffle existing players into a new formation without changing fundamentals. "We trained hard, but it seemed that every time we were to form up in teams, we would be reorganized. We tend to meet any new situation by reorganizing – and a wonderful method it can be for creating the illusion of progress ... while producing confusion, inefficiency, and demoralization." (Attributed

to Gaius Petronius Arbiter, Roman governor of Bithynia, AD60.)

Restructure A step up from reorganizing involving deeper changes, for example in response to a merger where, to accommodate the two parties, aspects of job design, work process, and so on, have changed. Often restructures, like reorganisations, fail to take account of the multiple interdependencies that need to form part of the restructure. This may result in employee cynicism of the type expressed well by Scott Adams, the originator of Dilbert cartoons: "Let's form proactive synergy restructuring teams."

Risk analysis Risks are the various factors that could influence the achievement of business objectives – the upside opportunities (often forgotten) and the downside hazards. In organisation design work, it is important to identify, assess and determine appropriate ways of responding to these, and use a risk-control framework to manage the risks during the project's life cycle.

Sacred cow In organisational terms, an assumption, an idea or a practice that is fiercely protected, often with no apparent reason, and thus becomes a barrier to change. (See Kriegel, R. and Brandt, D., *Sacred Cows Make the Best Burgers: Developing Change Ready People and Organizations*, Warner Books, reprinted 1997.)

Self-organising networks Associated with various scientific fields including physics, artificial intelligence and chemistry, but now used more loosely to describe the natural (ie, unmanaged) emergence of connected people into a recognised and coherent community, usually around a project, or topic of interest. (See Goldstein, J., "Emergence as a Construct: History and Issues", *Emergence: Complexity and Organization*, Vol. 1, 1999, pp. 49–72.)

Silo	Organisational silos are divisions and departments that work independently of each other, resisting co-operation and collaboration with other functions in the organisation. Lack of information sharing between them leads to duplication, overlap and slowdown in getting things done. More dangerously it can also lead to mistakes and failure to act when the occasion demands.
Silo mentality	A compartmentalised view of business operations, often encouraged by hierarchical structures and reinforced by reward and recognition systems. People with a silo mentality are reluctant to share information, make connections between their work and the work of other departments, or see where collaboration could bring mutual benefit.
Six Sigma	A method of improving the quality, efficiency and effectiveness of business processes through rigorous and methodical statistical and data analysis that aims to achieve ± six sigma (standard deviations) or 3.4 defects per million items.
Stakeholder	A person with a vested interest in something. In organisational design work, stakeholders are people who are affected, directly or indirectly, by the scope of a new design and/or who can influence the success or failure of the design.
Structures	The arrangements of people in an organisation that appear, in some form of hierarchy, on an organisation chart (see Chapter 3).
Systems	The infrastructures to carry the processes. So, for example, a human resources IT system will track the flow of a recruitment process. In most cases, systems are technology-based, but paper-based systems are still in evidence in some organisations.

Ten Flatteners

In his book *The World is Flat* (Farrar, Straus and Giroux, 2005), Thomas Friedman argues that there are a number of forces acting to take globalisation into what he calls "3.0" – globalisation 1.0 being the period from 1492 until around 1800 and globalisation 2.0 lasting roughly from 1800 to 2000. Globalisation 3.0 is being triggered by the "Ten Flatteners" which he lists as follows:

1 Fall of the Berlin Wall. The events of November 9th 1989 tilted the worldwide balance of power toward democracies and free markets.

2 Netscape IPO. The August 9th 1995 offering sparked massive investment in fibre-optic cables, creating a worldwide infrastructure for later technological innovation and development.

3 Work flow software. The rise of these applications enables more people in more places to design, display, manage and collaborate on business data resulting in work flowing within and between companies and continents faster than ever.

4 Uploading or open-sourcing. Self-organising communities of geeks working on programs like Apache launched a collaborative revolution that resulted in community developed software.

5 Outsourcing. Initially, migrating business functions to India saved money and fuelled a third-world economy. Outsourcing is now occurring across continents, including from other continents to the United States and regionally.

6 Offshoring. Contract manufacturing is now occurring in a number of nations. It has served to elevate China to economic prominence.

7 Supply-chaining. Robust networks of suppliers, retailers and customers increase business efficiency. Wal-Mart is the undisputed champion of supply chains.

8 Insourcing. Logistics giants took control of customer supply chains, helping mom-and-pop

shops go global. UPS and FedEx have made millions transforming themselves in this way.
9 Informing. Power searching allows everyone to use the internet as a "personal supply chain of knowledge". This was the emergence of Google.
10 Steroids. New technologies pump up all forms of collaboration, making it digital, mobile, virtual and personal.

Source: www.workforceinnovations.org/speaker_docs/world%20is%20flat%20synopsis%20Workforce%20Innovations%20v.2.doc

Transactional design	A design developed to achieve "better sameness" that might be needed to carry out the mission and strategy but is not in a response to changes in them.
Transformational design	A design developed in response to environmental forces either external or internal to the organisation that affect the mission, strategy and culture (such as a major, high-level and potentially life-threatening force).
Triple bottom line	As well as creating economic (financial) value, organisations are increasingly seeking to create social and environmental value (or a least to do no harm). These three elements – economic, social and environmental – comprise the triple bottom line for reporting organisational performance and results.
Virtual organisation	An organisation that encompasses ("organises") a workgroup or community that may be within an organisation, may span multiple organisations, or may be outside the boundaries of any formal organisation. Essential features of a virtual structure are identification with shared concerns or issues and temporal and geographic separation of members of the community. There are other features that may vary across various virtual organisations, such as absence of formal

controls, rewards and incentives, and presence of relationships based on goodwill and reciprocity. (Definition adapted from www.brint.com/wwwboard/messages/9894.html.)

Vision/visioning Creating a compelling statement of what the organisation aspires to be or do is one of the first steps in designing a new state. Vision is important because it is the most fundamental impetus in inspiring people to do their best. A well-constructed vision also acts as a guide to decision-making, aligning the organisation's parts so that they work towards a desirable goal.

Walk the talk This phrase has a similar intention to the injunction "practise what you preach". Leaders of organisation design programmes are in the spotlight, and if they are serious about getting support for their programmes they must be seen to be consistently acting as role models and doing what they are encouraging other people to do.

Index